Economic Analyses in Historical Perspective

This book brings together leading scholars on the history of economic thought to demonstrate the vitality and richness of a discipline that welcomes both practitioners of intellectual, contextual history and specialists in the historical explanation of the analytical and theoretical dimension of economic science. They shed new light on a variety of themes and problems and move the frontier of knowledge in the areas covered.

Economic Analyses in Historical Perspective is presented in three parts. The first deals with French traditions in economics, a field that Gilbert Faccarello has tilled for many years and to which he has made numerous contributions. The second turns to the dissemination and diffusion of economic ideas and theories across national borders and thus to the European and even global level. Finally, the third part deals with analytical developments in some selected fields of economics: public economics, monetary policy, trade theory and spatial economics.

This volume is of great importance to those who study history of economic thought, political economy and monetary economics. The chapters centre around the work of Gilbert Faccarello, making this book a fitting tribute to his academic career on the history of economic theory and ideas.

José Luís Cardoso is Research Professor and Director of the Institute of Social Sciences of the University of Lisbon, Portugal.

Heinz D. Kurz is Professor Emeritus of Economics at the University of Graz, Austria, and Fellow of the Graz Schumpeter Centre.

Philippe Steiner is Professor of Sociology at the University Paris-Sorbonne and Honorary Senior member of the Institut Universitaire de France.

Routledge Studies in the History of Economics

For a full list of titles in this series, please visit www.routledge.com /series/SE0341

192 Economics, Ethics, and Ancient Thought
Towards a Virtuous Public Policy
Donald G. Richards

193 Ricardo on Money
A Reappraisal
Ghislain Deleplace

194 Natural Law and the Origin of Political Economy
Samuel Pufendorf and the History of Economics
Arild Saether

195 Ricardo and International Trade
Edited by Shigeyoshi Senga, Masatomi Fujimoto, and Taichi Tabuchi

196 Economics, Entrepreneurship and Utopia
The Economics of Jeremy Bentham and Robert Owen
Estrella Trincado and Manuel Santos-Redondo

197 War in the History of Economic Thought
Economists and the Question of War
Edited by Yukihiro Ikeda and Annalisa Rosselli

198 Schumpeter's Price Theory
Harry Bloch

199 Economics and Literature
A Comparative and Interdisciplinary Approach
Edited by çınla Akdere and Christine Baron

200 Economic Analyses in Historical Perspective
Edited by José Luís Cardoso, Heinz D. Kurz and Philippe Steiner

Economic Analyses in Historical Perspective

Festschrift in Honour of Gilbert Faccarello

Edited by José Luís Cardoso, Heinz D. Kurz and Philippe Steiner

Routledge
Taylor & Francis Group
LONDON AND NEW YORK

First published 2018 by Routledge

2 Park Square, Milton Park, Abingdon, Oxfordshire OX14 4RN
52 Vanderbilt Avenue, New York, NY 10017

Routledge is an imprint of the Taylor & Francis Group, an informa business

First issued in paperback 2019

British Library Cataloguing-in-Publication Data
A catalogue record for this book is available from the British Library

Library of Congress Cataloging-in-Publication Data
A catalog record for this book has been requested.

ISBN: 978-1-138-50119-5 (hbk)
ISBN: 978-0-367-89069-8 (pbk)

Typeset in Times New Roman
by codeMantra

Contents

Notes on contributors

Yusuke Ando is Associate Professor of the History of European Political Thought at Rikkyo University, Japan. A specialist in French eighteenth-century political and economic thought, he published *Commerce, Despotism and Public Opinion* (in Japanese, Sobunsha, 2014), which was awarded the 32nd Shibusawa-Claudel Louis Vuitton Japan Prize in 2015 and the 13th JSHET Young Scholar Award in 2016.

Michaël Assous is full Professor of Economics at the University of Lumière-Lyon 2. Assous is most noted for his work in the history of macroeconomics with issues surrounding the modelling of (in)stability in Fisher's, Harrod's, Kalecki's, Lange's, Meade's, and Solow's works. In 2012, he was awarded the ESHET (European Society of the History of Economic Thought) young researcher award.

Alain Béraud is Emeritus Professor at the University of Cergy-Pontoise. He edited, with Gilbert Faccarello, the *Nouvelle histoire de la pensée économique.* He also published with him an article entitled "Nous marchons sur un autre terrain". The reception of Ricardo in the French language: episodes from a complex history in *The Reception of David Ricardo in Continental Europe and Japan,* edited by Gilbert Faccarello and Masashi Izumo, Routledge, 2014: 10-75. He has published numerous articles on the history of political economy, in particular on French economists (Say, Cournot, Dupuit, Walras, Allais).

Rebeca Gomez Betancourt is full Professor in Economics at the University of Lyon 2 and Researcher at Triangle, UMR-CNRS. She has been Visiting Professor at the Universities of los Andes, Bogota-Colombia and Universidade Federal Minas Gerais, Belo Horizonte-Brazil. She is currently the President of the French Association for the History of Economic Thought and the director of the Master's degree in Theories and History in Economics at University of Lyon. Her work focuses on the history of monetary thought, in particular on American Economists of the late XIXth Century to the beginning of the XXth century. She has published on the history of the Federal Reserve System, the quantity theory of money and the monetary regimes in the Andean countries and in India. She lives in Lyon, France.

José Luís Cardoso is Research Professor and Director of the Institute of Social Sciences of the University of Lisbon. He is author and editor of several books on the Portuguese history of economic thought from a comparative perspective, with special emphasis on the study of the processes of diffusion and assimilation of economic ideas. He has published articles in the main international journals on the history of economic thought. His research interests also include economic history and methodology of economics. He is the general editor of the series *Classics of Portuguese Economic Thought* (30 volumes), co-founder of *The European Journal of the History of Economic Thought* and co-editor of the *e-journal of Portuguese History*. He was President of ESHET in 2014–2016.

Thierry Demals is Associate Professor of economics at the University of Lille. His research interests are in the history of economic thought, with a special attention to pre-classical economic thought, the philosophy of economics and the relationship between economics and political thought. He has co-edited *La Diffusion internationale de la Physiocratie* (1993) and *Y a-t-il des lois en économie?* (2007).

Daniel Diatkine was Assistant Professor at University Paris 1 Panthéon – Sorbonne and is now Professor (emeritus) at Evry University. He was a member of the Executive Committee of the European Society for the History of Economic Thought. His research field concerns Adam Smith and David Hume.

Julie Ferrand is Assistant Professor of economics at the University of Saint-Etienne (IUT Roanne). She holds a PhD (2014) in economics from the University Paris 1 Panthéon-Sorbonne, "Droit naturel, sensualisme et libre-échange: l'économie politique de Gabriel Bonnot de Mably (1709–1785)". She was lecturer at the Sorbonne University Abu Dhabi and Visiting Professor at the American University in the Emirates (Dubai).

Pierre Force, Professor of French and History at Columbia University, works at the interface between the humanities and the social sciences and has published in the fields of early modern French literature, intellectual history and social history. He is the author of *Le Problème herméneutique chez Pascal* (Paris: Vrin, 1989), *Molière ou Le Prix des choses* (Paris: Nathan, 1994), *Self-Interest before Adam Smith. A Genealogy of Economic Science* (Cambridge University Press, 2003) and *Wealth and Disaster. Atlantic Migrations from a Pyrenean Town in the Eighteenth and Nineteenth Centuries* (Johns Hopkins University Press, 2016).

Ludovic Frobert is Senior Researcher (CNRS/ENS-Lyon). He published *Introduction à Albert Hirschman* (with C. Ferraton, Paris: La Découverte,

2017), and he edited the volume *De la République de Constantin Pecqueur (1801–1888)* (Besançon, PUFC, 2017) and published the 2nd edition of *Les Canuts ou La Démocratie turbulente, Lyon 1831–1834* (Lyon: Libel, 2017).

Marco E. L. Guidi is Professor of History of Economic Thought at the University of Pisa. His research interests range from the history of utilitarian ethics and economics, to the study of national traditions of economic thought from the perspective of the institutionalisation of economics and the international circulation of economic ideas.

Harald Hagemann is Professor em. of Economic Theory at the University of Hohenheim, Stuttgart, Germany. He is also a Life Member of Clare Hall, University of Cambridge. In 1999/2000, he was Theodor Heuss Professor at the Graduate Faculty of Political and Social Sciences at the New School for Social Research in New York, USA. He formerly taught at the Universities of Bremen and Kiel, the Free University of Berlin, and has been a Visiting Professor at the Universities of Bologna, Graz, Linz, and Lyon 2, Nice Sophia Antipolis GREDEG-CNRS, Paris I Pantheon-Sorbonne, Strasbourg BETA-CNRS and Sydney and Meiji University Tokyo. His main research covers Growth and Structural Change, Technological Change and Employment, Business Cycle Theory and the emigration of German-speaking economists in the Nazi period. He was President of ESHET in 2010–12. Since 2013, he has been the Chairman of the Keynes-Gesellschaft.

Masashi Izumo is Professor at Kanagawa University, Yokohama, Japan. He is an executive member of the JSHET (Japanese Society for the History of Economic Thought) and co-founder and committee member of the Ricardo Society Japan. He is the co-editor, with Gilbert Faccarello, of *The Reception of David Ricardo in Continental Europe and Japan*, Routledge, 2014.

Heinz D. Kurz is Professor em. of Economics at the University of Graz, Austria, and Fellow of the Graz Schumpeter Centre. In 1990/1991, he was Theodor Heuss Professor at the Graduate Faculty of Political and Social Sciences at the New School for Social Research in New York. He formerly taught at the Universities of Kiel and Bremen and was a Visiting Professor at numerous universities, including Rome, Pisa, Leicester, Paris, Bangkok, Bogotá, Osaka, Tokyo, Wuhan, Djakarta and Pune. He is an Honorary Professor of Nanjing University. His books include *Theory of Production* (with Neri Salvadori; Cambridge University Press), *Economic Thought: A Brief History* (Columbia University Press) and *Handbook on the History of Economic Thought* (edited together with Gilbert Faccarello; Edward Elgar). He is the General Editor of Piero Sraffa's unpublished papers, a project carried out on behalf of Cambridge University Press. He was President of ESHET in 2006–2008.

Maria Cristina Marcuzzo is Full Professor in Economics at the University of Rome "La Sapienza" and Fellow of the Italian Academy of Lincei. She has worked on classical monetary theory, the Cambridge School of Economics, Keynesian economics and more recently, Keynes investments in financial markets. She has published about 100 articles in journals and books in addition to authoring or editing 20 volumes.

Manuela Mosca, Full Professor of History of Economic Thought, teaches at the University of Salento (Lecce) and at the University of Bologna. She was the 2009 winner of the History of Economics Society best article prize ("On the origins of the concept of natural monopoly", *The European Journal of the History of Economic Thought*, XV (2), 2008, pp. 317–353). On De Viti de Marco, she also published a book (*Antonio de Viti de Marco. A Story Worth Remembering*, Palgrave-Macmillan) and a documentary video (available at http://vimeo.com/29599475). Her new book *Monopoly Power and Competition: The Italian Marginalist Perspective* is forthcoming (Edward Elgar).

Arnaud Orain is Professor of Economics at the European Studies Institute of the University Paris 8. He was Davis Fellow of the History Department of Princeton University in 2015–2016. He is currently completing a book devoted to a cultural history of the John Law's System in eighteenth-century France.

Cosimo Perrotta, former Full Professor at the Univ. of Salento, Italy, was Council Chair of ESHET. He is the author of *Consumption as an Investment* (2004) and *Unproductive Labour in Political Economy. History of an Idea* (forthcoming), both published by Routledge. He has also published articles in *History of Political Economy*, *The European Journal of the History of Economic Thought* and many other international journals. He is a referee and invited reviewer for many journals and publishers and has been key speaker of several international conferences or seminars (recently in Mexico City, Valencia, Rome, Tokyo, etc.).

Jean-Pierre Potier is Emeritus Professor of Economics in the University Lumière-Lyon 2 and a member of the CNRS research staff *Triangle-Action, discours, pensée politique et économique*. He is author of numerous essays concerning French and Italian economic thought in the 19th and 20th century. He is one of the editors of the *Oeuvres économiques complètes* of Auguste and Léon Walras and of the *Oeuvres complètes* of Jean-Baptiste Say.

Jérôme de Boyer des Roches is *Maître de Conférences* at Paris Dauphine University - PSL since 1986. He published *La Pensée Monétaire, Histoire et Analyse,* éd. Les Solos, Paris, 2002. He has written for *Les Cahiers d'Économie Politique, Économie et Sociétés, The European Journal of the History of Economic Thought, The Journal of the History of Economic*

Thought, la *Revue Économique, la Revue Française d'Économie* and *Studi Economici*. He wrote also for *Nouvelle Histoire de la Pensée Économique* (ed. by A. Béraud and G. Faccarello, 1992–2000) and for the *Handbook on the History of Economic Analysis* (ed. by G. Faccarello and H.D. Kurz, 2016).

Philippe Steiner is Professor of Sociology at the University Paris-Sorbonne and honorary member of the Institut universitaire de France. His recent research is devoted to the relation between markets and morals (*Calcul et morale. Coût du travail et valeur de l'émancipation*, with C. Oudin-Bastide, Paris: Albin Michel, 2015 and *Marchés contestés*, with M. Trespeuch, Toulouse: Presses universitaires du Mirail, 2015) and the history of social sciences (*Durkheim and the Birth of Economic Sociology*, Princeton University Press, 2011 and *Donner. Une histoire de l'altruisme*, Paris: Presses universitaires de France, 2016).

Richard Sturn is Joseph A. Schumpeter Professor of Economics at Graz University and chair of the Institute of Public Economics. He is managing editor of *The European Journal of the History of Economic Thought* and author of numerous articles and books, notably on thinkers of the Scottish enlightenment, the Austrian tradition and public economics.

Jacques-François Thisse, a Fellow of the Econometric Society and of the Regional Science Association International, is Professor Emeritus at CORE (Belgium). He has extensively published in economics, operations research and geography. He has co-authored *Discrete Choice Theory of Product Differentiation* (MIT Press), *Economics of Agglomeration* (Cambridge University Press) and *Economic Geography* (Princeton University Press). He holds several Honorary Doctorates.

Keith Tribe retired as Reader in Economics for the University of Keele in 2002 and has since then worked as an independent scholar and professional translator. A specialist in German, eighteenth- and nineteenth-century economic thought, he published *The Economy of the Word* in 2015; in 2017, he edited *Cameralism in Practice* with Marten Seppel and published a joint introduction to HET with Roger Backhouse, *The History of Economics. A Course for Students and Teachers.*

Part 1

Introduction

Introduction

José Luís Cardoso, Heinz D. Kurz and Philippe Steiner

The twenty-two essays presented here to Gilbert Faccarello, celebrating his sixty-fifth birthday, range widely across the history of economic analysis and pay fitting tribute to the breadth and depth of Gilbert's scholarship and published work. In our approach to the sheer extent of Gilbert's work, we made a tripartite division. It hardly needs to be said that the resulting boundaries will often seem somewhat artificial, not least because the history of economic analysis is itself a seamless whole.

The first group of essays deals with French traditions in economics, a field that Gilbert has tilled for many years and to which he has made numerous contributions. It is no exaggeration to say that he has put the important ideas of early French economists back on the agenda of the international community of scholars, these ideas having been obscured by the 'anglicisation' of the subject during the second half of the twentieth century.

The second group of essays turns to the dissemination and diffusion of economic ideas and theories across national borders and thus to the European and even global level. Gilbert has played an important role in bringing European scholarship in the history of economic thought into contact with scholarship in other parts of the world, especially in Asia.[1] Many of the students whose work he has supervised have originated from distant places and have proven themselves to be excellent promoters of a growing international scientific community. Gilbert's studies deliberately set themselves against the trend in which the history of economic analysis becomes increasingly marginalised in mainstream economics, a trend that has continued until quite recently. However, we are now beginning to witness a turning of the tide, something that should not be surprising given the often lamentable performance of some elements of contemporary economics in interpreting the economic world; there is at last a positive search for remedies to its mounting problems. Severe economic crises in both the economy and academic economics have forced the economics profession to reconsider its doctrines, abandon views that can no longer be sustained, return to views that provide important insights or create new ones appropriate to the current situation.

The third group of essays deals with analytical developments in some selected fields: public economics, monetary policy, trade theory and spatial economics. Gilbert has himself contributed to most of these areas. Furthermore, a notable feature of his work, and testimony to Gilbert's cooperative and friendly nature, is the important part played in that work by co-authorship and co-editorship, not least with Alain Béraud, José Luís Cardoso, Christian Gehrke, Heinz D. Kurz, Antoin Murphy, Richard Sturn and especially Philippe Steiner.

Our appreciation of Gilbert's work begins with a short piece by Heinz D. Kurz who offers some personal reminiscences of Gilbert as regards the foundation, together with José Luís Cardoso and Antoin Murphy of *The European Journal of the History of Economic Thought* and other collaborations with whom Gilbert has been involved.

Part 2 then deals with Gilbert's work on French traditions in economics. His interest here goes right back to the second dissertation he had to write to gain tenure. Having written a PhD thesis devoted to the issue of Marx's theory of value, he turned to Boisguilbert's theory of prices in a series of interrelated markets that were all plagued by problems related to rapidly changing expectations in the grain market. He then devoted time to the study of Turgot's views on value, stressing the originality of the approach taken by this great economist of the physiocratic school. He later returned to the eighteenth-century French political economy, writing a series of essays on what he and Philippe Steiner called "French *Philosophie économique*," clarifying the underpinnings of major French economists from Boisguilbert to Say, through Quesnay and Turgot. The contributions here almost entirely address this approach to French *Philosophie économique*.

Philippe Steiner begins by dealing with a *Philosophe économiste*. He examines Quesnay's writings to demonstrate that they contain the first two constitutive elements of *Philosophie économique*: a sensualist theory of knowledge and an emphasis on self-interested behaviour. Steiner places special emphasis on Quesnay's conception of the legislator, considering the connection between "oeconomic government" and administration with respect to the reform of the tax system – as formulated first by Quesnay and then Le Trosne, a major contributor on this key point of physiocratic doctrine.

Two contributions then examine issues raised by economists who did not belong to this current of thought or, more radically, who fiercely opposed the physiocratic approach to *Philosophie économique*. Arnaud Orain and Julie Ferrand consider the relationship between the brothers Gabriel Bonnot de Mably and Etienne Bonnot de Condillac, the famous sensualist philosopher and economist. Whereas Mably declared that his work made use of the sensationalist theory of Condillac, his political economy was rather different from that of his younger brother. However, Orain and Ferrand show that beyond these apparent differences, both men eventually advanced almost similar projects for the French Kingdom: renewal based on the defence of workers against idle men (landowners), the suppression of luxury and a new educational plan to shape "new citizens." Opposition to physiocratic theory and to Turgot's reforms are also studied by Yusuke Ando in an examination of key writings from Jacques Necker, the Genevan banker who became head of the government of Louis XVI after the downfall of Turgot. It is said that Necker attempted to make a bid for political power by publishing two works, *Éloge de Jean-Baptiste Colbert* (1773) and *Sur la législation et le commerce des grains* (1775). Notwithstanding politics, these two works have important analytical features: They explain why the liberalisation of the grain trade failed in the 1760s and also demonstrate the coherence of Necker's political economy. Necker laid emphasis upon opinion, time and institution for an understanding of market functioning, believing that institutions exist as a result of opinion and time, not of "evidence" and the "natural order." These notions of opinion and time are related closely to the position Necker took in his famous *Compte rendu au Roi* (1781).

In Faccarello's approach to French political economy, economic theory is never isolated from other social sciences and philosophy, theology included. The following two chapters deal with these domains. Pierre Force considers Say's *Petit volume contenant quelques aperçus de l'homme et de la société*, published in 1817, written in a style reminiscent of seventeenth-century French moralists such as La Rochefoucauld and La Bruyère. The book was a literary enterprise without any clear connection to Say's famous *Traité d'économie politique*. However, these considerations of human nature were directly related to his economic views. Force shows that this is particularly clear in the discussion of the difference between self-interest and vanity, a normative disambiguation of the broader concept of *amour propre*, which Say borrowed from seventeenth-century Augustinian thinkers. Ludovic Frobert then examines Pierre-Simon Ballanche's *Essais de Palingénésie sociale*. This book had a huge influence on the first generation of French Socialists and especially on the Saint-Simonians. At the crossroads of religion and economics, Ballanche offered the outlines of a general knowledge of social laws, a science and philosophy of "collective man" – both statically and dynamically – which later served as an inspiration for the more specifically economic reflections of many authors opposed to the liberal/republican insights offered by Say.

By the 1830s, the influence of *Philosophie économique* was fading, its philosophical underpinnings being challenged by socialist thinkers, while its theoretical basis was also under fire. Alain Béraud's chapter shows how Pellegrino Rossi, who succeeded Say as professor in the Collège de France, was not a respectful disciple of his predecessor. Instead, he was rather more influenced by the works of English economists, notably David Ricardo. While Say criticised Ricardo for arguing in terms of abstract principles, Rossi argued that to make political economy a useful science, it was necessary to develop pure theory. Endorsing the Ricardian idea that the determining cause of value is the cost of production, Rossi presented to his French audience the notion of intensive rent, faithfully expounding the doctrines of the English classical school in a country where they were little understood and even less appreciated.

Finally, Jean-Pierre Potier considers Charles Gide's interpretation of marginalism in *Histoire des doctrines économiques depuis les physiocrates jusqu'à nos jours*, a major handbook on the history of economic thought in France until the 1950s. According to Gide, marginalism is composed of two closely related tendencies: the "Mathematical school" and the "Psychological school." Interestingly enough, Gide's views were reviewed and criticised by Léon Walras and Vilfredo Pareto, so the chapter offers an interesting reflection upon theoreticians reacting to the historical interpretation of their works.

Part 3 deals with the European and global dimensions of Gilbert's work. His long-standing interest in topics on the history of the French political economy and in the development of economic thought in France has been combined with an interest in addressing French issues in a comparative way, joining *European and global economic conversations*. The title of Part 3 of this volume reflects this concern with dialogue carried on among political economists from different countries. The chapters included in this section provide innovative contributions to topics relevant to a better understanding of GilbertFaccarello's 's comprehensive research agenda.

The first chapter by Cosimo Perrota discusses individualism, a key category of modern culture shaped in the seventeenth century. Among Protestants, individualism was an instrument to be used against the Catholic hierarchy, which presented itself as the intermediary between God and man. In mercantilist literature, the individualism of entrepreneurship was balanced by collective national development projects. For freethinkers, individualism was the way to a materialist foundation of social relationships and to a new ethics of comfort and enrichment. This new attitude was synthesised in Mandeville's aphorism: "private vices, public benefits." Finally, turning to a topic to which Gilbert has contributed several works, Cosimo Perrota discusses the complex itinerary of the Jansenist who started out preaching a severe life of renunciation (Pascal, Arnauld) but who ended up interpreting social relationships as based on tempered self-love and reciprocal respect. It was Pierre Nicole who refounded the idea of modern society in this way, seeking also to learn from non-religious cultures.

Thierry Demals focuses on the reception of David Hume's *Political Discourses* (1752) in France, particularly through Gournay's network. After providing an overview of the first (quite laudatory) reviews of the book published in French journals, this chapter presents and explores the French translation of Hume's treatise by Le Blanc (1754) who also offers a comparative assessment of the relative merits of Hume's and Melon's essays. Apart from a broad consensus on the benefits of trade and luxury, Le Blanc revealed a disagreement on three topics – paper money, public credit and slavery – on which he took the side of Hume against Melon. Demals also examines the reaction of Forbonnais who initially (1754) shared Hume's view on trade and luxury but who later (1755) positioned himself alongside Melon and criticised Hume's concerns related to the excess of paper money as well as Hume's construction of the price-specie-flow mechanism.

The next contribution in this section is by José Luís Cardoso, bringing attention to Genovesi and to the role of the concept of *economia civile* in the shaping of the Enlightenment discourse on political economy. Genovesi represented the typical conviction of an eclectic, yet enlightened, political economist who believed that economy and society could be improved and that material life would be ameliorated if changes were made to the arrangement of institutions. These ideas were also embedded in the texts of many other enlightened authors who wrote on economic and policy issues throughout the eighteenth century. The chapter draws attention to the relevance of both the translation of Genovesi's texts and the texts that he himself translated, thus stressing one of the most interesting features of the Enlightenment as an intellectual movement cutting across national borders and encountering different languages.

Keith Tribe's chapter offers a fine combination of intellectual history and economic analysis, very close to Gilbert's essays on the political economy of the period under study. The analysis of Say's footnotes to the French translation of the first edition of Ricardo's *Principles of Political Economy* (1817) shows that Say raises objections to Ricardo's exposition of the labour theory of value. As Marx read Ricardo's *Principles* in the second French edition of this translation, Tribe argues that we can consider the degree to which Marx's reading of Ricardo might have been influenced by Say. Moreover, the standard edition of Ricardo is now a version that has been editorially constructed to support an argument regarding Ricardo's refinements of his own ideas. Therefore, by looking at Say's footnotes, we gain a fresh perspective on what Ricardo first wrote and to what precisely Say objected.

Harald Hagemann's chapter focuses on the history of German editions of Adam Smith's *Wealth of Nations*. It discusses the different qualities of the translations and their resonance in German economic discourse, highlighting how contemporary politics and the zeitgeist have influenced the reception of Smith's economic doctrines by German authors. The universities of Göttingen and Königsberg emerge as the main entrance gates for both Smithian ideas and the Scottish Enlightenment, both of which also had a certain impact on the Stein-Hardenberg reforms after Prussia's defeat by Napoleon. The contemporary appropriation of Smith's work is also an issue addressed by Hagemann in this chapter, showing how the bicentennial of the *Wealth of Nations* in 1976 was employed as an occasion that served differing motivations for two new, distinct translations in a Germany then divided between East and West.

The chapter by Masashi Izumo reviews the significant role and impact of John Ruskin, a leading Victorian thinker, in early twentieth-century Japan, especially for those involved in promoting ideas and movements sympathetic to anti-industrialisation and anti-capitalism. The chapter shows that the critical viewpoints of Ruskin and William Morris on modern industrial societies became an intellectual resource for Japanese contemporary criticism. Some intellectuals attempted to apply Ruskin's ideas in their own ways in Japan. Although mostly unsuccessful, their experience of failures and defeats offers a key to an understanding of serious problems that modern Japan, which is at a turning point again, still faces today.

The closing chapter of this section is by Marco Guidi, raising some basic methodological issues that arise from the translation of economic texts, considering these as an aspect of the international circulation of economic ideas. He argues that the translation of economic works is the product of individuals and intellectual circles who play key roles in institutions, economic activities and politics. This discussion differs from the foregoing chapters but offers a common rationale for the processes of diffusion and appropriation of economic ideas, theories and policies that shape global economic conversations.

Part 4 documents vividly Gilbert's interest in the history of economic analysis, to use Schumpeter's concept, that is, the development of economic theory or analytical economics. Whilst some historians of economic thought stay away from mathematics and model building, Gilbert always insisted that the formalisation of ideas and economic relationships is an essential part of our field that must not be neglected. As the history of economics shows, mathematics can be put to very productive use, but there is also the danger of what Paul Romer recently called 'mathiness' – the misuse of mathematics in economics, masquerading academic politics as science.

In his chapter, Richard Sturn confronts two approaches to public economics: Richard Abel Musgrave's functional approach, which distinguishes between an allocation, a distribution and a stabilisation function, and Arthur Cecil Pigou's much more conventional approach, which is made in terms of the distinction between public revenues and expenditures. These differences, Sturn argues, affect the way in which specific issues are tackled by the two authors. A principal concern is with the treatment of merit wants in Musgrave and a comparison with Pigou's distinction between desires and their satisfaction. Both authors see reason to question the widespread idea that consumer sovereignty is universally applicable.

In her chapter, Manuela Mosca turns to Antonio De Viti de Marco's lecture notes on public finance, which the author continually reworked and updated between 1886 and 1928. Mosca makes good use of the notes taken in dictation or in shorthand by De Viti's students. The emphasis here is on his discussion of competition and the role it played in his advocacy of free trade. While competition played an important role in the early lecture notes, by the beginning of the 1920s, it disappears, whereas it here begins to play an important role in De Viti's theory of democracy. Mosca considers that this might be seen as "the courageous assertion of an irreducible liberal" who was strictly opposed to fascism.

Jérôme de Boyer des Roches, in his chapter, deals with the American economists Edwin Walter Kemmerer and Irving Fisher who, in debates at the beginning of the twentieth century, argued against the Germans Karl

Helfferich and Georg Friedrich Knapp and the Swede Knut Wicksell that the "law of supply and demand" can be extended to money and determine the general price level. Much of the debate turned on the question of whether the number of equations is equal to, or falls short of, the number of variables whose values are to be ascertained. The author argues that Kemmerer confused the money price level and the accounting price level and that Fisher, who adopted Kemmerer's theory, proposed two equations to determine one price.

In the following chapter, Rebeca Gomez Betancourt deals with Kemmerer's role as the "money doctor" who gave advice to more than fifteen mostly Latin American countries on monetary institutions and policies during the first three decades of the twentieth century. Kemmerer advocated a metallic standard system, in particular a Gold Exchange Standard. He distinguished between three types of gold standards. The Gold Exchange Standard knows neither free coinage of gold nor domestic gold coin circulation; its main purpose is to ensure the stability of the exchange rate. The stabilisation fund that Kemmerer proposed was an exchange rate stabilisation fund but no currency board. Alas, while his recommendations at first fell on fertile ground, they were later abandoned.

Michaël Assous, in his chapter, provides a summary account of important aspects of Michal Kalecki's political economy. Assous first deals with Kalecki's early vision, influenced by discussions amongst Polish socialists in which he participated. These conversations focus attention on the "irrationality" of capitalism, mass unemployment and recurrent crises. Kalecki then argued that cycles occur because of the two-pronged nature of investment: It increases aggregate demand, which stimulates the economy, but then it increases productive capacity, which depresses it. Assous then turns to Kalecki's analysis of class struggle, which is seen to determine the markup on variable cost in the economy and the share of profits as well as his concept of the political business cycle.

In the following chapter, Maria Cristina Marcuzzo has a closer look at how John Maynard Keynes, at different stages in his intellectual development, viewed expenditures on consumption goods on the one hand and money-making as an end in itself on the other. While at first, the two activities were treated separately, as his work matured, they became two sides of a single coin. The latter was seen as preventing a sufficiently high level of aggregate effective demand and correspondingly, a high level of employment. Hence, the main problem Keynes faced in his economic policy recommendations was finding a way to somehow neutralise the negative impact of people's "love of money" on economic activity. This was a precondition for developed economies benefitting from high degrees of utilisation of their productive capacity.

Daniel Diatkine deals, in his chapter, with Smith's analysis of foreign trade and asks what is the difference between domestic and foreign trade. According to his reading of Smith, foreign trade is not international trade because in Smith, one does not encounter the concept of "nation," despite the title of the Scotsman's magnum opus. Diatkine contends that, while in Ricardo's *Principles*, the nation is the basic economic unit, this is not the case in Smith. Smith instead sees the "city" as the basic economic unit, and in his conceptualisation, foreign trade should therefore be taken to concern trade amongst cities. In accordance with this interpretation, Smith's argument about the non-equalisation of the profit rate is said to refer to different cities and not to nations.

Jacques Thisse then deals with some important issues in spatial economics. He shows that the assumption of competitive conditions employed in the Arrow-Debreu model of general equilibrium cannot be sustained if space is taken seriously. Starting from the work of David Starrett, he shows with a well-chosen and simple example that competitive conditions are inadequate for economic geography. He then expounds the "spatial impossibility theorem," which states that no competitive equilibrium involving trade exists when transporting goods across space is costly and in which space is taken to be homogeneous. He concludes by exploring the role of spatial non-homogeneities, both exogenous and endogenous, and argues that they may help to restore competitive conditions.

Finally, readers of this book will note that some "big names" often appear alongside "smaller" ones. Gilbert Faccarello has shown himself eager to act along the same lines, studying Karl Marx and Alexandre Vandermonde, John Maynard Keynes and Graslin, Piero Sraffa and Charles de Coux with the same level of scrutiny. We would like to stress the value of this approach and engage historians of economic thought in associating the study of the great masters with "the pursuit of the rarest birds," to quote the subtitle of Gilbert's interview published in the *Erasmus Journal of Philosophy and Economics*.[2]

Notes

1 Gilbert is highly knowledgeable about Asian philosophy, art and music and is a veritable collector of Buddhist art; he has a considerable collection of statues and figurines.

2 "In the pursuit of the rarest birds. An interview with Gilbert Faccarello," *Erasmus Journal of Philosophy and Economics*, 2014, 7(1), pp. 86–108.

2 Gilbert, the man with his head above the clouds

Personal reminiscences

Heinz D. Kurz

It was in Paris in early 1991 on the occasion of a workshop at the Université de Paris X-Nanterre to which Christian Bidard had invited me that I met Gilbert Faccarello for the first time. He wanted to see me after the workshop on the wonderfully located premises of the École Normale Superieure in St. Cloud, east of Paris, above the river Seine. It was a sunny day, and I was sitting on a bench outside the dormitory in which I stayed and from whose dining hall one had a marvellous view of the city. Gilbert came and informed about the plans to found a European journal devoted to the history of economic thought. He told me that there were plans to transform an existing Italian journal into a European one, which would be published in English or in some of Europe's most widely spoken languages: English, Spanish, French, German and Italian. He also told me which scholars were already involved in planning the project: Professors José Luís Cardoso of Lisbon and Antoin Murphy of Dublin were a part of the enterprise along with a number of Italian colleagues. Gilbert invited me to join the project.

I was taken by surprise, but because I thought that the basic idea was sound and that European traditions in economic analysis deserved to get a better hearing, I gratefully accepted the invitation. We then discussed some of the proposals that had been put forward in previous discussions with the other scholars involved. Would it be a good idea to stay with the publisher of the Italian journal, which, I was told, was an option and had been suggested by the Italian colleagues? Gilbert and I agreed quickly that an entirely new start was needed. Because the Italian publisher seemed to have had little international experience and lacked visibility outside Italy, it would perhaps be preferable, we felt, to approach a publishing house with an international reputation. In case such a publisher was to be found that was interested in the project, would the publisher also be willing to give the journal a truly European touch by publishing articles in several European languages? While I thought that a polyglot journal could, in principle, be a good thing, I was very sceptical that this was feasible. I knew that the Swiss journal *Kyklos* had difficulties in sticking to its multilanguage concept and actually dispensed with it. The fact that English had become the *lingua franca* in economics and that especially young scholars were keen to publish in that language and reach an international audience did not exactly speak in favour of a polyglot journal. We discussed the pros and cons of each solution but were clear that the issue could not be settled without the publisher's consent. Which international publisher to approach? We exchanged our experiences with regard to those each of us had dealt with in the past.

The next theme we touched upon was whom to invite to serve on the editorial and the advisory board of the new journal. Gilbert informed me that if the new journal would replace the Italian one, the Italian colleagues involved in the initiative thought that the people on the latter's board should be invited to become members on the board of the new journal. I objected, saying that in this case, hardly anyone else could be co-opted from other European countries, and if the orientation of the new journal would differ markedly from that of the old one, would it not be naive to presume that the members of the old board would be happy with the reorientation? Would they rather not insist on having a word to say on the new journal's orientation? And would this not lead to potentially disturbing convulsions? Gilbert fully agreed and stressed that this was a further reason in support of making a fresh start not constrained by past obligations. A truly European initiative, we felt, requested the involvement of scholars coming from several European countries. However, we were also convinced that it would be good to secure the support of major scholars from non-European countries for the project. We wanted the journal to become a leading outlet in the field, and this required the best brains available. We also discussed the names of a few scholars that ought to be approached when the time had come to do so. But first, there had to be a meeting with the other people involved in the project to sort out whether an agreement could be reached regarding the pending issues.

When I left Paris, I did so with the pleasant feeling of having made a new friend who was a dedicated scholar and a highly talented intellectual entrepreneur. Gilbert, I thought, was a man with his head above the clouds, seeing clearly what the problems and options were with regard to the project under consideration. Our cooperation thereafter fully confirmed this impression.

Antoin, Gilbert, José Luís, three Italian colleagues and I met in Lisbon in September 1991 to discuss in detail the initiative on behalf of the foundation of *The European Journal of the History of Economic Thought*. We had long and occasionally heated debates with two of our Italian colleagues. It turned out that the legacy of the past weighed too heavily on the project and limited our degrees of freedom in conceptualising the new journal as best as we could. Antoin, Gilbert, José Luís and I, supported by one of the Italian colleagues, quickly agreed that the new journal needed a new publisher and a freshly chosen editorial and advisory board. In our view, a halfway house between the Italian journal and the new one was not an attractive option. Antoin brought up the name of Alan Jarvis, whom he knew well, and named Routledge as a potential publisher. Although there was no formal final decision at the end of the Lisbon meeting, it was clear that there could be no agreement on the merging of two distinct editorial projects. A few months later, the Italian colleagues decided to pursue their own plans by transforming the old journal into a new one, staying with the Italian publisher.

Having reached clarity in this regard, the remaining 'gang of four' was able to continue to work on the project. Two crucial events are worth reporting. After the Lisbon meeting, Antoin contacted Alan Jarvis. Three of us had a meeting with Alan in London in March 1992. Alan showed a vivid interest in the proposal but was not unexpectedly opposed to the idea of a journal publishing papers in English, Spanish, French, Italian and German (or a subset of these languages). The journal had to be in English with important passages coming from other languages translated into English in the main text and perhaps given in the original tongue in endnotes. We reached an agreement with Alan and Routledge. The publisher then sent a contract, which the four of us signed in our capacity as the four managing editors of *The European Journal of the History of Economic Thought*. Routledge was keen to start the project soon with two issues per year and the option of increasing the number of issues later. It was decided that 1993 would be the year when the new journal should be launched.

The second event took place at a meeting in Paris on April 21, 1992 in which we decided on all the important organisational matters. When rereading the minutes of the meeting in the course of preparing this note, I was stunned by the perfectionist spirit it breathes. In one passage, it is stated, 'The need to minimise transport and accommodation costs dictates [!] that Paris be used as the centre for such meetings'. 'Not a bad dictate at all', I thought! As regards the location of the headquarters, there was the idea of having them in Paris at the Centre Alexandre Vandermonde of Gilbert's university, the Université Panthéon-Assass, provided that sufficient financial and other forms of support were made available by the university. The alternative was a research centre of the Institute of Economics at the Technical University of Lisbon (CISEP), in which case the headquarters would be transferred to José Luís. The Lisbon option turned out to be feasible, and so we decided, with Gilbert's and José Luís's explicit consent, in favour of Lisbon.

José Luís did a magnificent job over a period of twenty years until 2013 when he stepped down from the position of managing managing editor, a title he rightly deserved. He ran the journal in an efficient and smooth way and contributed massively to its success. The cooperation with him was always extremely pleasant and effective. In the same year, the other managing managing editors also stepped down and handed the journal over to Muriel Dalpont, Richard Sturn and Hans-Michael Trautwein with the journal's headquarters moving to Graz, Austria.

We were surprised by how easy recruiting members for the journal's board was and how even very prominent economists kindly accepted our invitations and wished to be involved as advisers, authors, referees and reviewers of books. The first double issue of the journal was published in the autumn of 1993. It was dedicated to the problem of how to affect the transition from a centrally planned economy to an economy in which markets play an important role. This problem was high on the agenda of former 'socialist' countries in Eastern Europe and elsewhere, and the challenge was to show what can be learned from the history of economic thought in this regard. After all, problems of the transition from forms of economic and political centralisation to forms of decentralisation have been a major concern of economists and economic philosophers ever since the inception of systematic economic analysis.

I was glad to be a part of this group of fine scholars with whom I quickly became friends. The collaboration with them over the years was extremely easy, fruitful and pleasant. This does not mean that we never had differences of opinion or conflicts. We did, but we always succeeded in resolving them quickly in a mutually respectful way.

The project, I dare say, became a success, and the cooperation with Gilbert, José Luís and Antoin intensified. Gilbert invited me several times as visiting professor to the Panthéon-Assas University in Paris. I encountered his colleagues and several of his talented PhD and master students at the Maison des Sciences Économiques, Boulevard de L'Hôpital, and we had numerous discussions about a great many themes, going well beyond economics and its history. Gilbert came to Graz and gave lectures to master students in the history of economic analysis, and he gave papers on the occasion of conferences and meetings in the Styrian capital.

Gilbert is knowledgeable and erudite in an astounding number of fields. He is an expert and connoisseur, especially of Asian arts. I admired the superb collection of Buddhist statues and figurines in his apartment, and we exchanged our experiences and impressions travelling to countries in the Far East. We visited numerous exhibitions in the Grand Palais, the Centre Pompidou and the museums with which Paris is so richly endowed. We also shared an interest in jazz music – and good cuisine.

Gilbert and I got involved in another huge project. On the occasion of the conference of the *American Economic Association* in San Francisco in 2009, Edward Elgar approached me, asking whether I could propose to him an interesting book project. Gilbert and I had already tinkered for some time with the idea of bringing out a collection of essays covering large parts of the history of economic analysis. After consultation with Gilbert, we proposed to Edward Elgar in April 2009 that we would contribute to his series of *Handbooks*, writing on the history of economic analysis. We planned a set of three volumes. The first volume was supposed to deal with the lives, contributions and impacts of some of the most important economists in the history of the subject, with the emphasis on 'Western' authors; the second volume with schools of economic thought and the third with the history of some major areas of economic investigation, reflecting the subject's internal division of labour.

When we signed the contract with the publisher, we did not know what difficulties were waiting for us, beginning with the health problems that each of us had at different times; the dropout of some of the more than 140 authors and the need to replace them; the language problems with some of the texts submitted by non-native English speakers; and the enormous amount of time needed to copyedit and streamline the various entries and create some uniformity of style, composition, and so on. The project dragged on for a long time, and there were moments in which I (at least) was close to despair. This had a lot to do with my lack of orderliness. While bearing the title of an 'ordentlicher Universitätsprofessor', which literally translates to 'orderly university professor', I was and am not exactly this. Which version of someone's entry was the most recent one? Who had not yet delivered his work? Had the authors incorporated the changes and corrections that Gilbert and I, along with the referees we had involved in the project and who kindly helped us, had asked for? Did the list of references contain all the important works on the subject matter under consideration? Had the authors added the relevant cross references to other entries? Were the affiliations of the authors correct? These and a myriad of other questions bothered me a great deal. Yet there was Gilbert who repeatedly helped me out of the impasse. In case the three volumes of the *Handbook on the History of Economic Analysis* (2016) should be considered a valuable contribution to the discipline, a large share of the credit belongs to him. His (almost) Prussian virtues (and the absence of any signs of Prussian vices) were of the utmost importance to the eventual accomplishment of the huge task. I am deeply grateful to him.

Having survived this huge challenge, we could not help getting involved in another one, which, although somewhat less demanding, required a lot of our attention, energy and time. Invited by Routledge to act as editors of its online project on the *History of Economic Thought* in the *Routledge Historical Series*, covering the period from 1700 up until 1914. The project provides a treasure trove of useful information that will be of great value to students and researchers in economics and its neighbouring fields, such as sociology, political science, philosophy and history. The subjects covered include the contributions of major economists, of important subjects or fields in economics and of currents or schools of thought. The database made available to readers covers a wide range of books and journals devoted to the history of economic thought, all in one place. It contains many of the primary source texts in electronic form for the first time. This allows students and researchers to explore the history of economic thought first-hand, and it simplifies tracing the location of ideas in the primary texts for research papers. We commissioned freshly written short essays from leading experts who introduce key subject areas. These essays provide crisp summary accounts of the areas under consideration and draw attention to the current frontiers of knowledge. The database offers rich opportunities for interdisciplinary work. The material contained in it transcends narrow economic confines and reaches out to several other disciplines. The cooperation with Gilbert was again smooth and effective. The task is basically accomplished. The project will be put online shortly.

The question therefore cannot possibly be avoided: What will be next? Wishing Gilbert 'ad multos annos' sounds like announcing a lot of work ahead.

Part 2

French traditions in economics

3 Freeing trade or freeing humans? Mably and Condillac on economic policies and the renewal of the French Kingdom[1]

Julie Ferrand and Arnaud Orain

The Bonnot's brothers

Gabriel Bonnot de Mably and Étienne Bonnot de Condillac were brothers, and their lives and careers were intertwined. They were very close in their youth and the elder brother, Mably, was greatly affected by the death of Condillac in 1780 (Galliani 1981, 121). In the 1740s, Mably introduces Condillac in the salons and supports his first work. But then Condillac's ideas – the "sensationism" – became more famous than Mably's, and at the end of his life, the latter states that he was merely "applying the philosophy of (his) brother to the principles of morals and politics" (Mably 1794–1795b, 26). Condillac, for his part, approved the historical conceptions of his brother: He encourages his pupil the prince Ferdinand of Parma to read the books of Mably and publishes Mably's *De l'étude de l'histoire* in his *Cours d'étude pour l'instruction du Prince de Parme* (Galliani 1981, 116).

Condillac stated in his treatises that the feelings of pleasure and pain are the unique principles that must raise man "gradually to all the knowledge of which he is capable" (Condillac 1754, 225a). But these feelings are also the forces that drive him: When he feels a pain, the sensationist individual seeks to remember (thanks to his memory and imagination) an idea – i.e. the idea of an object, of a feeling – that gave him pleasure previously in order to fulfil the need and delete the sensation of pain. Thanks to repeated experiences and to his reason, which Condillac preferred to call "judgment" or "reflection", this individual learns to choose, i.e. "instead of looking for the object that offers the most lively pleasure, he observes the one where there is the most pleasure with the least pain" (Condillac 1754, 316a). In this respect, the child, the isolated man, the savage, etc. act to satisfy their needs and, we could even say, their self-interests.

Mably was completely in agreement with such principles. He felt "a lot of pleasure" (Mably 1783, 268–9) in reading his brother's *Traité des sensations* (1754), in which these ideas concerning knowledge and self-interest are developed. Mably was clearly opposed to innate ideas (Mably 1794–1795b, 23), and so he also put forward that "our soul is condemned to see through our senses" (Ibid, 24). Thanks to memory (Mably 1783, 230), humans remember their former pleasures and pains, seeking the former and trying to avoid the latter (Ibid, 107–8). Thereafter, a lot of time is needed for "reason" or "judgment" to resist "the charm of pleasure" and "to learn to distrust their senses, which do not present them with objects as there really are" (Mably 1794–1795b, 26). But at the end of the process, as in Condillac's theory, the child, young people or isolated men are able to judge the best way to satisfy their needs in accordance with their self-interest.

Concerning humans living in societies, both brothers followed the same line of reasoning at first. In the State of nature, Condillac argues that "the obstacles they [men] had to face in order to insure their self-preservation were such that they had no choice but to unite" (Condillac 1775, 16a), and Mably argues that "I will defend your happiness if you defend mine. This is the treaty of perpetual alliance made necessary by nature, as she wants to reunite people in a society" (Mably 1763, 280). In this respect, it is in the interests of all men to cooperate and to create Society. There is here a "utilitarian association". But then Condillac creates a kind of "moral calculation" in order to maintain it: When we help or create pleasure for our fellow men or act for the Public Weal, we feel "moral pleasures", thanks to a sort of "sympathy" and thanks to the rewards of the State and of public opinion (see Orain 2011). Now, because these moral pleasures are infinitely more powerful than the physical ones, it is rational for our self-interest to act in a virtuous way: "*Our enlightened self-interest* [*Notre intérêt bien entendu*] leads us to correct our bad habits, and to maintain and even strengthen the good ones, and to acquire better ones still" (Condillac 1775, 375a). Mably also believed in "Pity" in our hearts. He even claimed that a sort of calculation, deriving from the rewards and punishments of the State, could produce collective happiness:

> it is truly a law of politics which benefits with skill from our needs (...) our passions and our tastes, to teach the love we have for ourselves, which learns through the wise distribution of rewards and punishments that it is useful to moderate oneself (...) to respect the self-esteem of others in order to make it the instrument of our own happiness.
>
> (Mably 1794–1795b, 30)

But Mably was less concerned with the logic of self-interest than his brother, stating that "if a man seeks happiness in a measured way (...) he can scarcely only seek private happiness, but must draw on the happiness of the Public Weal" (Ibid, 19). As a matter of fact, while Condillac believed in individual welfare, due to consumption and a moderate enrichment compatible with Public Weal, Mably was more critical of such an approach.

However, both brothers agreed that in their century, the judgement was less and less capable of leading individuals to act in accordance with the well-being of their fellow citizens. Mably claimed that in such "frivolous" times – where all are greedy for money, where the government and the dominant classes give bad examples – "the insatiable needs for our luxury and our idleness unceasingly tyrannise the unfortunate who are condemned to working the land" (Mably 1776, 32). The passions of the rich and their disordered imagination led society to decline. While Condillac accepted small inequalities, he also believed that the rich – especially the landowning class – had created new "frivolous needs" (Condillac 1776, 354b). Such needs for luxury would contribute to the ruin of good customs in society and destroy its economic bases. Society is starting to consume useless goods, the orientation of consumption "changes land use; and one can see that necessary goods for man's subsistence diminish in proportion as others increase" (Ibid, 303b). Was such a decline avoidable?

Different economic policies?

Both brothers had learnt political economy from the works of Cantillon (1755) and those of the Gournay circle (Orain 2004; Ferrand and Orain 2017). For Condillac, following Abeille (1768) (see Orain 2006), the policies against free trade were the main causes of disorders. What was true in every sector of production was particularly damaging concerning craft guilds and the grain trade. By concentrating supply in a few workshops devoted to luxury items, the guilds made the larger-scale manufacture of necessary goods harder. Prices were high, and unemployment was substantial. The problems of the grain trade were even worse. In complete accordance with the arguments for free trade, Condillac reasoned that with prohibitions on grain trade (especially export bans), prices would be very volatile: The system produced incorrect perceptions. On the one hand, landowners and farmers grew rich when grain was in short supply, selling it at high prices. As a consequence, there was no incentive to better the land and to increase production. Lastly, merchants benefited from erroneous legislation: As they knew that grain could not arrive from foreign countries (or could only arrive very rarely), they could hoard grain, wait for price rises and then sell stocks when prices were at a maximum. Merchants created what he called the "scarcity of opinions". These occur either when grain stocks remain unnoticed even though they do actually exist or when dishonest speculation abounds.

For Condillac, all these outcomes disappeared once free trade was allowed. The concept of a "true price" (*vrai prix*) was central in his arguments: Free trade would set every commodity at its "true price", i.e. a non-volatile but stable equilibrium price capable of reconciling sellers and buyers. The reasoning was well known: With the arbitration of the merchants who bought grain in the provinces or countries where they were plentiful harvests and sold it where harvests were poor, prices would increase in the former and decrease in the latter in order for these prices to be almost the same.

For Condillac, the advantages of such pricing in the grain market were enumerable. Stable sales prices would entail stable wages and in this respect, stable labour costs. Under these conditions, farmers would make profits every year, even more so during the good harvests. Thus, both landowners and farmers will have an incentive to better the land and to increase production due to the fact that rents and profits will rise automatically. It will also keep them from travelling to the cities to indulge in their vices, luxuries and social competitions. Instead of conspicuous spending, landowners will be forced to redirect their income towards the creation of better production conditions. This will benefit the wider population, which will be able to find employment (Condillac 1776, 326a). Finally, when liberalisation occurred, merchants would no longer be in a position to create scarcity: It would be impossible to grow rich through hoarding. It was by useful work (arbitrage) that they earned their livings.

But Condillac did not believe that this would suffice for societies to enjoy a state of well-being. Luxury, even limited luxury, would not be eradicated and would always be potentially ruinous for the countryside. For Condillac, political economy was a necessary but insufficient condition for establishing a happy society.

Mably too gave priority to examining and reforming the grain trade but not in the same terms as his brother (Ferrand 2013; Ferrand and Orain 2017). From the first edition (1746) of his *Droit public* to the latest (1764), even up to *Du commerce des grains* (1775), including *Principes des négociations* (1757), Mably defended the same policy: promotion of the "domestic commerce". He condemned a "bad" luxury for economic reasons mainly: It prevented the rise of real wealth. A populationist, Mably was always concerned by the cheap price of foodstuffs and manufactured goods. However, he was fully aware of the damage caused by the non-consumption and non-value of grain on agriculture – hence his continuous and unfaltering defence of free domestic trade and his constant opposition to prohibitions, monopolies and privileged companies (Mably 1764, II: 235–6). Throughout his life, he was also cautious of foreign trade: From 1746 onward, he was a clear opponent of bullionism, judging the European enterprises in the East to be vain and useless. As for trade on the Continent, he proposed to revoke the freedom of trade that the Dutch enjoyed in French ports.

According to him, the free exports of grain led to an even worse situation of inequality if there is only a small group of landowners in a kingdom. The starting point for Mably was that the first and main result of liberalising the grain trade was not a more stable, average price. Instead, free trade led uniquely to strong price rises for grain. Mably's judgement on such a policy was clear: "You want to enrich the landowners ruining everyone, nothing is more ridiculous" (Mably 1775, 258). Basing his ideas on the experience of the 1760s and the works of Ferdinando Galiani (1770) and Simon Linguet (1771), Mably argued that the wage earners and the small *rentiers* were the first losers in such a policy. This was because if the grain price increased, it would be false to argue that wages and rent would follow, especially in the first years. The standard of living of the working class in particular would decrease, and the *manouvriers* would end in misery. But Mably assumes that the landowners and farmers would be "touched by the tears of the unfortunate" (Mably 1775, 277) and consent to raise the wages of day labourers and other agricultural workers in order to maintain their purchasing power. In such a case, gross earnings rise with prices, but costs rise too and in the same proportions so that there is no effect on net product (Ibid). This is a zero-sum game.

The increase in production costs has necessarily to be passed on in the price of manufactured goods. Thus, marketable goods are more expensive than in any other country, and foreigners will not buy them from France because "clearly the people, whose wages and whose working days are less significant may provide these goods with a better market and those buyers will prefer them to all other traders" (Mably 1775, 279). This point of view was reinforced by much praise for Colbert's policy. As a matter of fact, while the latter "favoured useless arts and luxury manufacture too much", the minister understood that "trade should only take place in superfluous products, and not in staple goods" (Ibid, 282–3).

Mably also mobilised an argument by Cantillon, though he did not apply it to monetary issues in general, adapting it instead to the grain trade. It was well known that Cantillon had suggested that an excess in the balance of trade would lead to a large quantity of money in circulation in a Nation, and then prices would increase, and such a nation would become less competitive, and finally, manufactures would be ruined. A surplus in the balance of trade would inevitably lead to damage and devastation. Now according to Mably, the foreign trade of grain brought an additional quantity of money into the kingdom, thus leading to inflation. So, foreign liberalisation would lead to a rise in the exports of grain but at the same time, cause a fall in the exports of manufactured goods, following the rise of labour costs (Mably 1775, 289). Everything does not belong to the landowners in the State, society is not made for them only, so they do not have to urge the legislators to "sacrifice to [their] cupidity this countless multitude that have only its arms and its industry to subsist" (Ibid, 275). However, Mably is very subtle on the grain trade question:

> But I beg you, my dear Eudoxe, to pay close attention to one thing, which is that I would subject the grain trade to less strict rules in a country where there were many more landowners than in ours, and which was not inhabited almost generally by men who live only from their work.
> (Ibid, 273)

This point is crucial. Free exports of grain (Mably is favourable to free domestic grain trade) ratifies and even reinforces inequalities that arose before it. But it is not the liberalisation of grains in itself that is harmful but the fact that this enriches a small number of citizens (Ibid, 274). The institution of free export could even be a solution to the reduction of inequalities as Mably thought at first but only on the condition that the majority of inhabitants be landed labourers. Mably's economic policy does not imply freedom of trade, but neither does it exclude it in principle. As his brother Condillac, Mably would promote a healthy domestic commerce, that is to say, an improvement upon agriculture and the useful arts for the people of the countryside, a policy for a simple life.

Similar politics for the renewal of the kingdom of France

Now, where did luxury and what both brothers called "useless needs" *really* come from? What caused idleness and faulty judgement?

For Condillac, landowners lack necessary contact with "real objects", i.e. the realities of labour and also of nature (Condillac 1780, 399a). Here, the operation of the understanding that Condillac calls "imagination" (it is actually an uncontrolled memory) is too strong. What happens when there is too much imagination in a man's mind? This man no longer pushes aside ideas that have nothing to do with the need he tries to satisfy. His ideas are too easily linked, and in this case, he undergoes a change in his thinking process, he wishes for fancies or uses inappropriate means to achieve his purposes. Landowners have become denatured and, in a sense, mad because frivolity has become the rule. Condillac is perfectly clear on this point by stating that "the taste of luxury is in fact only a fault of imagination" (Condillac 1775, 112b).

Mably made exactly the same statement. Speaking about the rich, their idleness and their pleasures, the philosopher stated that

> To awaken feelings of pleasure in this state, unnecessary needs have to be created; boredom prevails and our imagination comes to our rescue: we fall into the worst excesses as more and more has to be done to rekindle sensations that have little to do with natural needs.
>
> (Mably 1794–1795c, 401)

There is here a kind of madness in human behaviour: "By what strange folly do we seek study and refine our needs, if inequality in wealth does not accustom us to view such ridiculous delicacy as evidence of superiority, and so has not led to a kind of consideration" (Mably 1776, 37).

Being far from work, pain and necessity, the rich create new needs in societies, and these needs give birth to luxury and then birth to all the troubles of societies: ambition, conspicuous consumption, envy, avidity for wealth, etc. Actually, the eschatology of both brothers is quite the same: They want to encourage agriculture and the "useful arts" against luxury, and they believe in the virtues of frugality (Condillac 1775, 108 ff.; Mably 1776, 10–11). Condillac transposed such an ideal of frugality into his framework of the simple life (*vie simple*): "the arts must make some progress to draw us from a coarse life; and they must halt after some progress, to prevent our falling into a soft existence" (Condillac 1776, 306a).

How could healthy judgement be restored that would lead individuals towards useful and necessary needs and not useless ones? How could the virtues be restored? Both the answers lay in education.

The educational plan of Condillac is twofold: It aims at reforming both education in general and the education of the sovereign in particular. Its purpose is to establish a new model of virtue for society as a whole, to make individuals' behaviour consistent with the model of society he intends to promote (Orain 2006).

Children's education is the basis of this reform. Tutors must first of all know perfectly the origin and the progress of human ideas. Unruly imagination must be counter-balanced by a return to an analytical approach. Analysis consists of "decomposing, comparing and grasping relationships" (Condillac 1775, 769a) between ideas. This is the only way that judgement can be restored. A healthy judgement will be capable of impeding the choice of frivolous goods and of catalysing a drive towards the kind of simplicity that Condillac dreamt of. The idea that it is possible to reach such a goal, i.e. to destroy all the instances of small madness permeating a society, could seem chimerical. However, Condillac was already of the belief that this was achievable when he got involved in the education of the young Prince of Parma (Condillac 1775, 400b). By fighting against the imagination in the spirit of the sovereign, he will be able to choose useful needs, useful arts, and create a simplicity of life, for the well-being of his subjects.

Mably sought to eradicate education that only cultivated memory and imagination (Mably 1767, 7). To the young Marquess who he taught in *Du cours et de la marche des passions dans la société*, Mably wrote,

> Continue to nourish your reasoning and thinking and question the promises of imagination; the multitude is never wise, and that is one of the main causes of the degrading and demeaning society. To govern your small Republic, get used to resisting prestigious imaginations (...) The advice I give you, I would give to all Princes, all magistrates and all ministers.
>
> (Mably 1794–1795c, 409)

But contrary to Condillac, Mably did not believe in the virtue of the so-called analysis of ideas. In his thinking, it was (good) passions that should be set against (bad) passions, which were led by imagination. In this respect, education during childhood had to implement and direct passions.

In the previous quotation, Mably addresses the dominant classes. But again, contrary to his younger brother, he wanted to promote public education of the people. In his thinking, private education led to dissensions in Society: Every class educates its young men with prejudices against the others, and the hierarchy of conditions leads to dissension. There is no common goal, no ideal beyond private interest, everyone is only "occupied with their domestic fortunes" (Mably 1776, 309–10). These public schools should be schools of morals. Thanks to Natural Law and History (especially that of Greece and the Roman Republic), pupils would find their models. In short, all education should strive to inculcate love for the Public Weal and horror for greed and ambition in the hearts of pupils. Creating passions for public virtue was the unique goal of such an education.

We have found the same established observations, the same goals and fairly similar causes in both brothers' ideas concerning the problems of their time. And while their economic policies differed, they both judged these policies to be insufficient and hence both turned to education.

Notes

1 A first version of this paper was presented to the International Conference "French Political Economy in the Age of Enlightenment," Rikkyo University (Tokyo, Japan), 8–9 September 2012.

References

Abeille, L.-P. 1768. *Principes sur la liberté du commerce des grains.* Amsterdam: Desaint.

Cantillon, R. (1997) 1755. *Essai sur la nature du commerce en général.* Paris: INED.

Condillac, E. Bonnot de. 1746. *Essai sur l'origine des connaissances humaines*, in E. B. de Condillac (1948–1951), *Œuvres philosophiques de Condillac*, Paris, PUF, 3 vols, vol. I.

———. 1749. *Traité des systèmes*, in E. B. de Condillac (1948–1951), *Œuvres philosophiques de Condillac*, Paris, PUF, 3 vols, vol. I.

———. 1754. *Traité des sensations*, in E. B. de Condillac (1948–1951), *Œuvres philosophiques de Condillac*, Paris, PUF, 3 vols, vol. I.

———. 1755. *Traité des animaux*, in E. B. de Condillac (1948–1951), *Œuvres philosophiques de Condillac*, Paris, PUF, 3 vols, vol. I.

———. 1775. *Cours d'études pour l'instruction du prince de Parme*, in E. B. de Condillac (1948–1951), *Œuvres philosophiques de Condillac*, Paris, PUF, 3 vols, vol. II.

———. 1776. *Le commerce et le gouvernement considérés relativement l'un à l'autre*, in E. B. de Condillac (1948–1951), *Œuvres philosophiques de Condillac*, Paris, PUF, 3 vols, vol. II.

———. 1780. *Logique ou les premiers développements de l'art de penser*, in E. B. de Condillac (1948–1951) *Œuvres philosophiques de Condillac*, Paris, PUF, 3 vols, vol. II.

Ferrand, J. 2013. Mably and the liberalization of the grain trade: an economically and socially inefficient policy. *The European Journal of the History of Economic Thought*, 20(6): 882–905.

Ferrand, J. and Orain, A. 2017. Abbé de Mably on Commerce, Luxury, and "Classical Republicanism." *Journal of the History of Economic Thought*, Vol. 39, n°2, pp. 199–221.

Galiani, F. (1984) 1770. *Dialogues sur le commerce des blés.* Paris: Fayard.

Galliani, R. 1981. Condillac et Mably. In J. Sgard (dir.), *Corpus Condillac.* Genêve and Paris: Slatkine, pp. 113–122.

Linguet, S.-N.-H. 1771. *Réponses aux Docteurs modernes, ou Apologie pour l'Auteur de la Théorie des loix, et des Lettres sur cette théorie. Avec la réfutation du systêmes des philosophes économistes*. Troisième partie.

Mably, G. Bonnot de. 1757. *Des Principes des négociations pour servir d'introduction au droit public de l'Europe fondé sur les traités*, in G. B. de Mably (1794–1795a), *Œuvres complètes de l'Abbé de Mably*. Lyon: Delamollière, 15 vols, vol. V.

———. 1763. *Entretiens de Phocion sur le rapport de la morale avec la politique*, in G. B. de Mably (1794–1795a), *Œuvres complètes de l'Abbé de Mably*. Lyon: Delamollière, 15 vols, vol. X.

———. 1764. *Le Droit public de l'Europe fondé sur les traitez conclus jusqu'en l'année 1740*, in G. B. de Mably (1794–1795a), *Œuvres complètes de l'Abbé de Mably*. Lyon: Delamollière, 15 vols, vols. V–VII.

———. 1767. *De l'étude de l'histoire à Monseigneur le Prince de Parme*, in G. B. de Mably (1794–1795a), *Œuvres complètes de l'Abbé de Mably*. Lyon: Delamollière, 15 vols, vol. XII.

———. 1775. *Du Commerce des Grains*, in G. B. de Mably (1794–1795a), *Œuvres complètes de l'Abbé de Mably*. Lyon: Delamollière, 15 vols, vol. XIII.

———. 1776. *De la Législation ou principes des loix*, in G. B. de Mably (1794–1795a), *Œuvres complètes de l'Abbé de Mably*. Lyon: Delamollière, 15 vols, vol. IX.

———. 1783. *Des Talens et du Beau*, in G. B. de Mably (1794–1795a), *Œuvres complètes de l'Abbé de Mably*. Lyon: Delamollière, 15 vols, vol. XIV.

———. 1794–1795b. *Du développement des progrès et des bornes de la raison*, in G. B. de Mably (1794–1795a), *Œuvres complètes de l'Abbé de Mably*. Lyon: Delamollière, 15 vols, vol. XV.

———. 1794–1795c. *Du cours et de la marche des passions dans la société*, in G. B. de Mably (1794–1795a), *Œuvres complètes de l'Abbé de Mably*. Lyon: Delamollière, 15 vols, vol. XV.

Orain, A. 2004. *Choix individuels, Morale et Théorie de la valeur dans l'œuvre de l'abbé de Condillac (1714–1780)*, Ph.D. diss., Université Paris 1.

———. 2006. Directing or reforming behaviors? A discussion of Condillac's theory of *vrai prix*. *History of Political Economy*, 38(3): 497–530.

———. 2011. The moral theory of Condillac: a path toward Utilitarianism. *Revue de Philosophie Economique/Review of Economic Philosophy*, 13(2): 93–117.

4 Physiocratic *Philosophie économique*

Philippe Steiner

I would like to stress how much the physiocratic approach to political economy set up a general view of society in which a theory of knowledge, a theory of agency and a theory of the legislator are bound together. This is what Gilbert Faccarello and I have called the "French *Philosophie économique*" (Faccarello and Steiner 2008), going from Pierre de Boisguilbert to Jean-Baptiste Say, through to François Quesnay and Anne-Robert-Jacques Turgot.

This chapter examines Quesnay's writings in order to demonstrate that they contain the first two constitutive elements of *Philosophie économique*: a sensualistic theory of knowledge, an emphasis on interested behavior. Then I put a special emphasis on his conception of the legislator, considering, the connection between "oeconomic government" and, the administration in the case of the reform of the tax system, according to Quesnay and then Gabriel-François Le Trosne.

Quesnay's philosophical underpinnings of *Philosophie économique*

The expression *Philosophie économique* conveys the idea according to which the 18th-century political economy was producing a general view of man, society and politics. The first constitutive part of Quesnay's *Philosophie économique* does not raise difficulties because the founder of the physiocratic movement was a clear advocate of Etienne Bonnot Abbé de Condillac's sensualistic philosophy. The second edition of Quesnay's last medical writing—*Essai sur l'œconomie animale* (1747)—and his article *Évidence* (1756), the first entry he wrote for the *Encyclopédie*, were two important expressions of this sensualistic philosophy. Later on, this philosophy was at the root of his approach to mathematics (Quesnay 1773), notably when he ruled out calculus on the ground that nothing could be based on magnitudes that one cannot experience through sensation.

In his *Essay Concerning Human Understanding*, John Locke opened the way to an empiricist conception of knowledge; his theory of knowledge changed the focus of enquiry because the issue was now in understanding the actual functioning of the human mind. Quesnay (1747) took up this point of view, which was also largely spread by Condillac in several important books published during the 1740s and 1750s. However, Quesnay parted company with Locke, whose theory of ideas he considered confusing and vague. He contented himself with taking a sensualist point of departure while maintaining a large part of Nicolas Malebranche's theory of ideas because he considered this theory a better one once the correct point of departure was taken up. Ten year later, he strongly endorsed the sensualistic view of this theory of knowledge in the entry *Évidence* (Quesnay 2005: p. 88, §25).

Quesnay considered that the mind makes a big divide between humans and animals and between simple freedom or "*liberté animale*" and enlightened freedom or "*liberté d'intelligence*" (Quesnay 1747: III, 278, 350–60; Quesnay 2005: p. 83, §52). Men are not machines, they are not passively driven by sensations (Ibid: p. 279) as far as they follow the evidence provided by the active parts of their minds; accordingly, Quesnay said, reason and freedom are to be considered. Reason is defined as "the human capacity to reach truth in human judgment and to choose the best, thanks to the intellectual faculties of the mind" (Ibid: p. 312), and freedom is defined as "the power to examine in order to determine according to reason whether to act or not" (Ibid: p. 350). Enlightened freedom, or rational action, is the result of the active faculties of the mind in which one examines various motives in order to determine what is the best action to be performed in a given context. What really determines a rational actor is the discovery of the best outcome thanks to his attention, his factual knowledge and his ability to grasp the truth or *évidence*. Quesnay offered an interesting illustration of his point of view when considering a merchant who has to choose between two goods (Ibid: pp. 350–1).

Quesnay thus had a theory of rational economic behavior that was grounded on the working of the enlightened freedom's *calculating* what was the best outcome of a given resource. However, Quesnay considered that men were often driven by their simple freedom or by their common sense. Men did not always scrutinize their basic sensations with the help of their attention to determine what was the best action; in many cases, common sense decisions were not only good but provided the same result as enlightened reason (Quesnay 1747, III: 266–7).

Quesnay's sensualistic approach to human knowledge offers an easy way to ground *Philosophie économique* upon interested behaviors; however, a sensualistic theory of knowledge does not imply that pain and pleasure are made the "sovereign master of mankind" as Jeremy Bentham will put it in the opening sentence of his *Principles of Morals and Legislation*. Quesnay's approach to interested behavior must be qualified by his belief in a "natural order", which includes a "natural economic order", created by God. This form of *Philosophie économique* brings together interested behavior and natural order, a point of the greatest importance when the understanding of physiocratic views of politics and economic policy is at stake. It means first, that human behavior is driven by interest and more particularly by economic interest, and second, it means that people can be governed by their interest. On this ground, Quesnay and the physiocrats have built a powerful view of the functioning of the economy and its management in which the legislator is in charge of putting together the knowledge of the natural order through his command over the economic table and the functioning of the circuit of wealth and the interested behavior of the different classes of the kingdom. The importance given to interested behavior is salient in Quesnay's *Maximes générales du gouvernement économique*, a major text written when he was in full command of his system of œconomic government. The first maxim made the political role given to interest crystal clear (Quesnay 2005: p. 566).

Quesnay emphasized the necessity to ground political power on the general interest that is also the particular interest of the (enlightened) citizens. This meant that the œconomic government should be able to resist the demand of some specific groups—"les intérêts particuliers"—and particularly the commercial interest. Hence, the maxim VIII required that the œconomic government "leaves to themselves the sterile spendings" (Quesnay 2005: p. 568), which meant that this part of economic activity should be submitted to the constraint of competition, the relevant form of constraint for bringing these *costs* to their minimum level.

Quesnay's theory of the legislator

The issue of taxes offers good opportunities for making Quesnay's theory of the legislator clear through the connection of interested behavior, a given economic policy and the theory of the legislator. This is the third constitutive dimension of *Philosophie économique*.

In Quesnay's writings, there are many sentences in which government, administration, nation, State or kingdom are invoked to explain a particular point in his political economy. The term "administration" is less common (about twelve occurrences) but of importance in understanding Quesnay's views regarding the changes needed to relieve the situation in which the kingdom finds itself. Administration is a menial part in the machinery of the government, and, in this sense, it contrasts to government as can be seen here: "The government of the revenues of the nation must not be abandoned to the discretion or to the authority of a subaltern and particular administration" (Quesnay 2005: p. 205). When Quesnay wants to give more weight to the subject, administration is described as "general" administration (Quesnay 2005: p. 259). What are the reasons behind such a lack of confidence in low-level administration? Quesnay fears that poor decisions could be made by civil servants because they are badly prepared to resist particular interests, notably the mercantile interest, which is contrary to the good government of the nation or to œconomic government. The limited importance of low-level administration can also be seen in the way that it is subordinate to and defined by the nature of the government, so if the government becomes despotic, the administration itself is unable to establish order. However, administration may have a positive sense when associated with government, with good government or, to use *the specific term created by Quesnay, with œconomic government.*

There are about fifteen occurrences of this linguistic innovation in the entries written for the *Encyclopédie*; the first one associates œconomic government with the name of Sully and also with the core of the physiocratic theory:

> [...] this great minister had grasped the true principles of œconomic government of the kingdom, establishing the wealth of the king, the strength of the State, the happiness of the people, in the revenue of the land, that is to say in agriculture and the external commerce of its products.
>
> (Quesnay 2005: p. 183)

Œconomic government is devoted to the management of real wealth, the net product generated by the agricultural sector of the economy: "Thus, œconomic government must take care of the growth and the perpetuity of this revenue, all the other advantages that depend upon it will develop and sustain themselves" (Quesnay 2005: p. 244; see as well pp. 220, 256). In the entry on taxes, Quesnay offers a different twist to this statement, pointing out that taxes should not encroach on farmers' capital: "The most important and inviolable rule of œconomic government is thus to make sure that taxes do not endanger the progress of agriculture" (Quesnay 2005: p. 232). In the entry on population, the same idea is maintained, noting what population should be that is necessary for the effective functioning of the agricultural sector:

> The condition of the population and of the employment of men are thus the principal objects of œconomic government in any State, because it is from the work and industry of men that the fertility of the land stems, the monetary value of its production, and the good use of monetary wealth. Here are the four sources of abundance; they each concur in their mutual growth, but they cannot do so without the general administration of men, of goods, of productions.
>
> (Quesnay 2005: p. 259)

This sentence can be read as a definition of political economy, an expression that Quesnay does not use, apart from the subtitle given to the entries written for the *Encyclopédie*. The emphasis on the agricultural sector gives hand to the critique of the mercantile interest or the "mercantile system (*système des commerçants*)" (Quesnay 2005: p. 302), which was always prone to leading the government astray (Quesnay 2005: p. 297).

The link between administration and œconomic government is particularly strong where the reform of the taxation system is at stake. Quesnay's theory of wealth and consequently, his theory of value and price follow from the question of who should pay taxes and how these taxes should be paid. The administrative dimension of the issue is of significance to Quesnay as he stated explicitly when commenting on Jean-Baptiste Naveau's *Financier citoyen*:

> It is not so much the excessive gains of financiers, but the immense sum paid to the lower ranks of the administration, the injustices and trouble in commerce, that prevent the beneficial progress that the author imagines [...] This multitude of clerks busy with levying taxes upon goods is, in itself, a loss of men to the State: all these men paid by the nation do not produce by their work any wealth for the State, thus this expenditure and these men are nothing but a sheer loss to the kingdom.
>
> (Quesnay 2005: p. 230)

However, Quesnay explains that the kingdom can improve if the administration does its proper job (Quesnay 2005: p. 231). In that case, thanks to its contribution to œconomic government, the government belongs to the productive class, as is the case when landowners manage their property well:

> Landowners can be considered as men who produce through management and the improvement of their property; the sovereign himself and his ministers contribute directly and generally to the growth of wealth through the œconomic government of the State. Upon this depends the prosperity of the nation, but it is necessary that the administration does not lose sight of the true source of the revenues of the kingdom.
>
> (Quesnay 2005: p. 305)

Taxes were obviously among the major issues considered by Quesnay in the series of papers that he planned to publish in the *Encyclopédie*. Tax was an issue in the entry "Fermiers", then developed in "Grains" and in "Hommes"; however, the entry "Impôt" was especially devoted to what was a highly controversial topic during the Seven Years' War. The war was hugely expensive, the French monarchy being hampered by its relative lack of access to the international financial market as compared with the British. The domestic political situation was also difficult. In such circumstances, how could physiocratic reform make any headway? The answer to this conundrum is provided by the *Théorie de l'impôt*, a book published in 1760 under Victor Riqueti, marquis de Mirabeau's name only, even though it is clear that Quesnay's ideas were vital to its writings.

At the root of the physiocratic proposal is the concept of net product, that is to say, the difference between the value of agricultural production and its cost. The logical solution to taxation is therefore to levy a single tax directly upon the net product, which amounts to saying that commercial and financial revenues will be ignored by the new fiscal administration. This straightforward solution clarifies matters because objections to inquisitive administrative practices become irrelevant. However, this net product raises a more difficult problem: How is it possible to know not the value produced on a piece of land but the net product obtained on that piece of land without relying on local administration and its politically unacceptable behavior? Mirabeau has an answer to this problem: There is no need to impose upon the people and seek access to the "secrets of the households" to establish the exact amount of the net product; existing leases provide all the information that is needed:

> In a word, a lease is the only reliable basis for the government when assessment of the net product, that is to say the revenue of the country, is at stake. It is only from this revenue that the government can take its share; the total of the leases is the total amount of the revenues of the nation, and it is on this sum that the share of the State can be levied, according to the rule set by necessity; this is the only way to achieve an enlightened agreement between the king and the nation, the necessary basis for good administration in the domain of finance.
>
> (Mirabeau 1761: p. 248)

The market agreement between the landowner and the farmer is the solution because the agreement states explicitly the amount of rent to be paid by the farmer to the landowner. Is this solution a decisive step toward ending the obstruction of administration? Is not Mirabeau naïve in believing that the actual leases will be accessible to fiscal administration?

Mirabeau makes clear to the reader that he is fully aware that leases were already the basis of fiscal administration when the "vingtièmes" and the "dixièmes" were levied. And he knows that the real leases were hidden, with false ones given to the fiscal administration. Hence, there were frauds on the one side and disappointments on the other because the amount of taxes accruing to the government was smaller than expected. Nevertheless, Mirabeau claims that the single tax on the net product, assessed through the leases, offers a solution because it is in the direct interest of farmers' practicing "grande culture" or the capitalist form of husbandry—furthermore, according to the physiocratic theory of the incidence of taxation, it is also in the direct interest of the landowners. These capitalistic farmers, with whom Quesnay dealt in his entry "Fermiers", would not jeopardize their wealth by using counterfeit leases; they would have no interest in cheating because the taxes would be paid by the landowner and not by themselves: "[farmers] would not conceal the agreement, notably because they have no interest in the diminution of a tax which does not concern them in any sense" (Mirabeau 1761: p. 252).

Would the farmers be ready to cheat and then share with the landlord a portion of the taxes due to the government? Mirabeau's answer is negative. Such a strategy of tax avoidance would imply a complex system in which a counterfeit lease would have to be written to diminish the rent paid to landowners and thereby their taxes, and a part of that sum—a third in Mirabeau's example—would be left in the hands of the farmer. In exchange for that, Mirabeau supposes that the concealed part of the lease would be paid in advance to the landowner, so that the latter would be sure to get his full share. Such a system would cost farmers too much capital, and, consequently, Mirabeau claims that the leases used would be the real ones, thus providing an accurate basis for the single tax.

Later on, this issue is considered in great detail in Gabriel-François Le Trosne's *De l'administration provinciale et de la réforme des impôts*. No claim to originality is made for this book; nevertheless, the author offers a synthesis of two different strands of the physiocratic doctrine of taxation, administration and politics (Charles and Steiner 1999).

Following Quesnay and Mirabeau, Le Trosne stresses the very great cost of the present system of taxation because, according to his calculation, indirect taxes cost the nation twice the amount received by the king (Le Trosne 1779: I, pp. 67–8). This cost is a severe obstacle to the growth of the net product and to the strength of the nation. How is it possible to end the deficiencies of administration that have brought this situation about? In line with Quesnay's later views and the views advocated by Le Mercier de la Rivière (1767), Le Trosne mentions the positive role played by public opinion, which is the true legislator in the physiocratic view of politics (Steiner 1998: pp. 96–116). However, one cannot rely on this political force in the case of taxation: First, because public opinion is mainly Parisian, and people with an interest in the vagaries of the present inefficient administration are numerous in that city (Le Trosne 1779: I, p. 128). Second, it will take a long time before men of letters are inducted into the true principles of the administration of taxes, and thus it will take too long before public opinion is able to play its role fully (Le Trosne 1779: I, p. 139). Happily enough, there is a more straightforward solution: "Nobody but an authority enlightened as to its true and well calculated interest can intervene in private interests" (Le Trosne 1779: I, p. 129).

So, in line with the physiocratic theory of legal despotism, Le Trosne's solution is emphatically associated with an enlightened government and thus with an active role given to (economic) experts. However, this example of a top-down system of administration is associated with local administration, which had been strongly advocated by Mirabeau since the beginning of his intellectual career.[1] Thus, Le Trosne (1779: I, p. 177) suggests maintaining local administration in the Pays d'État and to creating an administration of this kind in the Pays d'Élection. The role of this administration would be to distribute the tax burden among the landowners, whatever their social status (nobility, clergy or the third estate). Who will do this?

The landowners themselves, and they will do it for free. Why? Le Trosne reassesses the physiocratic credo, according to which proper administration of the tax system will increase the revenue of the landowners so that their interest is aligned with the proper administration of the tax system. This common interest explains why the landowners would do it for free; a further argument comes from the fact that provincial assemblies will decide how to use a part of the product of the taxes. Finally, Le Trosne also mentions the symbolic remuneration associated with the honor of being elected as a member of the provincial assembly and, potentially, as a delegate to the national council, which is composed of members of provincial assemblies who meet once a year to discuss, with the King or with the Contrôleur général, issues related to fiscal administration (Le Trosne 1779: I, pp. 538–40 and 567–71). Following Quesnay's ideas, this administration would base the tax burden upon the leases agreed between landowners and farmers. These leases would be held by a trustee, or a notary, so that the progress of cultivation and the revenue accruing to the landowner would be known every nine years when the leases were renegotiated. The new structure of fiscal administration would not be costly because landowners would work for free, and the former local administration would simply be suppressed (Le Trosne 1779: I, p. 159). According to his calculations, the total cost will be about six million French livres, which means a massive reduction of the cost of levying taxes, compared to the 167 million that indirect taxes cost.

Le Trosne is adamant in making clear that his administrative system should stay entirely under the command of the central administration or government: Notably, provincial assemblies would not have the power to ratify either taxes or the rate of taxation (Le Trosne 1779: I, pp. 205 and 530). In the same line of thinking, as it is important to proceed to a general and uniform change in fiscal administration, the reform must be made by the government so that members of the provincial assemblies would have nothing to do but implement the reform as designed by the government:

> provincial administrations will be in charge of implementation, no more. It is not enough to send them a general plan; it is necessary to send them all the details, with instructions and examples, in such a way that the planned reform and the way to implement it would be the same everywhere.
>
> (Le Trosne 1779: II, p. 217)

Central expertise in the government therefore remains crucial, even when local administration is recruited to the reformation of the tax system.

Conclusion

The philosophical and political dimensions of Quesnay's writings, together with many writings of the physiocrats, provide all the elements required to sort physiocracy within the domain of *Philosophie économique.*

In following the administrative dimension of Quesnay's approach, it is possible to disentangle Quesnay's theory of the legislator's legal despotism. Thereby, his position within *Philosophie économique* is more strongly ascertained.

Notes

1 See Mirabeau's *Précis de l'organisation ou Mémoire sur l'administration provinciale* and his *Réponse aux objections contre le mémoire sur les états provinciaux*, published as the fourth part of *L'Ami des hommes*. Quesnay was not opposed to a synthesis between the enlightened central administration and provincial administration, as this is plainly stated in the end of the entry "Impôt": "If the administration is placed in difficulty by the detail and the difficulty of proportional taxation, it can avoid this detail and difficulty by asking the provinces to assess taxes in their part of the country: they would do a better job than dedicated administrators, and this task is too important to be badly done" (Quesnay 2005: p. 256). And in the following sentence, Quesnay suggests reading the *Mémoire de l'administration provinciale*.

References

Charles, Loïc and Steiner, Philippe. 1999. Entre Montesquieu et Rousseau: la Physiocratie aux origines de la Révolution française. *Études Jean-Jacques Rousseau*, 11: 83–159.

Faccarello, Gilbert and Steiner, Philippe. 2008. Interest, sensationism and the science of the legislator: French *Philosophie économique* 1695–1830. *The European Journal of the History of Economic Thought*, 15(1): 1–23.

Le Mercier de la Rivière, Pierre-Paul. (2001) 1767. *L'ordre naturel et essentiel des sociétés politiques*. Paris: Fayard.

Le Trosne, Gabriel-François. (1788) 1779. *De l'administration provinciale et la réforme de l'impôt*. Bâle and Paris: Duplain.

Mirabeau, Victor-Riquetti marquis de. 1761. *Théorie de l'impôt*. s.l.

Quesnay, François. 1747. *Essai physique sur l'œconomie animale*. Paris: Cavelier.

———. 1773. *Recherches philosophiques sur l'origine des vérités géométriques*. Amsterdam and Paris: Knaper et Delagnette.

———. 2005. *Œuvres économiques complètes et autres textes*. Paris: Ined.

Steiner, Philippe. 1998. *La "Science nouvelle" de l'économie politique*. Paris: Presses universitaires de France.

5 Opinion, time and institution

Necker's critique of 'new science'[1]

Yusuke Ando

> There is a great defect in the abstractions of political economy: that the effects of opinion and imagination are never taken into consideration; and also that one adopts the same sight of the present and the future. One grasps the kingdom en masse and in a space without time.
>
> (Necker 1784, p. 265)

Introduction

'New science' is a term coined by Du Pont de Nemours in 1768 to designate the political economy of François Quesnay (1694–1774), the leader of the physiocrats. This science was designated as new because it was distinguished from traditional economic discourse in the following ways: (1) the use of calculation and clarity of language in argument and demonstration, (2) a small number of reduced principles linked to one another, and consequently, (3) the abstraction of a higher order (Steiner 1998a, pp. 17–28). As the quotation at the beginning of this chapter shows, it is on this third issue that Jacques Necker (1732–1804) found himself in opposition against the physiocrats.

Necker, a Genevan banker, is often considered a political opponent of the physiocrats because he was involved with the French East India Company whose exclusive privilege they attacked. Moreover, Necker took the post of Director-General of Finances after the downfall of Turgot, who was backed strongly by the disciples of Quesnay.[2] For this reason especially, Necker attempted to make a bid for political power by publishing two works, *Éloge de Jean-Baptiste Colbert* (1773) and *Sur la législation et le commerce des grains* (1775).[3] Notwithstanding politics, both works contain analytical aspects. They explain why the liberalization of the grain trade failed in the 1760s and also prove Necker's coherent discourse in political economy, which differs completely from that of the physiocrats.[4] The key notions that we highlight here, in order to understand his political economy, are opinion, time and institution; institution exists as a result of opinion and time, not of 'evidence' and the 'natural order'. These notions of opinion and time are closely related with the position Necker took in his famous *Compte rendu au Roi* (1781).

This chapter then discusses Necker's concepts of opinion, time and institution, which are at the heart of his political economy.

First, we will start by examining how Necker took into account the effects of opinion and imagination with regard to functioning of market (Section 1). Second, we shall deal with Necker's conception of time as the interval between the present and the future (Section 2). Third, we shall turn to the importance of institution as opinion stabilized over time (Section 3). Finally, in conclusion, we will be able to grasp Necker's coherent discourse in political economy ranging from *Éloge de Jean-Baptiste Colbert* to *Compte rendu au Roi.*

The effects of opinion and imagination

The concept of *bon prix* (good price) is central to the 'new science' of the physiocrats. According to their arguments, *bon prix* refers to a high price that brings about the greatest amount of agricultural production, which should be carried out when internal and external trade is completely free. However, such a price has a limit because international competition would force the price continually toward the average level among trading nations. That is, the price will automatically adjust itself with what the physiocrats call the natural order.[5]

However, Necker considered the possibility that grain prices rise regardless of the actual relationship between quantities sold and the sum of needs. In his account, it is impossible to grasp directly the reality of phenomena that concern the whole society: 'One can never see in a sensible way the chain that links primary causes with their effects' (Necker 1775, p. 62). The ordinary man, in particular, tends to fix his attention solely on that around him.[6] When 'the relationship between quantities and needs is ignored, one cannot help producing an idea about it by conjecture' (Necker 1775, p. 322). Thus, Necker doubted the establishment of the *bon prix* as a high price that is always useful and advantageous to the whole society. He wrote,

> [For the physiocrats,] high price is established only by the effect of relationship inherent in the nature of things, which is impossible to thwart; but this idea does not seem correct … Prices are a compound of reality and imagination … In several circumstances, prices may even be construed as opinions.
>
> (Necker 1775, pp. 322–323)

As the social world is fundamentally different from that of nature, we cannot expect that 'natural laws' function in society as well as in the natural world. Therefore, Necker did not acknowledge that 'prices … are quite similar to degrees of a thermometer in the observations of the physicist' (Necker 1775, p. 62).

Under what circumstances, then, does the disturbance to natural laws of society occur? How are prices influenced by the effects of opinion or imagination? On this issue, Necker provided a concrete example. If traders concentrate a large quantity of wheat in a certain place by monopolizing the commodity, people have an impression that the total amount is reduced, despite the existence of a higher quantity. As a result, the fear of famine spreads among consumers, and prices soar as consumers promptly stock up on the product (Necker 1775, p. 165). In this case, even fear and anxiety can sufficiently 'produce revolutions in prices, which the spirit of imitation strengthens' (Necker 1775, pp. 165–166). Thus, Necker highlighted the fact that man is influenced by some visible occurrence or other.

> It is in vain that we rely on the power of reasoning, because occurrence will always conduct the opinion of men; it is a teacher to whom everyone listens, which excites neither hatred nor jealousy, and with which everyone always imagines he has forged connections by his foresight.
>
> (Necker 1775, p. 326)

This brings to mind the phenomenon that occurs when depositors rush to a bank to withdraw their money at the start of an economic crisis.[7] In the worst outcome, everyone acts hastily in the same way as others – what Necker meant by 'the spirit of imitation' – and consequently, the prediction is realized. In particular, in a nontransparent situation in which one cannot obtain all information, people tend to interpret small gestures as sinister signs. Necker said that 'all unknown motives are magnified by the imagination' (Necker 1775, p. 301).

It can be said that Necker had a unique talent for analyzing opinion. In particular, concerning the grain trade, he was of the view that economic indicators, such as prices, are not always determined by the natural order but rather by several circumstances in which each actor perceives some or other information and by the influence of sentiment or imagination developed in interaction with others. This means that, for Necker, the effects of opinion and imagination have a great influence on the stability or instability of the market, as we discuss in Section 3.

Time – the present and the future

Based on the presupposition of the physiocrats, the liberalization of the grain trade maintains the *valeur vénale* (market value) at a certain level; as the market value exceeds the cost of production, the income and gain, which make up the *produit net* (net product), are provided to landowners and farmers; the more net product increases, the more *avances* (capitals) become available to improve and expand the culture; as a result, the physiocrats' ideal situation, known as *abondance et cherté* (abundance and high price), occurs. According to this ideal scenario, France as the agricultural kingdom would enjoy as much wealth as possible, and scarcity and famines were also expected to disappear completely.[8]

But Necker did not approve of this series of proposals, however clear they were in theory. Rather, he pointed out an error of 'new science': that it does not take into account time. In other words, the interval between the present and the future. He commented about this in no uncertain terms:

> From one century to another, we assign subsistence and public tranquillity to the power of freedom, to the power of self-interest, and to many other abstract principles that we can respect; however, given a distance of one month, but one week away, everything changes, and we leap for an appealing remedy, which in practice means the most safe and the most immediate.
>
> (Necker 1775, pp. 236–237)

Why do we find ourselves in this dilemma concerning time? To understand this, it is necessary to refer to Necker's analysis of class society. In his account, some people are forced to live from hand to mouth, while others are not: This is the opposition of interests between laborers and landowners. Necker clarified the difference between these two classes: 'the former live for today, the latter often to maintain their luxury or their amenities'; on one side, we see 'men who live by their laboring', and on the other side, 'the lords of land … can, in their calculations, determine common price, and balance one year with another' (Necker 1775, pp. 55, 305). Insofar as there exists such an asymmetry, we can never treat these two classes in the same way. Regarding the liberalization of the grain trade, 'the working class man puts his life and that of his family at stake, and the landowner [risks] a mere delay in the increase of his luxury' (Necker 1775, p. 74).

However, Necker did not refute free trade of all kinds. At issue for him was the case of grain, exclusively. Celebrating the administrative talent of Colbert, Louis XIV's Controller-General of Finances, who had 'reflected on the power of free trade and that of competition', Necker pointed out the importance of time in the emergence of market equilibrium:

> Colbert was no doubt aware that competition, which is given so much power, sooner or later restores the levels it disturbs; however, he also knew that it arrives only at the end of a given time: an indifferent and almost imperceptible interval when applied to luxury goods or convenient goods; but a terrible interval when it comes to a foodstuff whose loss we cannot bear for a day; a mere doubt becomes a danger, or anxiety in a moment can shake a province, weaken the springs of confidence, and produce still greater evils.
>
> (Necker 1773, pp. 36–37)

Even if we agree to some extent with the benefits of free trade and competition, it is only in the future that we can enjoy the effects of liberalization.

However, the majority of people who are laborers do not have enough resources or means to wait for such a long period. They must live in the present. Thus, Necker criticized an inadequate conception of time in the 'new science' of the physiocrats; he said that if it was permitted to simply discuss the pure linkages of one formula with another 'with the precision of exact sciences', this would mean that 'men present and future are merely X in algebra' (Necker 1775, p. 60).

Institution as opinion stabilized over time

What was visible and evident in the failure of liberalization during the 1760s was the fatal gap between the natural order and the existence of society. French society refused the principle of free grain trade, and this was accompanied by many riots and uprisings throughout the kingdom where most of the people were loyal to traditional conceptions such as *just prix* (just price) or *taxation populaire* (popular taxation).[9] However, faced with this reaction, the physiocrats denounced the society itself without reconsidering their doctrine[10] because, for them, the liberalization of the grain trade was based on a 'natural order [that was] the most advantageous to mankind' (Quesnay 2005, p. 1018) and the 'new science' of political economy revealed the '*necessary* laws of Government made for man and proper for men of all climates and all countries' (Du Pont de Nemours 1768, p. 604).

Necker, meanwhile, defended the existing society, in other words, the set of human institutions that had been established historically. For him, society works well with rules or norms to which its members give their consent, either explicitly or implicitly, and not with transcendent truths or principles that are demonstrated perfectly. On this issue, Necker wrote,

> I have found ... there was often more truth in public opinion than in the new systems. This perhaps applies to the principles of political economy turned into customs, as the moral transmuted into proverbs ... These are the results produced over time and by a series of observations; nobody showed the process, but it has nevertheless existed.
>
> (Necker 1773, p. 71)

Here, again, what draws our attention is the very important place occupied by opinion and time in Necker's political economy. The social order exists as the aggregate of human institutions, which consist of opinions attaining a sort of equilibrium point over a long period.[11] In other words, the social order depends on 'public opinion', which is present as 'the result of the thinking of nations and centuries', and which 'exercises its empire over the society and even within the families' (Necker 1775, p. 184). Thus, trying to change by force the institutions to which people are accustomed, which they have justified in their lives, causes a destructive result for the society itself.

Furthermore, at a time when popular anxiety about provisioning – fear of famine or monopolies – was strong, the institutions historically established between the ruler and the ruled, such as *économie morale* (moral economy) or *pacte de subsistence* (pact of subsistence), were held to be much more acceptable than the new system of freedom. Paying all his attention to the institutions that were highly justified among the people, Necker believed the set of governmental interventions and regulations on grain trade should be supported rather than abolished. In arriving at this conclusion, he described the essentials of his political economy as art rather than as science:

> There is ... one truth in political economy as well as in every other science; but who can be sure of getting there? Who can submit to his single thought this restless mass of sentiments, passions, and wills? Ah! How many cautions, cares and sacrifices are not yet required to the administrator convinced, when he wants to make men out of their habit? Precipitation was suitable to the legislators of a savage country living under barbaric customs; but in civilized states of Europe, especially in France, there are few economic institutions where some benefits are not attached to the disadvantages.
> (Necker 1775, p. 327)

In this way, Necker appreciated historically formed institutions, including the mind-set shared among people and the practices established between the ruler and the ruled to coordinate particular conduct and reduce uncertainty in the whole society. Above all, he was convinced that a new system, whatever it is, could never be established without conforming to public opinion. On this point, he was not completely opposed to reform but rather warned of the importance of public opinion in accompanying institutional change[12]: 'The public opinion', he insisted, 'strengthens or weakens all human institutions' (Necker 1775, p. 327).

Necker concluded as follows: Instead of 'making a new law on grain trade' based on the 'new science',

> it is much better to modify slightly the existing one, and mitigate its abuse by the administrative authority, and grasp, for the establishment of a new law, the circumstances which can help it amidst public opinion, or at least defend it in its birth against the insults of the occurrence.
> (Necker 1775, p. 326)

Conclusion

By carefully analyzing Necker's two works opposing the liberalization of the trade in grain, we have been able to ascertain the analytical elements therein. Far from the abstraction and formalization of the 'new science' of the physiocrats, Necker developed his analysis with respect to opinion, time and institution, the last notion existing as a result of the first two. In particular, opinion contains two important concepts in the view of Necker: First, that which is stabilized over time and directed to institutions; second, that which is destabilized in unexpected situations due to institutional change.

We note the possibility that his analyses derived from his career as a banker who was well versed in both credit and confidence. In summary, his views on these topics are expressed as follows: (1) regarding the effects of opinion and imagination, he realized that the functioning of the market is often far from actual economic performance because of the expansion or contraction of confidence; (2) regarding time, he believed that, while credit or confidence facilitate a transaction in an interval between the present and the future, the same does not apply to the liberalization of the grain trade; and (3) regarding institutions, he knew that it is very costly to dissolve or break the confidence in an historically established institution, that is, an opinion that had stabilized over a long time.

Moreover, we can say that these conceptions deriving from Necker's career were more or less retained in his *Compte rendu au Roi*. Indeed, when he published the revenues and expenditures of the Royal Treasury, Necker sought to change unstable opinions into well-established confidence among potential creditors, except that the figures may or may not have been correct.[13] Taking advantage of the interval between the present and the future, Necker, as Director-General of Finances, issued more national bonds for France's commitment to the war in North American colonies. Necker and the physiocrats were in stark opposition again because the latter sought to reconstruct France's finances by means of a single tax on land, while Necker took recourse to issuing public debt.

Notes

1 The first version of this paper, written in French, was presented at the international conference *L'anti-physiocratie: critiques et oppositions au mouvement physiocrate, de la fin des années 1750 au milieu du 19 siècle* (Université de Lyon 2, April 2013). I would like to thank the organizers and participants for their comments, time and effort.
2 See, for example, Lüthy (1961 t.2, pp. 381, 394, 407–412). In addition, there were more than 150 pamphlets arguing against Necker during his tenure (Burnand 2009).
3 See Grange (1974, pp. 23, 33) and Burnand (2004, pp. 19–20).
4 On this subject, some studies focus on theoretical confrontations between the physiocrats and Necker: For example, the rivalry between the formal rationalization and substantial rationalization of economic knowledge (Steiner 1998b, Chap. 2) and the opposition between national economic growth and people's subsistence minimum (Grange 1974, pp. 178–184).
5 See, for example, the following analyses by Quesnay: 'The more prices are subject to the natural order, the higher they are constantly, and the more profitable they are in trade with foreign countries, the more they stimulate agriculture' (Quesnay 2005, p. 558); 'With the freedom and facility of foreign trade, including both export and import, grains have a more consistently equal price, since the most equal price is one that prevails among trading nations' (Quesnay 2005, p. 589).

6 However, at the same time, Necker sharply contrasted 'the private man ... guided by a torch which illuminates him alone' with the 'man of public good' who was capable of paying attention to the whole society (Necker 1775, pp. 62–63). He afforded a privileged role to legislator in order to reconcile the different interests in society (Steiner 2006, pp. 269–270).

7 Indeed, Necker remarked that 'anxiety' often becomes 'a real evil' (Necker 1775, p. 255), which is quite similar to what Robert Merton later called the 'self-fulfilling prophecy' (Merton 1948).

8 For these formulas of the physiocrats, see the maxims proposed by Quesnay: '*Abondance et cherté* is opulence'; 'The abundance of production is obtained by great advances; consumption and trade sustain the flow and the market value of production; the market value is a measure of the wealth of nation'; 'it is consumption, flow, facility and freedom of internal and external trade that ensure the market value which forms revenue' (Quesnay, 2005, pp. 570, 584, 594).

9 For historical research on the liberalization of the grain trade and the political and social events that occurred at that time, see Kaplan (1976, 1982, 1984). In addition, for research that applies E.P. Thompson's point of view to the eighteenth-century French context, see Gauthier and Ikni (1988).

10 Necker commented on this curious reversal as follows: 'with a single thing, perfect freedom, they will govern the world without any pain; ... if the society becomes distressed and refuses this experience, they accuse it of impatience, the society alone is to be blamed, and the principle maintains its glory or its pretensions' (Necker 1773, pp. 42–43).

11 On the contrary, Quesnay had great contempt for history. 'Don't look for lessons', he said, 'in the history of nations or aberrations of men, history presents just an abyss of disorder' (Quesnay 2005, p. 1015). Le Mercier de la Rivière confirmed the doctrine of his master: '[Social order] is far from the work of men; it is, instead, established by the Author of nature, like all other branches of the physical' (Le Mercier de la Rivière 1767, p. 49).

12 Concerning the possibility that Necker took a 'strategy of prudence' in order to implement liberal economic reforms, see Faccarello (1998, pp. 144–149). Regarding the reforms led by Necker in his ministry, see Harris (1979) and Hardman (1995, pp. 133–143, 162–167).

13 On this point, see Burnand (2004, pp. 59–61).

References

Burnand, L. (2004). *Necker et l'opinion publique*. Paris: H. Champion.

———. (2009). *Les pamphlets contre Necker: médias et imaginaire politique au XVIIIe siècle*. Paris: Classiques Garnier.

Du Pont de Nemours, P.-S. (1768). *De l'origine et des progrès d'une science nouvelle*, in *Œuvres politiques et économiques de Du Pont de Nemours*, vol. 1. Nendeln: KTO Press, 1979.

Faccarello, G. (1998). Galiani, Necker and Turgot: a debate on economic reform and policy in eighteenth-century France, in *Studies in the History of French Political Economy: From Bodin to Walras*, G. Faccarello (ed.), London; New York: Routledge.

Gauthier, F. and Ikni, G. R. (1988). *La Guerre du blé au XVIIIe siècle: la critique contre le libéralisme économique au XVIIIe siècle*. Montreuil: La Passion.

Grange, H. (1974). *Les idées de Necker*. Paris: C. Klincksieck.

Hardman, J. (1995). *French Politics 1774–1789*. London: Longman.

Harris, R. D. (1979). *Necker, Reform Statesman of the Ancien Régime*. Berkeley: University of California Press.

Kaplan, S. L. (1976). *Bread, Politics and Political Economy in the Reign of Louis XV*, 2 vols. The Hague: Martinus Nijhoff.

———. (1982). *Le complot de famine: histoire d'une rumeur au XVIIIe siècle*. Paris: Librairie A. Colin.

———. (1984). *Provisioning Paris: Merchants and Millers in the Grain and Flour Trade during the Eighteenth Century*. Ithaca: Cornell University Press.

Le Mercier de la Rivière, P.-P. (1767). *L'ordre naturel et essentiel des sociétés politiques*. texte revu par F. Markovits, Paris: Fayard, 2001.

Lüthy, H. (1961). *La banque protestante en France*, 2 vols. Paris: S.V.E.P.E.N.

Merton, R. K. (1948). The self-fulfilling prophecy, *The Antioch Review*, 8(2): 193–210.

Necker, J. (1773). *Éloge de Jean-Baptiste Colbert*, in Necker (1820–1821), XV: 3–126.

———. (1775). *Sur la législation et le commerce des grains*, in Necker (1820–1821), I: 1–336.

———. (1781). *Compte rendu au Roi*, in Necker (1820–1821), II: 1–157.

———. (1784). *De l'administration des finances de la France*, in Necker (1820–1821), IV: 1–578.

———. (1820–1821). *Œuvres complètes de M. Necker*, M. le Baron de Staël (ed.), 15 vols. Paris: Treuttel et Würtz.

Quesnay, F. (2005). *Œuvres économiques complètes et autres textes*, C. Théré, L. Charles and J.C. Perrot (eds), 2 vols. Paris: Institut National d'Etudes Démographiques.

Steiner, Ph. (1998a). *La « science nouvelle » de l'économie politique*. Paris: Presses Universitaires de France.

———. (1998b). *Sociologie de la connaissance économique*. Paris: Presses Universitaires de France.

———. (2006). Le débat sur la liberté du commerce des grains (1750–1775), in *Histoire du libéralisme en Europe*, Ph. Nemo and J. Petitot (eds). Paris: Presses Universitaires de France.

6 Jean-Baptiste Say as a classical moralist

Pierre Force

One of Gilbert Faccarello's main scholarly contributions has been his study of the connections between early modern Augustinianism and the emergence of classical political economy. Such connections appear, for instance, in the work of Pierre de Boisguilbert,[1] who was indebted in part to Pierre Nicole's *Moral Essays* and the theory of "enlightened self-love." Here, I would like to show an example of similar connections well after the rise of political economy, made by an author who, at first sight, had few affinities with seventeenth-century French moralists: Jean-Baptiste Say.

The *Petit volume contenant quelques aperçus de l'homme et de la société* (Small Volume Including Some Observations About Man and Society) was published with Deterville, Say's usual publisher, in 1817.[2] It presented itself as a work written "in the manner of La Bruyère and La Rochefoucauld" and added that the subject matter ("man and society, our tastes and our flaws, our ridicules and our vices, our interests and our actions") "will never be exhausted."[3] The word "*aperçus*" in the title was an implicit reference to La Bruyère, who had presented his work as a series of *remarques* (observations) in the tradition of humanist *notationes*, which did not have the generalizing aim of La Rochefoucauld's maxims and were not necessarily short and pithy like maxims. The book was filled with references to classical moralists: Montaigne, Pascal, and La Rochefoucauld are mentioned three times each, Molière and La Bruyère, twice each. One might be tempted to read this volume as a belated attempt to produce "literature" in the *Grand Siècle* tradition in a way that is entirely disconnected from the "scientific" aims of the *Traité d'économie politique* (Treatise on Political Economy).[4] I would like to show that, quite to the contrary, these considerations about human nature, expressed in the vocabulary of classical moralists, are directly linked to Say's economic thinking. I will do this with a single example by showing how a particular remark echoes earlier debates that were economic and moral at the same time. The remark is about the difference between self-interest and vanity:

> Self-interest, in spite of all the calumnies directed at it, leads to far fewer and far less dangerous mistakes than vanity, which was called an

> anti-social vice by a contemporary philosopher. A man's self-interest does not always, and in fact does rarely go against another man's self-interest. All useful professions are beneficial to those who exercise them and those for whom they are exercised. However, the vanity of one man necessarily goes against the vanity of another because the one will not rule unless the other lets himself be ruled.[5]

According to this line of thinking, self-interest is a beneficial impulse because it promotes cooperation, while its nefarious cousin, vanity, leads to the war of all against all because it makes each of us a potential tyrant who will be satisfied only when others bend to our will. The definition of vanity as an "anti-social vice" is credited to an unnamed "contemporary philosopher." Who is this philosopher with whom Say agrees?

In all likelihood, this vocal critic of vanity was Condorcet. In the preface to his 1776 work *Réflexions sur le commerce des blés* (Reflections on the Grain Trade), Condorcet criticized an earlier author who had praised vanity as a social virtue:

> A modern author asserted in print that vanity is a social virtue because it puts our happiness in the hands of others (*Praise of Colbert*, page 34). However, since vanity is always invested in the possession of material goods, of which most men are deprived, it follows that vanity needs others only as victims, and is precisely an anti-social vice.[6]

We can see from this reference that Condorcet coined the expression "anti-social vice" as the exact opposite of an earlier author's expression ("social virtue"): vice against virtue, anti-social against social. An earlier view had been that vanity promoted cooperation among humans (and therefore economic activity and prosperity). Condorcet saw vanity as the impulse behind extreme social inequality and oppression of the poor by the rich.

The literary conventions of the time leaned against naming contemporary authors even when they were being quoted verbatim. Here, Condorcet does not name his polemical target, but he quotes the title of the book, which makes identification easy. The *Éloge de Colbert* (Praise of Colbert) had been published just three years before by Jacques Necker as the winning entry in an essay competition organized by the *Académie française*. In Necker's book, the praise of vanity occurs in the context of Colbert's efforts in fostering economic growth:

> From every corner under his ministry new occupations and new businesses arose, through the creation of countless manufactures; he encouraged some with subsidies, some by borrowing techniques from abroad, some by honorific distinctions, and all by paying attention and showing interest. This is how the sovereign or his minister exercise power over a receptive nation, which is motivated by vanity, a weakness that

> should be called a social virtue because it feeds on the opinion of others and in doing so puts one's happiness in their hands and forms between men an endless chain of relationships, pleasures, and reciprocal needs.[7]

According to Necker, Colbert was a great minister because he knew how to use vanity to foster economic growth. Vanity, which is a vice from an individual point of view, is a virtue when it comes to the interests of society as a whole and is therefore deemed to be a "social virtue." This is the classic apology for luxury, which peaked in public discourse in France in the 1730s and 1740s and was based on a combination of Colbertist and *mondain* arguments.[8] The philosophical-theological underpinnings of these arguments were largely Augustinian and revolved around the paradox of a vice's seemingly virtuous effects. The most deliberately shocking form of the paradox was Mandeville's *Fable of the Bees*. A more reasonable-sounding version could be found in the *Moral Essays*, in which Pierre Nicole explained that the effects of *amour-propre* (self-love) were hardly distinguishable from the effects of charity. The key question, however, was exactly how this transmutation of a vice into a virtue was taking place. Augustinians like Nicole gave various psychological explanations and ultimately ascribed the transmutations to the work of divine Providence. In the *Fable of the Bees*, Providence was invoked as well, perhaps ironically, as was the work of "the dexterous management of a skilful politician"[9] who was turning private vices into public benefits. It is the latter aspect that is emphasized in Necker's *Éloge de Colbert*. Necker invoked not the mysteries of Providence but the *arcana imperii*. Vanity is an engine of economic growth because the sovereign knows how to put its effects to good use. A clever minister knows how to use the vanity of the king's subjects to get them to work more and more efficiently in order to produce the wealth that will make the country strong.

John Shovlin has shown that starting in the 1750s, there was a backlash against the apology for luxury as well as various attempts to moralize modern commercial society and make it compatible with civic virtue. If we examine Condorcet's thinking, we will see that his main objection against the apology for luxury was a political one. In the *Sketch for a Historical Picture of the Progress of the Human Mind*, Condorcet acknowledged that "manners have become less violent...through the influence of the spirit of industry and commerce which is inimical to unrest and violence as the natural enemies of wealth."[10] However, the clever manipulation of the passions and interests of the citizens by the sovereign was both wrong and ultimately doomed to fail because it divided society into two camps: "the one fated to rule, the other to obey, the one to deceive, the other to be deceived."[11] Such a division overlooked the fact "that all men have an equal right to be informed on all that concerns them, and that none of the authorities established by men over themselves has the right to hide from them a single truth."[12]

A similar political argument can be found in the work of Say, who was writing in the same civic-minded tradition. In the *Petit volume*, Say tells the story of a conversation he had with Napoleon. The economist sums up the courage to criticize the emperor for corrupting the nation. The emperor replies that the economist is naïve:

> I once ventured to chastise Napoleon on the grounds that he was depraving the nation. Nothing can depict the exquisite disdain with which he replied: Haven't you heard that one governs men better with their vices than their virtues? Where did his purported cleverness lead him? What is the use of having the vicious and the fools on your side, when their rule is temporary, while being against good sense, enlightenment, and good faith, which grow in authority every day, and whose reign is the strongest because it is based on the interests of the majority?[13]

This anecdote, published in 1817, two years after the fall of the emperor, highlights the failure of political cleverness. It should be added that Napoleon's posture was not a particularly shocking or cynical one. It was the expression of an eighteenth-century conventional wisdom that Hume once summarized in the following way:

> Political writers have established it as a maxim, that in contriving any system of government, and fixing the several checks and controls of the constitution, every man ought to be supposed a knave, and to have no other end, in all his actions, but private interest. By this interest we must govern him, and, by means of it, make him cooperate to public good, notwithstanding his insatiable avarice and ambition.[14]

As Richard Whatmore has shown, Say's dislike of Napoleon's politics was based on the same principle as his dislike of British politics: "Britain was a modern republic in the same sense as Bonaparte's Empire: leaders ruled in the name of the people, but in practice against the interests of the people."[15] Against the clever rule of the few in the name of the many, Say proposed a democratic conception of politics based, as we have just seen, on "good sense, enlightenment, and good faith, which grow in authority every day, and whose reign is the strongest because it is based on the interests of the majority." The concept of *intérêt du plus grand nombre* (interests of the majority) was directly borrowed from Helvétius.[16] It assumed that a stable and moral system of government would come only if the citizens had a clear understanding of their own interests.

These debates ultimately revolved around questions of moral psychology, which Say, following Helvetius, still understood as informed by a dialogue with seventeenth-century French moralists. The key question was whether the impulse that La Rochefoucauld, Nicole, Bayle and many others called *amour-propre* promoted conflict or cooperation. In the *Moral Essays*, Nicole had shown how self-love became enlightened for reasons of internal necessity that could ultimately be tied to divine Providence. However, for Augustinians like La Rochefoucauld or Bayle, if self-love had a way of putting checks on itself, the results were not always reliable or consistent. As Bayle puts it, "monarchs do not always orient their passions by the wind of their interest" and sometimes "give up their glory, their prudence, and their most fundamental interests."[17] Similarly, for La Rochefoucauld, the military enterprises of Augustus and Marc Anthony could be described as rational, self-interested behavior or, just as plausibly, the result of childish vanity:

> Great and striking actions which dazzle the eyes are represented by politicians as the effect of great designs, instead of which they are commonly caused by the temper and the passions. Thus the war between Augustus and Anthony, which is ascribed to the ambition they entertained of making themselves masters of the world, was probably but an effect of jealousy.[18]

War and ambition as expressions of vanity are a recurrent theme in the *Petit Volume*. Children as well as kings often engage in irrational and self-destructive behavior based on an inflated sense of their own importance:

> Moral philosophers seem to believe that the love of self, or self-interest, governs the actions of men more than self-love, or vanity. I believe on the contrary that in general vanity has a greater influence on them than love of self. One just needs to observe how often men follow their vanity against their own interests: take the child who starves himself in protest of a punishment he received or the potentate you could flatter into making so many mistakes, and who destroys his country, which is the foundation of his own power, to avenge himself of an insult he read in the newspaper.[19]

The descriptions of human behavior that we find in the *Petit volume* explicitly present themselves as continuations of La Bruyère and La Rochefoucauld, and Say, like La Rochefoucauld, highlights the many discrepancies between actual behavior and what a rational, normative sense of one's interests would dictate. The main difference is the following: In La Rochefoucauld, all behavior, rational or irrational, is ascribed to *amour-propre*, a mysterious entity that generates self-awareness and self-delusion at the same time. Say, on the other hand, has different names for each end of the spectrum: Self-delusion is called *vanité* and self-awareness is called *intérêt*. The former leads to conflict, the latter leads to cooperation. As I have shown elsewhere, the word *amour-propre* had been used to describe and explain a wide spectrum of behavior, rational and irrational. In Say's work, the word took on the narrower meaning it still carries in French today and was used as a synonym for vanity.[20] One may argue that some of the richness of Augustinian anthropology was lost in the process. On the other hand, the disambiguation was necessary for the promotion of self-interest to the status of an axiom in economic thinking.

Notes

1 Gilbert Faccarello, *Foundations of Laissez-Faire: The Economics of Pierre de Boisguilbert*, London: Routledge, 1999.
2 Jean-Baptiste Say, *Petit volume contenant quelques aperçus de l'homme et de la société*, Paris: Deterville, 1817, 1.
3 "On a fait bien des écrits dans le genre de La Bruyère et de La Rochefoucauld; on en fera beaucoup encore, et la matière ne sera pas épuisée. Quelle matière que l'homme et la société, nos goûts et nos travers, nos ridicules et nos vices, nos intérêts et nos actions!" Ibid.
4 Jean-Baptiste Say, *Traité d'économie politique*, Paris: Deterville, 1803.
5 "L'intérêt, tant calomnié, ne nous fait pas faire de si grosses, de si dangereuses sottises que la vanité, qu'un philosophe de nos jours a nommé un vice anti-social. L'intérêt d'un homme n'est pas toujours, et même n'est pas souvent, en opposition avec l'intérêt d'un autre homme. Toutes les professions utiles sont profitables à ceux qui les exercent et à ceux pour qui elles sont exercées; mais la vanité d'un homme, est nécessairement en opposition avec la vanité d'un autre, parce que l'un, ne peut dominer, que l'autre ne se soumette." *Petit volume*, 89.
6 "Un auteur moderne a imprimé que la vanité est une vertu sociale, parce qu'elle met son bonheur entre les mains des autres. (Eloge de Colbert, page 34). Mais comme la vanité se place toujours dans la jouissance des choses, dont une grande partie des hommes est privée, il s'ensuit que la vanité n'a besoin des autres que pour en faire ses victimes, et qu'ainsi elle est précisément un vice anti-social." *Condorcet, Réflexions sur le commerce des blés. Avertissement, Œuvres complètes*, vol. 19, Paris: Cramer, 1804, 187, note 1 [London, 1776].
7 "On vit s'élever de toutes parts sous son ministère de nouvelles occupations et de nouveaux objets d'industrie, par l'établissement d'un nombre infini de manufactures; il excitait les unes par des secours d'argent, les autres par des instructions prises chez les étrangers, quelquefois par des marques d'honneur, et toujours par cette attention et cet air d'intérêt qui ont tant de pouvoir de la part du souverain ou de son ministre, sur une nation sensible, et qu'on peut exciter par la vanité, par cette faiblesse qu'on devrait appeler une vertu sociale, puisqu'en se nourrissant d'opinion elle met son bonheur entre les mains des autres, et forme entre les hommes une chaîne éternelle de rapports, de plaisirs, et de besoins réciproques." Jacques Necker, *Eloge de Jean-Baptiste Colbert. Discours qui a remporté le prix de l'Académie française en 1773*, Paris: Brunet, 1773, 42.
8 See John Shovlin, *The Political Economy of Virtue. Luxury, Patriotism, and the Origins of the French Revolution*, Ithaca: Cornell University Press, 2006, 13–48.
9 Bernard Mandeville, *The Fable of the Bees*, edited by F. B. Kaye, Oxford: Clarendon Press, 1924, vol. 1, 369 [sixth edition, London: J. Tonson, 1732].
10 Jean-Antoine-Nicolas de Caritat, marquis de Condorcet, *Sketch for a Historical Picture of the Progress of the Human Mind*, London: Weidenfeld and Nicolson, 1955, 127. "Les mœurs se sont adoucies …par l'influence de cet esprit de commerce et d'industrie, ennemi des violences et des troubles qui font fuir la richesse." *Esquisse d'un tableau historique des progrès de l'esprit humain*, Paris: Boivin, 1933 [Paris: Agasse, 1794], 148.
11 *Sketch for a Historical Picture of the Progress of the Human Mind*, 129. "…l'une est destinée à gouverner, l'autre à obéir; l'une à mentir, l'autre à être trompée" *Esquisse d'un tableau historique des progrès de l'esprit humain*, 151.

12 *Sketch for a Historical Picture of the Progress of the Human Mind*, p. 129. "…que tous ont un droit égal de s'éclairer sur tous leurs intérêts, de connaître toutes les vérités; et qu'aucun des pouvoirs établis par eux sur eux-mêmes, ne peut avoir le droit de leur en cacher aucune." *Esquisse d'un tableau historique des progrès de l'esprit humain*, 151.

13 "Je me suis hasardé, une fois, de reprocher à Napoléon qu'il dépravait la nation. Rien ne peut rendre la finesse du dédain avec lequel il me répondit: Vous ne savez donc pas encore que l'on gouverne mieux les hommes par leurs vices que par leur vertu ? Où cette prétendue habileté l'a-t-elle conduit ? Quel est l'avantage d'avoir pour soi les pervers et les sots dont le règne n'a qu'un tems, parce que tout l'ébranle; et d'avoir contre soi le bon sens, les lumières et la bonne foi, dont chaque nouvelle circonstance avance l'autorité, et dont le règne est le plus inébranlable parce qu'il est fondé sur l'intérêt du plus grand nombre ?" *Petit volume*, 61.

14 David Hume, "Of the independency of Parliament," in *Political Essays*, edited by Knud Haakonssen, Cambridge: Cambridge University Press, 1994, 24 [*Political Discourses*, Edinburgh: A. Kincaid and A. Donaldson, 1752].

15 Richard Whatmore, "Democrats and Republicans in Restoration France," *European Journal of Political Theory* 3:37 (2004), 47.

16 Claude Adrien Helvétius, *De l'homme: de ses facultés intellectuelles et de son éducation*, London: Société Typographique, 1773, 89, 91, 216, 433.

17 Pierre Bayle, *Dictionnaire historique et critique*, Amsterdam: P. Brunel, 1740, "Louis XI" article [Amsterdam: Reinier Leers, 1697]. "Cela montre que les monarques ne tournent pas toujours leurs passions selon le vent de leur intérêt … leur gloire, leur prudence, leurs intérêts les plus capitaux."

18 "Ces grandes et éclatantes actions qui éblouissent les yeux sont représentées par les politiques comme les effets des grands desseins, au lieu que ce sont d'ordinaire les effets de l'humeur et des passions. Ainsi la guerre d'Auguste et d'Antoine, qu'on rapporte à l'ambition qu'ils avaient de se rendre maîtres du monde, n'était peut-être qu'un effet de jalousie." François de La Rochefoucauld, *Maximes et réflexions diverses*, edited by Jean Lafond, Paris: Gallimard, 1976, maxim 7.

19 "Les philosophes moralistes paraissent croire que l'amour de soi, l'intérêt, dirige les actions des hommes plus que ne le fait l'amour propre, la vanité. Je pense au contraire que la vanité exerce sur eux plus d'empire, généralement parlant, que l'amour de soi. Il suffit d'observer dans combien de cas les hommes agissent par vanité d'une manière opposée à leurs intérêts, depuis l'enfant qui blessé d'une mortification qu'on lui a fait essuyer, boude contre son ventre, jusqu'au potentat à qui l'on fait faire tant de sottises en le flattant, et qui détruit son pays, c'est-à-dire le fondement de sa puissance, pour se venger d'une insulte de gazette." *Petit volume*, p. 83.

20 "First Principles in Translation: The Axiom of Self-Interest from Adam Smith to Jean-Baptiste Say," *History of Political Economy* 38:2 (2006), 319–338.

7 Theology and knowledge of the "collective man" in the writings of Pierre-Simon Ballanche

Ludovic Frobert

The issue of the relationships between political economics and theology lies at the heart of several recent historical studies undertaken by Gilbert Faccarello.[1] The period immediately following the French Revolution as well as the first third of the 19th century stand out among the salient episodes of this history. In the wake of Jean-Baptiste Say's *Traité d'économie politique* (1803), political economics laid claim to its positivity and to its status as a leading science of a new era by ridding themselves of the domain of beliefs and opinions and by advocating for the foundation of the nascent industrial society upon the criterion of usefulness and individual interest. However, the reflection upon industrialisation immediately became more complicated at the turn of the 1820s. Liberal thinkers such as Benjamin Constant, Germaine de Staël and the nebulous Saint-Simonian group, which deployed after the death of its inspiration, the author of *Le Nouveau Christianisme* (1825), considered individual interest alone insufficient and so called for more soul for the new industrial world. In their article entitled "Religion and Political Economy in Early 19th Century France", Gilbert Faccarello and Philippe Steiner took great care to distinguish the three industrialist versions – associated with the names Say, Constant and Saint-Simon – from a line of reactionary and counter-revolutionary thinking that they associated with the names of Joseph de Maistre, Louis de Bonald and Pierre-Simon Ballanche.[2] This may be exact in general terms but should be nuanced concerning Ballanche. Rather than being a reactionary, he belonged to the category of "enlightened traditionalists."[3] He insisted that "Christianity, the so perfect law of religious humanity, is eminently disagreeable to the initiatory law of theocracy." As Paul Bénichou underlined, in Ballanche's eyes, one should reconcile tradition and the Enlightenment by proposing "this idea of a Christianity responding to the present, although faithful to itself, and subject to the law of progress."[4] This short note will provide an opportunity to revisit the author of the *Essais de Palingénésie sociale* (1827) and demonstrate that, in that work, Ballanche proposed not actual economic reflection but rather the outlines of a general knowledge of social laws, a science and philosophy of the "collective man" – both statically and dynamically – which later served as an inspiration for the more specifically economic reflections of other authors.

Ballanche

The son of a great printer and publisher, Ballanche was born in Lyon in 1776. His childhood was marked by the sight of physical and moral suffering, particularly the traumatic 1793 destruction of Lyon by the revolutionary armies.[5] As every commentator of his life and works has remarked, the themes of mourning, pain, the supremacy of suffering and, above all, the law of ordeals and purification were at the heart of his philosophy. In his youth, he was influenced by Catholicism, the Lyon Neoplatonic tradition and freemasonry. His work of reflection upon the French Revolution, however, was essentially based upon two apparently antagonistic foundations that he wished to reconcile. On the one hand, there was his respect for Catholicism and traditional monarchy and his criticism of the theocrats. On the other hand, there was his promotion of liberalism, which he increasingly assumed in the civil, political and social areas while criticising secular liberalism. He was influenced by Joseph de Maistre and his work, *Considérations sur la France* (1796). However, Ballanche was also an attentive reader of Jean-Jacques Rousseau and an admirer of Madame de Staël and had extensive knowledge of the debates of the group centred on Coppet. He was very close to Juliette Récamier, and, around 1810, his friends, such as Camille Jordan, Joseph-Marie de Gérando, André-Marie Ampère and Claude-Julien Bredin, were the young leaders of the new liberal generation in Lyon. Ballanche published his major works between 1818 and 1829. A first series was published during the first Restoration. His *Essai sur les institutions sociales* (1818), *Le vieillard et le jeune homme* (1819) and *L'Homme sans nom* (1820) praised the *Charte* and the liberal Restoration of Louis XVIII and underlined that the Revolution – which he called the "blaze of all the crimes" – had ravaged the old institutions while also inaugurating a new era of liberties. The hardening of the regime in the early 1820s as well as the moral and political bankruptcy of the reactionary reign of Charles X drove Ballanche to undertake his great work: the *Essais de Palingénésie sociale*. The volumes of this "cyclic epic"[6] appeared between 1827 and 1829. In this work, Ballanche presented a theory of the evolution of humanity, of "the plebeian evolution, successive initiations [and the] complete development of humanity," an evolution regulated by the directing values of "Christianity (...) [an] eminently plebeian religion, the true religion of humanity."[7] After the *Trois Glorieuses* of July 1830, Ballanche worked on another great work, his *La Ville des expiations*, which was still unfinished when he died in 1847.

More often than not, clarity was not the strongest feature of Ballanche's works, and it is impossible to find a rigorous presentation of his philosophy. According to Alan Busst, however, a synthetic formula to be found in a letter to Juliette Récamier contained the main elements:

> "I do admit [that there is] something progressive in Christianity, but only in the sense that as the human faculty becomes more apt to understand,

> it penetrates further into the comprehension of the dogma; and that the dogma, form the origin, contains everything which successively enters human intelligence" (1838).[8]

The point here is not the detailed presentation of this "philosophy" but an attempt to indicate the presence of intellectual material in the writings of Ballanche, which, through later transformations by other authors, could inspire the nascent economic reflection, particularly among those authors who were groping their way around such terms as "social", "society", "associated" and finally "socialism". This philosophy could reveal itself to be heuristically fertile for the first socialist and Christian political economics at four levels: the analysis of behaviours; the spotlighting of inequality and conflict as driving forces for change; the necessarily rhythmic character of change; and finally, the relationships of normative and positive elements in the study of institutions and their evolution.

Intelligence

The conception of behaviour developed by Ballanche borrowed elements from the theses of both the counter-revolutionaries and the liberals. In both cases, however, these borrowings were accompanied by strong criticism, while Ballanche attempted to follow a middle way between these two ideological positions. From the counter-revolutionaries, such as Joseph de Maistre, Louis de Bonald, and Lamennais, he borrowed the theory of social relationships[9] and the thesis of the pre-eminence of the social over the individual. Ballanche explained that "society [is] a natural institution". He also wrote that "property is a divine institution... language, society [and] property are identical things". However, he stood out from the reactionary thinkers by (1) radically transforming the transmitted meaning of these social constraints of divine origin and by (2) imagining a more flexible conception of this social constraint.

1 The reactionaries considered that natural social relationships imposed the need for hierarchies of races, ranks and the justice of punishments. Turned towards the past as it was, their conception consecrated the return to the society of the *Ancien Régime*. Ballanche explained, on the contrary, that the institutions bore within them a quite different divine message, transmitted by Christianity, and that this message should be interpreted in terms of solidarity, equality and dignity for all, values that were only to be progressively achieved in the future.
2 Moreover, the reactionaries presented a strong variant of the idea of social constraint: The individual, through his instincts, sentiments and beliefs alone, was completely controlled by natural institutions. Ballanche opposed a completely different conception of this: "man, that is, intelligence, the human essence" (32), he wrote, is "an intelligent creature,

by his nature as an intelligent creature, [he] is a free and independent power, a power within the general order" (94). But intelligence was not exactly reason in the writings of Ballanche, who was an untiring critic of the 18th century, Rousseau, Voltaire and Diderot, stating that "the philosophy of the 18th century is thus to be entirely overturned" (269)[10]. Here, he borrowed the arguments of the counter-revolutionary critique of the Enlightenment and of the autonomy of individual reason – the bases of the social contract. According to Ballanche, the liberty of man was correlated to his intelligence because intelligence, in which sentiment also participated, enabled man to recognise and develop the natural (divine) values present in the institutions of his time. Man discovered God through the institutions. Ballanche thus attempted to simultaneously account for reason and sentiment:

> to know and to love, that is man in his entirety. He is thus called upon to develop both, or successively through society, his intelligence and his moral sentiment. I even believe that the development of the moral sentiment cannot be complete, cannot approach being complete unless [it is] through the greatest possible development of intelligence.
>
> (240)

In summarising his point of view on this matter, Ballanche noted,

> society develops man. Man perfects society. The perfecting improvements of society then become the perfecting improvements of man. An uninterrupted chain of primitive causes producing effects, which, in their turn, become causes.
>
> Man has always found himself in a social milieu. Consequently, all his knowledge is based upon traditions of contemporary teachings.
>
> He has intelligence to understand, and moral sentiment to choose.
>
> Man perfects himself by means of the social milieu in which he finds himself placed.
>
> (257)

Palingenesis

As can be seen in the above quotation, the adjustment between man and institutions was, however, neither automatic nor instantaneous: "what is manifest is the development, the evolution" (96). Here, Ballanche presented a nuanced philosophy of history, explaining, in particular, that "human affairs are contingent, but they are neither fatal nor fortuitous" (122). He borrowed from various sources, such as myths, poetry and the ongoing scientific debates about transformism,[11] and proposed a philosophy of history in terms of the development of humanity, in which a germ was progressively transformed in the sense of blooming and growing through characteristic cycles of fall and recovery. This was the idea of social palingenesis.[12] In the writings of Ballanche, this characteristic rhythm of history resulted from his ideas on behaviour and institutions or, even more, from his vision of the relationships between man and God:

> the liberty of intelligent beings has been provided for in the laws which govern the Universe. God imposed upon Himself, if is permissible to speak thus, the duty to respect it; but, at the same time, He reserved for Himself the faculty of repressing it, since it could have gone so far as to trouble the harmony of the world.
>
> (88)

In opposition to those who he baptised as retrograde "men of destiny", the followers of a "philosophy of discouragement and despair" (Maistre) and in opposition to the arrogant Prometheanism of the liberals, Ballanche reminded his readers that when all was said and done, man was only the "co-legislator of a world" (27) to be constructed – no mean feat in itself. History was not characterised by a long fall nor by linear progress but by a succession of ordeals overcome by human societies, ordeals that gradually initiated them into the very meaning of an evolution willed by God.[13] Ballanche thus evoked the "dogma, one and identical, of the fall and rehabilitation" in order to signify the "duration of the successive ordeals" (89) and the "successive developments" (213) necessary for the progressive initiation of men. This conception placed "life considered as an ordeal"[14] at the heart of a philosophy of history associating cycles and progress: "the education of the human race is always hard, because it always contains the double condition of expiation and progress bought by effort, even by pain" (188).

Conflicts

What was the genetic form of this ordeal through which humanity progressed along the path of successive initiations? Ballanche clarified this especially after 1824 and the discovery of the work of Giambattista Vico: "for there to be progress, there must be conflict" between "the patrician principle and the plebeian principle." Here, Vico's *Scienza Nuova* transmitted both the idea of a spiral development, through *corsi i ricorsi*, and the development of the plebeian as a driving force and therefore the economic and social factors of history within this conquest and the idea that "the most important social questions can only be decided by force" (230). Ballanche also sought his "general formula of the history of every people" in the history of Rome, the history of its beginnings, the chronicles of "Roman seditions" and the "picture of the ancient struggle between plebeian and patrician" (126). The rhythm of history was thus marked by a whole succession of liberties snatched by the plebeians from the patricians: "speech, personal freedom, civil liberty thus form different degrees of plebeian evolution" (152). However, in this vision of conflict, which Ballanche borrowed from Vico, the fundamental element remained the idea that, given its specific, natural or providential properties, political and social conflict between patrician and plebeian constituted a fertile conflict.[15] Although it was turned towards the picture of political and social struggles in ancient Rome, Ballanche's palingenesis was above all intended to speak about a present that was dominated by the reactionary ideas of "the man of ancient doctrines", the "prophet of the past", namely, Joseph de Maistre. Jules de Polignac (1829–1830) and his Ultra government marked the apogee of a "genius of retardation... concentrated in the small number, but the small number armed with social power, with the force of organization" (197). Anticipating the struggles of the 1830–1848 period, Ballanche also warned of the "necessity of having the people enter into participation in power" (158) and even added an extra degree to emancipation:

> the participation of the people in power is not yet sufficient in the current state of ideas and opinions. Society must arise out of the people itself. Once instituted, society marches towards the independent: one day, it has to produce the power which must rule it.
>
> (160)

Solidarity

For Ballanche, society was "a natural institution", and its state achieved the enabled man – every man – to experience the "doctrine of solidarity" (257), meaning the progressive and rhythmically timed achievement of liberty and equality.

If the constraints that enabled human arrogance to be reduced were to be evoked, a place also had to be made for individuality. On this point, Ballanche specified,

> one becomes irritated at *individuality*. One fears that society might be reduced to individualities. However, there always remains a moral force which everyone obeys, which is the link of all, which sets out from a common shared centre, and which then returns from the circumference to the centre.

This was far removed from the panopticon. He continued,

> it is the state, it is opinion, it is society which govern themselves. It is no longer the small number which presses down upon the multitude; it is everyone exercising an influence upon each [person]. The opinion of all governs; the opinion of each [person] is formed, is modelled upon the opinion of all, freely acquiesces to it, or submits to it freely, without, however, completely

> acquiescing to it. Finally, there remains the sympathetic instinct, an admirable link, which unites all the men of all times and all places.
>
> (243)

But above all, the success or, at least, the progress of the palingenetic movement enabled the anticipation of the inexorable decline of inequality. Yet again, the theocrats and their opinions about "distinct natures"[16] were strongly criticised by Ballanche. He reminded his readers that the plebeianism that had been realised was "humanity making itself", a political and social state that, through the generalisation of intelligence (with its attendant reason and moral sentiment) to all, would reach "the full emancipation of man" (114). These options dictated major developments, which Ballanche devoted to education, and which culminated in his texts about prison and the death penalty. Equality and full liberty were to be found at the end of the long, asymptotic struggle of the plebeians against the patricians throughout history[17]. The fact that "all men reach human dignity" (252) was the objective that constituted the true yardstick of progress, and, as such, it was merely what "Christian equality" had always striven to achieve. Given this, Ballanche concluded, "Christianity is the eminently plebeian religion, the true religion of humanity" (116).

In revolutionary France at the turn of the 1830s, Ballanche's work had a large audience. His palingenetic vision influenced the young school of *L'Avenir* in which Montalembert, Lamennais, Lacordaire and de Coux defended "God and liberty". Ballanche's vision left its mark on authors of his time, such as Chateaubriand and Saint-Beuve, later authors such as Victor Hugo, a crop of young poets and even young painters (like Paul Chenavard in Lyon). Above all, however, the intuitions of Ballanche inspired the first developments of Saint-Simonianism. The *Essais* (1827) were read by the Saint-Simonians while the discussions of the *Exposition* were still in session, pre-schism discussions that were attended by all the circles of the Church, from Saint-Amand Bazard to Pierre Leroux and Jean Reynaud, Philippe Buchez and even the future Fourierists of the *Phalanstère* (Jules Lechevalier and Abel Transon). In a letter to Ballanche, Barthélémy-Prosper Enfantin admitted the influence of "the regenerating idea of palingenesis".[18] Palingenesis was indeed discussed during the *Exposition* and had influence, even in economics, upon the whole "adolescent socialism" that was to develop in post-1830 France.

Acknowledgements

The author would like to thank Nigel Briggs, Senior Translator, Cabinet, ENS de Lyon for his assistance in elaborating the English version of this text.

Notes

1 Gilbert Faccarello, "Economics and Theology in France in the 18th and 19th Centuries", in Paul Oslington (ed.), *The Oxford Handbook of Christianity and Economics*, Oxford University Press, 2013.

2 Gilbert Faccarello and Philippe Steiner, "Religion and Political Economy in Early 19th Century France", *History of Political Economy*, vol. 40, 2008, pp. 26–61.

3 The expression was proposed in Marin Ferraz, *Histoire de la philosophie en France au 19e siècle, traditionalisme et ultramontanisme*, Paris, 1880, p. 270.

4 Paul Bénichou, *Le Temps des prophètes. Doctrines de l'âge romantique*, Paris, Gallimard, 1977, p. 74.

5 Concerning Ballanche, here, I have made particular use of: Arlette Michel, "Introduction" to P. S. Ballanche, *Le vieillard et le jeune homme*, Paris, Garnier, 1981; Alan J. Busst, "Introduction" to P. S. Ballanche, *La vision d'Hébal*, Paris, Minard, 1969; by the same author, *L'Orphée de Ballanche, genèse et signification. Contribution au rayonnement de la pensée de Giambattista Vico*, Berne, Peter Lang, 1999; Georges Navet, "De l'Aventin à la Croix-Rousse. PS. Ballanche et le héros plébéien", *Le Cahier* (Collège international de philosophie), avril 1988, pp. 29–41; the chapters devoted to Ballanche in the above-quoted work by P. Bénichou as well as those in Louis Trénard, *Lyon, De l'Encyclopédie au Préromantisme*, Paris, PUF, 1958; and finally, Arthur McCalla, *A Romantic Historiosophy. The Philosophy of History of Pierre-Simon Ballanche*, Brill, 1998.

6 Pierre-Simon Ballanche, *Essais de Palingénésie sociale*, tome premier, *Prolégomènes*, Paris, Didot, 1827, p. 13.

7 Ibid, p. 114 and p. 116.

8 Allan J. L. Busst, "Introduction" to P. S. Ballanche, *La vision d'Hébal*, Genève, Droz and Paris, Minard, 1969, pp. 71–72.

9 See, here, Pierre Macherey, "Aux sources des rapports sociaux: Bonald, Saint-Simon, Guizot", *Genèse*, octobre 1992; Frédéric Brahami, "Individu, pouvoir, société dans la pensée contre-révolutionnaire", in Blaise Bachofen (ed.), *Le libéralisme au miroir du droit*, Lyon, ENS-Editions, 2008.

10 For example, Ballanche reproached Montesquieu, Rousseau or Voltaire, having ignored the fact that "the only possible development for man is in society, and society is a religious work" (126).

11 George Canguihem, *Du développement à l'évolution au 19e siècle*, Paris, Puf, 1985.

12 p. 37: "Everything is evolution and development. Everything has palingenetic movement".

13 p. 10: "The Providence of God who has never ceased to watch over human destinies wanted them to be a series of mysterious and painful initiations for them to be meritorious as faith and labour".

14 Ballanche evoked (p. 82): "the fundamental idea of the successive perfectibility of the human soul, subject to trials".

15 A. Busst clarified this in the following terms: "The plebeian always preferred immediate emancipation to gradual initiation; whereas the desire of the patrician is to slow down initiation and to prolong imprisonment. In this theory of the conflict of classes, Ballanche quite closely follows the *Scienza Nueva* by Vico; but to the Vico conception of the struggle engaged by the plebeians to obtain civil and religious rights, Ballanche adds the notion of initiation. "Providence watches over this conflict between Will and Destiny and ensures the harmonious functioning of the two principles. Although Providence does not identify itself with either one or the other principle, it can in turns take sides with one and the other; for if one of the principles begins to dominate the other in such a way as the initiating movement should stop, then God must intervene in favour of the weakened principle to re-establish the equilibrium", A. Busst, introduction to Ballanche, *La Vision d'Hébal*, op. cit., p. 26.

16 He continued, "to continue to say that there is a noble nature and a plebeian nature, or, in other words, two human essences, is a theory marked by obsolescence… There are only noble individuals not [noble] races, and these noble individuals are those who raise themselves to the level of social progress; there are no longer any plebeians but the individuals [who are lagging] behind this progress" (250).

17 Here, it is worth quoting A. Busst: "In Ballanche's system, terrestrial man is always fallen and always rehabilitated. In other words, his stay here below, which is an ordeal and an initiation as well as a punishment, bears witness to both his rehabilitation and his fall. And every obstacle opposed to human will, amongst which social inequality seemed to be the most unjust to the liberals, is above all aimed at the correcting of human will. As this [human will, as] incarnated in the plebs, advances along the path of rehabilitation, the rigours of inequality are softened, until the moment when, human will being perfectly rehabilitated, all men will be equal. The conflict between the classes, which will end in perfect social equality, is thus the most important manifestation of this struggle of the volitive and progressive principle against the fatal and stationary principle, [a struggle] through which man is destined to perfect himself. And the perfecting of man will have the effect of abolishing all the divisions which this struggle produces", *Vision d'Hébal*, p. 66.

18 Letter from Enfantin to Ballanche, reproduced in Saint-Simon and Enfantin, *Œuvres de Saint-Simon et Enfantin*, vol. 13.

8 Pellegrino Rossi

A Ricardian at the Collège de France?

Alain Béraud

With the death of Jean-Baptiste Say on 14 November 1832, the Chair of Political Economy at the Collège de France fell vacant. There were two candidates for the post: his son-in-law Charles Comte and Pellegrino Rossi, Professor of Law at Geneva.[1] François Guizot, the Minister of Public Instruction, opted in favour of Rossi who was, however, less well known than his rival. However, Guizot thought that it was necessary to teach, at the University, the constitutional law. He created a chair devoted to the subject in the Paris Faculty of Law and appointed Rossi. Guizot (1860, t. 3: p. 121) explains clearly his decisions in his memoirs. He shared Rossi's conviction that teaching had to be reformed in line with the needs of the nation, that one must train economists to forestall the formation of "levellers" and constitutionalists to prevent the emergence of Jacobins – that it was necessary to train "a generation of enlightened citizens so that the same men might not first become fractious, and in time rebels" (Rossi [1820] 1857, t. 2: p. 407). So that Rossi agreed to teach the constitutional law, Guizot also appointed him as Professor of Economics to the Collège de France.

Rossi was badly received at the Faculty of Law, both by his colleagues and by the students. The economists were more benevolent. An account of his first course was printed in the *Revue mensuelle d'économie politique* (Rossi 1834). On 6 April 1842, he was elected President of the first Société de l'économie politique and chaired the first meetings of the second. He was not merely the successor of Say at the Collège de France; he also succeeded Say as the leader of the French economists, even if some of them criticised him for more than once sacrificing economic science to the claims of political expedience (Puynode 1868: p. 439).

There is a marked lack of agreement in assessments of the manner in which Rossi's economic writings relate to those of his predecessors. Ivo Rens (1980: p. 199) presents him as a disciple of Say. Luc Marco (1988: p. 293) suggests that as an economist, Rossi was eclectic. Puynode (1868: pp. 428, 442) reproached Rossi for the way that he borrowed from ideas put forward by Ricardo. Antoine-Élisée Cherbuliez, by contrast, thought that Rossi's strength was to have known how to make good use of classical English teaching:

> Compatriot of Gioia and successor to Say, his political economy repeat neither the errors of the Italian school, nor those of the French; he turned to the English economists. He deliberately took up their doctrines, their ideas on the aim, character and limits of political economy, and of the central questions of this science; it is these doctrines and ideas that he faithfully taught as a professor in a country ... in which there was little understanding for them, and even less taste.
>
> (Cherbuliez 1867: p. 492)

It is this proposition that I want to examine here. We shall not be held, however, in the only relations between Rossi and Ricardo. Certainly, Rossi also did make use of other English classical economists, in particular Adam Smith and Thomas Robert Malthus. But French liberals had long read, debated and adopted ideas put forward by Smith as well as by Malthus in his *Essay on the Principle of Population*. The problem was with Ricardo: with his method, his theory of value, and his analysis of distribution.

Method

In Say's eyes, Smith had had the merit of employing a method appropriate for political economy: He moved "from regularly observed facts to general laws that were their consequence" ([1814] 2006: p. 34). He criticised Ricardo for doing the exact opposite, "sometimes arguing in terms of abstract principles to which [Ricardo] ascribed too great a generality" ([1819] 2006: p. 47). Say criticised neither the logical coherence of Ricardo's analysis nor the hypotheses on which it was based. But he thought that the results that he derived from them taught us nothing.

Rossi rejected this line of argument. To make political economy a useful science, it was necessary, first of all, to elaborate on a pure theory. He argued that one must distinguish three kinds of facts and ideas. One could be interested in wealth from both a theoretical and a practical point of view; moral and political considerations were of importance if one wished to understand social problems and propose solutions. Three types of knowledge corresponded to these three considerations: *pure*, or *rational, economics; applied economics*; and *social economics*.[2] Their aims and methods are different. The object of rational economics is truth. It is based on a small number of general facts and proceeds deductively. This is more of a science of reasoning than an observational one. Applied economics was directed to action, science simply being a means, seeking to integrate analytically a series of particular facts that pure economics neglects. It constantly strives to make use of observation. Finally, social economics links other disciplines with political economy, in particular ethics and politics. One should not seek the solution to a social question by using one economic principle, but other dimensions of the problem had to be taken into account and other principles employed.

By confirming that political economy, considered as a science of wealth, is a rational science that is a science of reasoning, which begins with general facts and deduces from them a series of propositions, Rossi in fact endorses the approach that Ricardo followed in his *Principles of Political Economy*. Once hypotheses had been formed, it was not at all necessary to make a comparison between results and experience at each stage of the argument, as Say had claimed ([1819] 2006: p. 47). The principle that Rossi defended here was shared more or less explicitly by a number of economists, in particular by Léon Walras[3] ([1874] 1988: p. 52): Pure economics was the foundation for both applied and social economics.

Value

In the first lectures that Rossi gave at the Collège de France, he made use of Smith's distinction between use and exchange value (1834: p. 337). Like Say, he maintained that "use value is the foundation of exchange value", but he understood this in the same way that Ricardo did: "that which was no use to anyone is not something that can be exchanged."

He altered his analysis over the course of 1836–37. To satisfy our needs, a thing can be used in two ways. It can be consumed. Utility of this kind is value in use. It can be sold, and another good can be acquired that is capable of satisfying our needs. This indirect utility is its value in exchange. The exchange value of a diamond is not therefore disproportionate to its use value:

> The value of the diamond is perfectly proportionate to its utility, using this word in the way that economists might do. Utility as the property of satisfying a need, real or fictive ... is not of great importance. Where does the value of the diamond come from? From the intensity and the vivacity of the need that the diamond satisfies... the diamond has an exchange value proportioned to the service that is meant to give.
>
> (Rossi [1836–1837] 1884, t. 1: p. 65)

His analysis differs from those of both Say and Ricardo. It is not a new idea, and Rossi reminds us that it can already be found in Aristotle (1857, t. 2: pp. 120, 125). This is important. Jules Dupuit referred to this in explaining why the price of a thing does not measure the utility that it has for the seller ([1849] 2009, t. 1: p. 245). When Carl Menger distinguished use value from exchange value, he argued in the same way as Rossi ([1871] 1976: p. 228). Dupuit and Menger did not take the ideas that made them famous from Rossi; but when, much later, they read him, they realised that he had anticipated them in forming the notions that lay at the base of their own work.

To say that prices are determined by supply and demand only "conceals the depths and difficulties of the question" (Rossi [1836–1837] 1884, t. 1: p. 78):

> We seek the law of price: it is said to be positively related to demand and negatively to supply. Yes, but what governs demand, what governs supply? What makes that the supply or the demand is rather such as such other one? What is the law of supply and demand?
>
> (Ibid, : p. 58)

In place of the proposition that prices are determined by supply and demand, Rossi substitutes the idea that the determining cause of the value of things is their cost of production.

In his lecture course in 1836–37, Rossi maintained that the costs of production could be broken down into three elements: wages, the amortisation of capital, and profits (Ibid: p. 89). He explicitly excluded rent from the costs of production. However, the following year he noted that profit is a consequence and not expenditure. Abandoning his earlier formulation, he maintained that price is the outcome of labour and capitalised savings. However, while he changed his words, he did not change his argument; by capitalised saving, he did not mean the simple addition of successive advances: He took account of the interest on the sums invested.

The argument that costs of production determine prices depends on two restrictive hypotheses: that markets are competitive and that means of production are mobile[4].

> It plainly belongs to an abstract and purely rational political economy; it is as true as a law of rational mechanics. ... It supposes a state of affairs exceedingly different from the real state of affairs. ... When one states that the formula presupposes free competition, that it presupposes the entire absence of all perturbing causes, and, in particular, the complete absence of monopoly ... one has a hypothesis not one part of which can be realised.
>
> (Rossi [1837–1838] 1884, t. 3: pp. 70–71)

Ricardo was well aware that his theory rested upon restrictive hypotheses. But Rossi blamed Ricardo for considering his theory to be more general than it really was.

Rossi rejected the idea that prices are determined by the relation of supply and demand as misleading. He adopted the Ricardian argument and interpreted it as a theory of production prices, not as a labour theory of value. He was insistent that this proposition was a part of rational political economy. If one sought to apply this to the study of concrete problems, it was necessary to keep in mind the restrictive nature of the hypotheses on which it depended.

The theory of distribution

When considering the distribution of the product, we should start from the issue of rent. Workers and capitalists share the product obtained with the aid of land and capital that yields no rent. Even if, for the sake of simplicity, wages are dealt with first and then profits, this is "one and the same question, having two aspects" (Ibid: p. 281).

Rent

Criticising the Ricardian theory of rent, Say noted that the worst lands always yield a rent. If that is so, it is because the productive qualities of the soil are limited, securing a rental payment to the owners of the worst land. Rent is not differential revenue. To overcome this objection, Rossi rests on the notion of intensive rent. When the demand for agricultural products increases, the additional demand can be satisfied by applying capital and labour to land that was already under cultivation. Even if all land is cultivated, production can still be increased; the returns would, however, steadily diminish. More intensive methods of cultivation would only be adopted if the price increased. But this price covers only the cost incurred with additional capital and does not bear upon rent.

Say considered that, because all cultivated land returned a rent, it was possible to break with the Ricardian theory of rent. Rossi tells us that this argument is mistaken:

> Why is it of any importance that all land yields a rent? The real issue is to know if there is a rent for each portion of capital applied to the exploitation of territory, for each portion of the product derived from land. The question is to know if each portion of the agricultural product brought to market provides for the wage of the labourer, the profit of the capitalist, more in all cases, a rental payment to the landed proprietor. That is clearly not the case.
>
> ([1836–1837] 1884, t. 1: p. 131)

At the time that Rossi was writing, the Ricardian theory of rent was treated as the most characteristic part of his work (Kubo 2013: p. 1). Few French economists endorsed this theory; worse, they seem not to have understood it. Rossi therefore marked himself out quite clearly from this reception.

Malthus argued that the prime cause of rent is the fertility of land (1815: p. 13). Ricardo rejected this argument ([1817] 1951: p. 402). Here, Rossi took up the argument that Malthus had made:

> The rate of profit depends on two circumstances: 1. on the productive power of the land in absolute terms …; 2. on the power of the land in question … in comparison with other land.
>
> ([1837–1838] 1884, t. 3: p. 104)

Because land that was entirely infertile could not give rise to rent, Rossi claimed that one could argue that land produced a rent because of its absolute fertility. In a rather less ambiguous way, he stated that the effect of technical progress proved his point. The example of the sugar beet showed that every discovery that improved the fertility of land also increased its rent. But he did not go so far as to establish that this result would necessarily be the outcome.

Wages and profit

Ricardo contrasted market wages and natural wages; in the same way, Rossi contrasted *salaire courant* to *salaire nécessaire*, the latter being defined as the minimum wage that would allow the worker "to live according to his condition, and moreover, leave after him a man" (Ibid: p. 150). For rather different reasons, he conceded that wages fluctuated. Ricardo referred to habit and custom. Rossi laid emphasis on the fact that the worker was not a means of production like any other:

> Enjoying his freedom, he either works or does not work, he works with greater or less intelligence, care, enthusiasm, and devotion; he engages himself for a longer or a shorter period; he argues over the price of his work; he gets married, or remains single; he eats more or less, according as he is prudent or imprudent, economical or wasteful.
>
> ([1844] 1857, t. 1: p. 285)

The going wage depends upon the supply and demand for labour and the price of the commodities that workers use. But to give this formulation a meaning, it was necessary to explain what determined supply and demand. Like Ricardo, for the supply Rossi relied on the law of population. But on what did demand depend? Ricardo wrote that it depended on the gross product of the nation ([1821] 1951: p. 390). Rossi referred to wealth and, like Ricardo, to revenue, but he conceded that these propositions were not strictly exact.

How did the introduction of machinery affect the demand for labour? Ricardo argued that the use of machinery reduced this demand. Rossi thought that this conclusion was beyond criticism ([1837–1838] 1884, t. 1: p. 196). The problem was to know whether this reduction was lasting or transitory. Like Ricardo, Rossi thought that in the long run, employment would increase: High profits and low prices for products increased the capacity for capitalists to save. One could only hope that the accumulation of capital would become faster, prompting a higher level of employment. The analyses of Ricardo and Rossi appear to be similar on this point.

However, Rossi maintained that while Ricardo's argument is correct and rational, it has hardly any practical application. What is the difference between their arguments ? Rossi regarded the initial fall in employment as so obvious that he did not examine it. No doubt, he was only thinking of a reduction that could be observed in which machines directly replaced labour.

But for Ricardo, there is a second effect: The consumption of workers in this industry falls, bringing about a contraction in the activity of those sectors producing wage goods. Thus, Rossi underestimated the initial fall in the demand for labour.

Rossi thought that profits depend on three factors: the condition of productive forces, the relationship between capital and the population, and the conditions of production of workers' means of existence. On this basis, he developed a very classical form of dynamic analysis. Rossi observed to his students that "There has nearly always been an era in societies when capital underwent a major expansion. What then happened?" (Ibid: p. 341). The volume of goods increased, and prices fell. Real salaries rose, prompting an increase in the size of the population. To feed this population, new lands had to be taken into cultivation or more intensive farming techniques had to be made use of. The cost of the most necessary commodities increased, and real wages fell. "If, as soon as the relationship between wages and capital settles, population ... begins to increase too quickly, there is no human power that can bring about an efficacious remedy to this state of affairs." (Ibid: p. 353). It is only foresight that enables men to begin to better their lot.

There is, however, one problem: the interpretation of the notion of real wage and of the nature of the relationship between wages and profits. Nassau W. Senior maintained that Ricardo thought that wages were high or low according to the part they had in the product. He also argued that when Ricardo wrote that anything that increased wages diminished profits, he meant to say that anything that increased the share of wages diminished the share of profits. The inverse relationship between wages and profits would be a simple truism. Unfortunately, Rossi accepted Senior's interpretation ([1837–1838] 1884, t. 3: p. 136). He forgot that Ricardo expressed wages as an invariable standard of value. Every rise in the rate of wages would thus imply a fall in the rate of profit. Rossi did not discuss this problem; he simply ignored it.

Conclusion

Cherbuliez (1867: p. 496) wrote that the real merit of Rossi was to have exposed "the doctrines of the English school, of Ricardo especially and also of Malthus, who seem to have been his favourite teachers." He added that "the small alternations, the innovations in principle or detail that he sought to introduce here... were of no great importance, and are in general of doubtful validity." This judgement is right but too severe.

It is right that Rossi, when studying the formation of prices and the distribution of revenue, drew on the analyses that Ricardo had developed. Breaking with the idea that prices are formed by the relation of supply and demand, he argued that they were determined by production costs. Cherbuliez considered the lectures given by Rossi in 1837–38 on the distribution of revenue to be a model of the genre. Here, one found a faithful exposition of the Ricardian theory of rent. This part of Ricardo's work had been met by French economists with a considerable number of faulty interpretations. They remained misunderstood. The impact of Rossi here cannot be denied.

The innovations made by Rossi are not, as Cherbuliez would have us believe, all of limited importance. Among the issues with which we have here dealt, three deserve emphasis. By contrasting pure and applied theory and arguing for the need to develop a rational political economy, Rossi showed that there was no point in criticising the abstract nature of Ricardian theory. By proposing a new interpretation of the opposition between use value and exchange value, he gave the idea of use value a place that it had not had before in the Smithian tradition. By emphasising that labour is not a commodity like any other because the worker is free, he suggested that its price was not determined in the same way as the prices of other goods. He went hardly any further than this, but, at the very least, he put forward a point of departure.

Notes

1 Rossi (1787–1848) led a turbulent life, first as an Italian, then as a Swiss, and finally as a French citizen. He held important political posts in all three countries and was assassinated while minister to Pope Pius IX – see Dufour's biography (1998) and the dissertation by Ledermann (1929).

2 Rossi did not explicitly introduce this last term, which was later employed by Léon Walras, but the basic idea is quite definitely there.

3 Walras unfairly criticised Rossi of only distinguishing theory and practice, thinking that in so doing, he had distinguished pure from applied science, whereas he had only added to the confusion between them (Walras 1879: pp. 23, 229).

4 Claire Baldin and Ludovic Ragni (2015) emphasize the role that the imperfect competition plays in Rossi's theory of value.

References

Baldin, Claire and Ludovic Ragni (2015). "L'apport de Pellegrino Rossi à la théorie de l'offre et de la demande: une tentative d'interprétation." *Œconomia*, 5(2) :193–227.

Cherbuliez, Antoine-Élisée (1867). "Pellegrino Rossi et ses œuvres posthumes." *Bibliothèque Universelle et Revue Suisse*, 30: 161–190 et pp. 481–505.

Dufour, Alfred (1998). *Hommage à Pellegrino Rossi (1787–1848), Genevois et Suisse à vocation européenne.* Bâle, Genève, and Munich: Helbing & Lichtenhahn.

Dupuit, Jules (1849). "De l'influence des péages sur l'utilité des voies de communications." *Annales des Ponts et Chaussées*, série 2, 17: 170–248, reproduit in *Œuvres économiques complètes*, Paris: Economica, 2009.

Guizot, François (1860). *Mémoires pour servir à l'histoire de mon temps*, t. 3. Paris: Michel Levy.

Kubo, Shin (2013). "The figure of Ricardo in mid-nineteenth-century Cambridge." Conference *New developments on Ricardo and the Ricardian traditions* 10–12 September, ENS de Lyon & Université Lyon 2.

Ledermann, László (1929). *Pellegrino Rossi, L'homme et l'économiste, une grande carrière internationale au XIXe siècle.* Paris: Recueil Sirey.

Malthus, Thomas Robert (1815). *An inquiry into the nature and progress of rent and the principles by which it is regulated.* London: John Murray.

Marco, Luc (1988). "Un économiste éclectique: Pellegrino Rossi (1787–1848)." *Revue d'économie politique*, 98(2): 293–302.

Menger, Carl (1871). *Grundsätze der Volkswirtschaftslehre.* Wien: Wilhelm Braumüller, English translation, New York and London: New York University Press, 1976.

Puynode, Gustave De (1868). *Études sur les principaux économistes: Turgot, Adam Smith, Ricardo, Malthus, J. B. Say, Rossi.* Paris: Guillaumin.

Rens, Ivo (1980). "Rossi économiste," in *Des libertés et des peines*, actes du Colloque Pellegrino Rossi, Genève: Georg, pp. 195–211.

Ricardo, David (1817–21). *On the principles of political economy and taxation.* London: John Murray, reprint in Piero Sraffa (ed.) *The works and correspondence of David Ricardo*, t. 1, Cambridge: Cambridge University Press, 1951.

Rossi, Pellegrino (1820). "De l'étude du droit dans ses rapports avec la civilisation et l'état actuel de la science," *Annales de Législation et de Jurisprudence*, 1 pp. 1–69 et pp. 357–428, reproduit in Rossi (1857), t. 2.

Rossi, Pellegrino (1834). "Cours d'économie politique au Collège de France." *Revue mensuelle d'économie politique*, 2: 330–345, 3: 91–109 et 354–367.

Rossi, Pellegrino (1836–7). *Cours d'économie politique*, t. 1, Paris: Joubert, 1840, t. 2; Paris: Joubert et Thorel, 2 volumes, 1840–1841, 5ème édition, in *Œuvres complètes de P. Rossi*, Paris: Guillaumin, 1884.

Rossi, Pellegrino (1837–8). *Cours d'économie Politique*, t. 3, Paris: Thorel, 1851, t. 4, Paris: Guillaumin, 1854, nouvelle édition, in *Œuvres complètes de P. Rossi*, Paris: Guillaumin, 1884.

Rossi, Pellegrino (1844). "De la méthode en économie politique – De la nature et définition du travail." *Journal des Économistes*, t. 8, 2: 113–122, reproduit in Rossi (1857).

Rossi, Pellegrino (1857). *Mélanges d'économie politique, d'histoire et de philosophie.* Paris: Guillaumin.

Say, Jean-Baptiste (1803, 1814, 1817, 1819, 1826, 1841). *Traité d'économie politique*, réédition variorum des six éditions, Paris: Economica, 2006.

Walras, Léon (1874). *Éléments d'économie politique pure*, réédition in Auguste et Léon Walras, *Œuvres économiques complètes.* Paris: Economica, 1988.

Walras, Léon (1879). "De la culture et de l'enseignement des sciences morales et politiques." *Bibliothèque Universelle et Revue Suisse*, 3(7–9): 5–32 et 223–251.

9 Charles Gide and marginalism in *Histoire des doctrines économiques*

Jean-Pierre Potier

In this study, we attempt to present Charles Gide's interpretation of marginalism in *Histoire des doctrines économiques depuis les physiocrates jusqu'à nos jours* in his chapter "The Hedonists" (Book V), focusing on the first edition (1909)[1]. We also take into account some modifications made in subsequent editions, particularly following the critical remarks of Léon Walras and Vilfredo Pareto.

For Gide, the German Historical School criticized the Classical School, its abstract method and its permanent and natural laws of nature, but it reduced political economy to a classification of observed facts. Thus,

> It would not have been difficult to predict that the pendulum would swing in accordance with that rhythm which is such a feature of the history of thought would cause a reversion to the abstract method at a favorable hour.
>
> (1909, p. 592)

Marginalism presented by Charles Gide

Effectively, what Gide chooses to name the "Hedonic school" emerges around 1871–74. For its representatives, economic science must be based on the "Hedonic principle", according to which man searches for the maximum of pleasure and the minimum of pain, a principle that is known in pure mechanics as the "principle of least effort" or the "economy of forces" (1909, p. 605). Human motives are thus reduced to the essential, and the *homo oeconomicus* is honored. In this context, "Men are considered only as forces and represented by arrows, as they are in manuals on mechanics" (1909, p. 593; also see p. 605). According to the author, who cannot resist the metaphor,

> We may laugh as much as we like at the *homo oeconomicus*, who is by this time only a skeleton, but it is this skeleton that has helped the science to stand upright and make progress. It is here in the evolution of economic

> science that we can find a process comparable to the biological evolution which marks the passage from the invertebrate to the vertebrate.
>
> (1909, p. 622)

However, for Gide, the Hedonic camp is in reality made up of two "schools" or rather, two "very closely related" sub-schools; on one side, the "Mathematical school" and on the other, the "Psychological school", which we can distinguish by their use of the mathematical method versus the psychological method. The former views relationships between people as relationships of equilibrium as well as of mechanics, whilst the latter focuses on the study of human desires. Respecting the order adopted in the first edition of *Histoire des doctrines économiques*, we will now individually review these two schools[2].

The Mathematical school

According to Gide, this school was brought to life by A.-A. Cournot. Amongst the pioneers, we have H. H. Gossen (*Entwickelung*, 1854), who must also be mentioned as a part of the origins of the Psychological school. Amongst the Mathematical school's representatives in 1871–74, Gide lists W. S. Jevons (whilst indicating that he also belongs to the other school) and L. Walras. He adds,

> Today the Mathematical method can claim representatives in every country: Marshall and Edgeworth in England, Launhardt, Auspitz, and Lieben in Germany, Vilfredo Pareto and Barone in Italy, Irving Fisher in the United States, and Bortkevitch in Russia. France, however, has no Mathematical economists, unless we mention Aupetit's, *Théorie de la monnaie* [an outstanding doctoral dissertation].[3]
>
> (1909, p. 597, note 1)

Subscribers to the Mathematical method are concerned by the exchange theory or rather, by a "*mécanique* of exchange". Questions of production, distribution and consumption can be found fully integrated into the exchange theory. Throughout his developments, Gide makes note of a graphic representation of two convex curves of supply and demand of a commodity, which are accompanied by very laborious explanations.

Gide pays particular respects to Walras[4] as he "endeavoured to bring every aspect of the economic world within his formula, a task almost as formidable as that attempted by Laplace in his universal system", and he quotes a brochure about this written by Pareto (*L'Economie pure*, 1902), which compares the *Eléments* to Isaac Newton's *Principia* (1909, p. 693). He also attempts to sum up the Walrasian theory of production with the Paris Bourse's famous trading day. The subtleties of *tâtonnement* are clearly ignored. Gide notes that the price and the cost of production necessarily overlap in a free and absolute competition regime, and, as a result, the

Walrasian *entrepreneur* does not get any "profit". Nevertheless, in the real world, profit exists like oscillations around a fixed point or like waves rolling into shore. Finally, Gide compares the Walrasian theory of production, which is made up of a closed circuit to F. Quesnay's "Tableau", which is "only closer to reality" (1909, p. 604).

The Psychological school

The main conception of this school can be attributed to Jules Dupuit, with articles on utility's measurement of public works (1844) and the utility of ways of communication (1849). In his presentation, Gide proposes a somewhat "Jevonsian" reading. The Classics' notion of "value in use" found itself revived but "very transformed" in the new theory. The distinction between final utility and total utility allowed for the diamond-water paradox, a question that had long tormented economists, to be resolved. As well as being able to graphically represent demand curves, we can also plot the curves of need (desire) decreasing in intensity, corresponding to a law that is at once physiological and psychological. Gide also makes an implicit allusion to William S. Jevons' "trading bodies" (1909, p. 610, note 1). Let us imagine that two individuals exchange wine for wheat. The exchange presupposes the equality of the two products' final utilities for each exchanger and not the equality of final utilities of each commodity for the two co-exchangers: in effect, a "no bridge" exists between their desires (1909, pp. 609–610, and note 2 on p. 610). Elsewhere, Gide alludes to the equality of marginal utilities weighted by prices and to Alfred Marshall's "consumer rent" and briefly elicits the theory of marginal productivity applied to several factors of production (J. B. Clark).

Gide completed his chapter by focusing on the "critique of Hedonic doctrines". Whilst the Hedonists were able to develop their ideas in a number of countries,

> up to the present France seems altogether closed to them. Not only was Walras, the doyen of the new school, forced to leave France to find in foreign lands a more congenial environment for the promotion of his teachings, but until recently it would have been quite impossible to mention a single book or a single course of lectures given either in a university or anywhere else in which these doctrines were taught or even criticized.
>
> (1909, p. 615)

Gide gives an overview of a few criticisms that could be directed towards Hedonists. First of all, he intends to dismiss the most humdrum attacks, such as those commited by Paul Leroy-Beaulieu, who declares the turn towards mathematics in economics in his *Traité théorique et pratique d'économie politique* as such: "It's a pipe dream, a real deceit [...]. It's for this reason that the so-called Mathematical school has neither a scientific foundation nor any practical application; it's purely a mind game" (1896, vol. III, p. 62). Some critics claim that human desires or needs are not measurable and that liberty cannot be put into an equation. And yet, the Mathematical school does not hold these pretentions. To this end, Gide (1909, p. 617, note 1) quotes a passage from the 22nd lesson from *Eléments d'économie politique pure* in which Walras indicates, "Actually we have never attempted to calculate decisions of human freedom; we have only tried to mathematically express the effects of such decisions" (1988, p. 334).

Gide discusses the criticisms made by the various schools in more detail, including those of Historical, Interventionist, Solidarist, Socialist – which see Hedonism as an "attempt to restore" the Manchester School: individualism, selfishness, harmony of self-interest and collective interest and above all, justification of the existing social order as the best possible system. In reality, Hedonists do not aim to justify the existing social order in an apologetic or normative respect but to explain it; Gide recalls Charles Rist's article "Economie optimiste et économie scientifique" - *Revue de métaphysique et de morale*, July 1904 and September 1907 (1909, p. 618), as a profound refutation of this criticism. The greatest possible advantage taken from free market exchange "does not imply any idea of distributive justice, any preoccupation with existing conditions nor the possible consequences of exchange" (1909, p. 618). Gide goes even further by claiming, "In sum, the Hedonic school does not have and does not want to have any theory of distribution: it does not know of co-owners ('co-partageants') but only of productive services whose value it calculates" (1909, p. 619).

Regarding the *laissez–faire* question and state intervention, Gide notes that Hedonic economists are divided. Thus, Jevons is "very resolutely interventionist", whilst "M. Walras leans towards the avant-garde agrarian socialists" (p. 620). Pareto, although an "ultra-individualist of opinion and vehemently hostile towards interventionism and solidarism", thinks that the maximum of welfare can theoretically be attained under a collectivist regime just as well as it can in a system of free competition.

Vis-à-vis the objection concerning applications that can be drawn from Hedonism, Gide observes,

> The result would at any rate be as unlike reality as the new society outlined by Fourier, the Saint-Simonians, or the anarchists, and its realization quite as improbable, unless we pre-suppose an equally miraculous revolution. The Hedonists forthrightly recognise this, and in this respect they show themselves superior to the Classical economists, who when they talk about free competition believe that it 'actually exists'.
>
> (1909, p. 622)

He soon adds,

> But if the Hedonists are very reserved towards possibilities of over realising their economic world, on the contrary they are very positive,

> perhaps too much so, concerning the virtues of their method and are not free of a dogmatic pride on this point, which recalls that of the socialist Utopians. We can hear the voice of Fourier when reading that 'what we have already found in political economy is nothing compared to what we could discover in the future' – understood through the scientific method [...].
>
> (1909, p. 623)

Here, Gide references an article by Pareto that appeared in the *Giornale degli Economisti* in September 1901.

Finally, on the question of the application of mathematics to political economy, Gide concludes his chapter on the Hedonists by citing a very anti-Walrasian point of view – that of Alfred Marshall:

> The most helpful applications of mathematics to economics are those which are short and simple, which employ few symbols; and which aim at throwing a bright light on some small part of the great economic movement rather than at representing its endless complexities.
>
> (Marshall, 1898, p. 313, quoted *in* 1909, p. 623)

Marginalists' reactions to Gide's presentation

How did marginalism's main representatives react? Walras and Pareto's reactions are particularly interesting.

The case of Léon Walras

On April 18, 1909, Gide informs Walras of the impending publication of *Histoire des doctrines économiques*:

> You will find, either in the chapter on the Hedonists which is by me, or in that on Land Rent by Rist, a large amount of space devoted to your doctrines - certainly much more than has ever been published in a French-language book. It will be delayed justice. However I must inform you that it is nothing but an elementary teaching book and therefore it can only be the subject of a very general statement.[5]

By way of postscript, Gide adds, "We will be greatly obliged if you could please indicate what you perceive to be inexact or erroneous - we will endeavor to correct it should it be republished". Here, we can see that he is advancing with great caution! Walras answers as soon as April 20: "I am awaiting your *Histoire des doctrines* and I will read it with great interest"[6]. Nonetheless, in his "Notes d'humeur", undoubtedly written sometime later, he indicates,

> "*We will be greatly obliged if you could please* indicate what you perceive to be inexact or erroneous - we will endeavor to correct it should it be republished". Ch. Gide, letter April 18, 09. Hédonistes (Gide), Rente (Rist). This will be long and difficult. They must be taught mathematics.
>
> (underlined by Léon Walras, 2000, p. 541)

But on May 15, he addresses the following note to the authors:

> L. W. very absorbed in the preparation of his Jubilee speech can only briefly express to M. Gide, as to M. Rist, the admiration that the vastly erudite work immediately inspires in him and the patient critique that makes up *Histoire des doctrines économiques* and the gratitude he owes them for the truly magnificent place he occupies in this work[7].

However, after plunging himself into reading *Histoire des doctrines économiques*, Walras writes to Gide on October 23, 1909:

> I have been reading this work for the past six months with the greatest care and the mostly lively satisfaction and have found only two points that I would like to present to you seriously: naturally, they are two mathematical points. I have indicated them on the included sheet. The second is a rather delicate point that I think I have established in Nos. 3 and 4 of my *Appendice* I in *Eléments*[8]. In case you should accept this observation, I have allowed myself to provide you with the text and the figure that you ought to replace the note on p. 602 with. Your two chapters, *Hédonistes* and *Théorie de la rente* seem to me to be a justification for the 'nationalization of land' which will be difficult to resist.
>
> (*Correspondence*, III, l. 1775, pp. 436–437)[9]

Firstly, Walras signals missing brackets in Gide's equations. Next, he formulates an objection to the graph of supply and demand. Gide had shown the curves of supply and demand as convex. Walras proposes a quasi-concave supply curve with a comment.

In the 2nd edition (1913) of *Histoire des doctrines économiques*, Gide corrects the missing brackets in the equations (p. 610, note 1). Beginning with Walras' indications, he modified the graph. However, his comment relative to the position of prices and quantities remains contradictory (pp. 623–624, note 1); the contradiction will eventually be removed, following Jacques Moret's critical remarks (4th edit., 1922, pp. 634–635, note 1)[10]. The difficulty in this matter is that while Walras argues for pure exchange, from the 2nd edition onwards, Gide discusses a process of production.

Walras's last article "Doctrines économiques" was published in the *Gazette de Lausanne* on January 6, 1910; he had passed away the previous day. It reads,

> [...]. M. Gide and M. Rist accomplished this immense task, which naturally presupposes a profound knowledge of English and German, and does not leave out any approach [...].
>
> (1987, pp. 515–516)

This confirmed the favorable public appreciation given by Walras.

Vilfredo Pareto's reaction

A "heated" reaction from Pareto exists in a letter to Maffeo Pantaleoni dated June 21, 1909:

> Il Gide ha scritto ora tali sciocchezze sulla economia matematica, che potrei fare un articolo da fare ridere a spese sue mezzo mondo. Ma per ciò mi ci vuole un poco di tempo, e per ora ho cose più serie da fare.
>
> (1984, vol. 3, p. 140)

Three years later, in a letter to Felice Vinci dated January 16, 1912, Pareto wrote a response in five points to his correspondent, indicating

> [...] 2) Non è il caso di discorrere di una 'scuola matematica'. L'uso della matematica è un fatto accidentale e non può essere fondamento di una classificazione. C'è maggior diffferenza tra gli economisti detti matematici, che tra essi e quelli di altre scuole. 3) La differenza fondamentale sta nell'uso più o meno esteso del metodo sperimentale. Ad esempio io sono più vicino ad Adam Smith che al Walras, dal quale pure ho ricavato il primo concetto dell'equilibrio economico. Sono poi più lontano dal Marshall, che da molti altri economisti che non adoperano la matematica. 4) E' dunque ridicolo ciò che fanno tanti, come il Gide e il Rist, cioè il pormi insieme al Walras e ad altri simili, mentre il dissidio tra noi è fondamentale. Io voglio fare dell'economia una scienza precisamente come la chimica, la fisica, l'astronomia. Essi vogliono che sia un'arte mista di metafisica che guidi verso l'ideale che si sono prefissi [...].
>
> (1975, vol. 2, p. 757)

In the *Traité de sociologie générale*, Pareto openly surrenders to the controversy. He writes,

> Prof. Charles Gide, who had in front of him the *Manuel* published in 1906, wrote this in 1909 in *Histoire des doctrines économiques*: '(p. 623) But [*if*] the Hedonists [among whom the author names V. Pareto. Why? Tell me] are very reserved towards possibilities of over realizing of their economic world, on the contrary they are very positive, perhaps too much so, concerning the virtues of their method and are not free

> of a dogmatic pride on this point, which recalls that of the socialist Utopians. We can hear the voice of Fourier when reading that 'what we have already found in political economy is nothing compared to what we could discover in the future' – understood through the scientific method -' And it is quoted as such: 'V. Pareto. *Giornale degli economisti*, September 1901'. Even more so if the quotation were exact. M. Gide would at least have been able to remark that the author changed his opinion, and adopted what we see clearly expressed in *Manuel*. But the quotation is not exact because M. Gide applies what the author says about the *pure theory* to practice! We could truly say that M. Gide has not read the article he quotes. We find this in the following passages [...] It is a matter of science, of pure science, not practical, as insinuated by the comparison with Fourier! Here is the end of the quotation that M. Gide separated from the rest of the article by abbreviating it even more [...]. In the rest of his book, Prof. Charles Gide continues to attribute opinions and theories to me that do not seem to have ever been mine, that I have even often fought against, because they were altogether contrary to my own [...].
>
> (1917, § 87, note 1, pp. 38–39)

Following the French publication of *Traité*, Pareto sent it to Gide by registered post. An exchange of letters between the two economists in December 1917, however, allowed the significance of the polemic to be minimized. In the 3rd edition of *Histoire des doctrines économiques* (1920), Gide attempts to justify his classification:

> Can we say there is a Mathematical school? Should we not rather say that the mathematical method has no necessary connection with Hedonic doctrines, no more than any other doctrine - but that it is simply an instrument which may be employed by the most dissimilar schools, and as a consequence, there is no place to open a special compartment in our classification for it? Nevertheless, the use of the mathematical method seems to be made up of a rather particular conception of political economy: that which is made up of restoring it intact to the act of exchange.
>
> (Underlined by C. G., 1920, p. 626)

In this quotation (just after "classification for it?"), in a footnote, Gide recalls the attacks he was subjected to, but he wishes to end the polemic. About this, he writes,

> This criticism was notably addressed to us by M. Vilfredo Pareto in his work, *Traité de Sociologie*, I, 87, note. M. V. Pareto protests against a passage in the first edition of this book in which we class him as a Hedonist and as alongside Walras. He declares that he does not belong to any school and does not have a method other than to make political

economy 'a science, exactly like chemistry, physics or astronomy'. But our classification is not significant other than grouping those who wish to make political economy an 'exact science' under the same heading.

(1920, p. 626, note 1)

Conclusive remarks

The treatment of "Hedonists" poses a real problem from the point of view of Gide's approach in *Histoire des doctrines économiques*. In effect, according to him, each "doctrine" is made up of "principles" but also of an applications' "system" for these principles. And yet, in the case of "Hedonists", we certainly have the principle but without an identifiable applications' system[11]. In addition, the classification that separates the two (sub)-schools, Mathematical and Psychological, seems debatable. In effect, it forces some authors, and particularly Jevons and Walras, to be mentioned in both camps. Indeed, from the 2nd edition on, Gide thought it a good idea to add a note to the beginning of the section dedicated to the Mathematical school: "The word school applied to mathematical economists does not at all suggest that they follow a common program: not at all, it is a matter of a methodology community" (1913, p. 619, note 1).

Elsewhere, if we can understand Gide's difficulties in fully understanding the Mathematical school's contribution, we can be amazed that he did not think it worthwhile to appeal to the Vienna School's, and particularly Carl Menger's, "literary" representation of marginalism. Gide thus stays silent on Menger and his disciples' "satisfaction of needs tables".

Notes

1 For some reflections about the teaching of marginalism in France, see Gide, 1890 and 1907.
2 From the 2nd edition (1913) on, Gide reversed the presentation "for clarity of display": firstly, the Psychological school followed by the Mathematical school.
3 *Essai sur la théorie générale de la monnaie*, (Paris: Guillaumin, 1901).
4 About the relations between Gide and Walras, see Montet, 1982 and Pénin, 1997.
5 C. Gide to L. Walras, 18 April 1909, *in*: *Correspondence*, III, l. 1739, p. 404.
6 L. Walras to C. Gide, 20 April 1909, conserved by the fonds Walras de Lausanne under the shelf-mark I, 220.
7 Noted dated 15 May 1909, preserved in the fonds Walras de Lausanne under the shelf-mark I, 220.
8 See "Théorie géométrique de la détermination des prix, I – De l'échange de plusieurs marchandises entre elles", (1988, 696–699).
9 William Jaffé published the sheet attached to this letter (*op. cit.*, 437).
10 Between 1920 and 1922, Gide receives numerous criticisms from Jacques Moret, author of a doctoral thesis on *L'emploi des mathématiques en économie politique* (Paris: V. Giard et E. Brière, 1915). In the 4th edition (1922, p. 635, note 1), Gide thanks him "for rectifying a few errors" in the chapter on the Hedonists.
11 See also Schmidt, 1983, p. 853–854.

References

Gide Charles, 1890. "The economic schools and the teaching of political economy in France", *Political Science Quarterly*, vol. V, no 4, pp. 603–635.
Gide Charles, 1907. "Economic literature in France at the beginning of the twentieth century", *The Economic Journal*, vol. XVII, June 1907, pp. 192–212.
Gide Charles and Rist Charles, 1909. *Histoire des doctrines économiques depuis les physiocrates jusqu'à nos jours*, 1st ed., Paris: L. Larose and L. Tenin; 2nd ed., 1913; 3rd ed., 1920; 4th ed., 1922; 5th ed., Sirey, 1926; 6th ed., Sirey, 1944, republished Paris: Dalloz, 2000.
Jaffé William, 1965. *Correspondence of Léon Walras and Related Papers*, Amsterdam: North Holland, (cited *Correspondence*), vol. I (1857–1883), vol. II (1884–1897), vol. III (1898–1909).
Leroy-Beaulieu Paul, 1986. *Traité théorique et pratique d'économie politique*. Paris: Guillaumin.
Marshall Alfred, 1898. "Distribution and exchange", *The Economic Journal*, extracts *in* A. C. Pigou, *Memorials of Alfred Marshall*, London: Macmillan, 1925, pp. 312–318.
Montet Christian, 1982. "Le rôle de Charles Gide dans le développement de la pensée walrasienne en France", *Revue des études coopératives*, 4th quarter, pp. 44–62.
Pareto Vilfredo, 1917. *Traité de sociologie générale*. Geneva: Droz, 1968.
Pareto Vilfredo, 1975. *Correspondance. 1890–1923*, 2 vol., Geneva: Droz.
Pareto Vilfredo, 1984. *Lettere a Maffeo Pantaleoni, 1890–1925*, 3 vol., Geneva: Droz.
Pénin Marc, 1997. *Charles Gide, 1847–1932. L'esprit critique*, Paris: L'Harmattan.
Schmidt Christian, 1983. "De Charles Gide à Mark Blaug: éléments pour une histoire de l'histoire de la pensée économique", *Revue d'économie politique*, vol. 93, no 6, pp. 847–868.
Walras Léon, 1874–77. *Eléments d'économie politique pure*, in *Œuvres économiques complètes*, Paris: Economica, 1988.
Walras Léon, 1910. "Doctrines économiques", *in*: *Mélanges d'économie politique et sociale*, vol. VII of *Œuvres économiques complètes* by Auguste and Léon Walras, Paris: Economica, 1987, pp. 515–517.
Walras Léon, 2000. "Notes d'humeur", *in*: *Œuvres diverses*, vol. XIII of *Œuvres économiques complètes* by Auguste and Léon Walras, Paris: Economica, pp. 539–541.

Part 3

European and global economic conversations

10 The individual, society and the economy in 17th-century thought

Cosimo Perrotta

The rise of individualism

The social conception centred on the individual is the keystone of modern culture. According to the medieval vision, mankind was only a part of the universal hierarchy in which individuals had no autonomy. They were unable to determine the destiny of society.

The breakdown of the medieval vision and the rise of the individual as the protagonist of social processes were the consequences of the new capitalist economy, which was based on individual initiative. Trading, entrepreneurship, risk-taking and the search for profit required personal engagement and autonomous decision-making processes.

The same features were also present in the long struggle for labour's autonomy. In the new economy, one's own job was no longer a social duty deriving from birth and social class. When the serfs ran away from feudal constraints and fought for their liberty to become artisans, they were creating a new culture based on individual autonomy.

Humanists, during their upward phase, transformed the new tendencies into new social values. They praised those attitudes that the medieval culture had despised, such as the search for riches, comforts and an active life (both economical and political), hereby enhancing worldly interests.[1] Man, in humanists' minds, was no longer a subordinate part of creation. He was the centre of the universe, reproducing macrocosm in his personal microcosm. Besides, macrocosm was no longer the limited universe of Aristotle. It was infinite, comprising an infinite number of worlds (see Giordano Bruno), while the microcosm of human individual had infinite potentials for development.

In this context, the conception of the individual as the basis of modern society was slowly being forged. No doubt the process was a long and complex one, reaching its accomplishment only at the end of the 17th century. Only then, when the relationship between individuals and social processes had been clarified, economics – specifically the analysis of the capitalist economy – acquired its theoretical status.

We can call individualism the tendency to analyse society by starting from the individual. In the early modern age, there were two different approaches: religious individualism and materialist individualism. Up to the middle of the 17th century, these approaches developed independently from one another.

Protestant individualism

In the 16th–17th centuries, religious individualism had only one root: St. Augustine (4th century; see in particular his *Confessions*), whose doctrine is based on grace. The latter is arbitrarily gifted by God to some men and women in order to save them (the doctrine of predestination). Augustine stresses the wretchedness and impotence of the individual who is unable to save himself because of original sin. Without grace, the individual is not even able to choose between the good and the evil. Earthly society, that is the *devil's city*, is nothing other than a chaotic mixture of bad actions having no end or meaning.[2]

This approach establishes a direct relationship between God and the individual without the mediation of the Church. The Augustinian monk Martin Luther started his rebellion against the corruption of the Church in 1516 by providing an extreme version of grace as the only possible way to salvation. His approach made the sacrament of confession useless. Thus, the mediation of the Church between believers and God was not necessary.[3]

In a famous study, Max Weber linked the doctrine of predestination with the capitalistic entrepreneurial spirit. The individual is completely alone before God, always feeling uncertain whether he is among the elect. This pushes him to strive harder in his work because his success, that is, his enrichment, is the sign of his predestination and salvation. Especially within the Calvinist communities, entrepreneurs are committed to work, profit and reinvestment; but at the same time, they are committed to an austere life.[4]

Despite many critical analyses,[5] Max Weber's thesis is still persuasive. Other famous historians have given an effective description of the small Calvinist communities in which the hope for salvation pushed their members not only to a hard-working and austere life but also to a sense of self-sufficiency and hostility towards the political power. They developed an elitist attitude, while they considered themselves to be a community of saints.[6]

These characteristics shaped the Protestant world, especially in Great Britain. They also animated the many religious American communities, born from the persecuted extremist sects who fled to the New World. American Puritanism was the result of such a culture. Its communities wavered between anarchism and a communist governance on the economic, social and cultural level. They had no interest in society as a whole.

So, we can say that Calvinism and Puritanism provided capitalist development with their cultural motivation, but they cannot be said to have been the actual driving forces for capitalist expansion. For the latter, not only individual motivations were needed but also collective projects.

Collective (mercantilist) projects of capitalist expansion

Contrary to what the neoclassical view suggests, the take-off of capitalist development in the 16th and 17th centuries was not only due to the private initiative of individuals: It was also the consequence of specific projects, theorised by mercantilists and implemented by the states. The capitalist market and development are not spontaneous. Although they require a multitude of individuals ready to produce and exchange, they are also the result of norms and initiatives put forward by the community and by the state.

First of all, the agents of the new economy protected themselves through professional associations, such as guilds. The latter gave individuals common tasks and rules for uniform behaviour. Individual interests were not denied but were merged and balanced. These associations represented the interests of economic groups before society and its institutions. The state was organised as a community (a commonwealth) in which particular interests were balanced, harmonised and directed towards a common aim.

Let's give some examples. In 16th-century England, a debate arose concerning the best economic policies needed to enrich the country. It started with a dispute about enclosures, that is, the illegal privatisation of the common lands promoted by landlords. The latter wanted to increase pasture: English wool was highly appreciated abroad, so they could export raw wool at a high price.

But these enclosures deprived villages of their resources for survival. Peasants were expelled from their own land and became beggars and crowded the towns. The government tolerated these enclosures because the privatisation of feudal properties modernised agricultural production and could help to create manufactures. The Tudors, above all, Henry VIII and his daughter Elizabeth I, obliged parishes to take care of the poor: to gather them together in workhouses and put them to work and to finance workhouses with the contributions of the community. At first, the contributions of the parishioners were voluntary, but gradually, they became compulsory, soon becoming a tax for the relief of the poor.[7]

Meanwhile, the sovereigns forbade the landlords to export raw wool (beyond a small quantity) and obliged them to devote a certain extension of their fields to growing other crops suitable for cloth mills, such as hemp, flax, etc. Raw wool and the other raw materials were sent to the workhouses for the production of cloth.[8]

As early as 1530, Thomas Starkey theorised such a policy and called for implementing national manufactures. He lamented that England was exporting its raw product to Florence and the Flemish and then reimporting, at a much higher price, the cloths made with her own material. By keeping this material in England, he wrote, the country can put the English poor to work and prevent begging.[9]

Starkey pleaded for an import substitution policy (see esp. p. 115), which from then on became one of the basic principles of mercantilism. Tudor sovereigns managed to govern several problems: the modernisation of agriculture, a check on the increase of beggars, import substitution and the extension of domestic manufactures, and the take-off of capitalist development.

Nearly a century after Starkey, Thomas Mun asked for the prohibition of Dutch fishing in English waters and the prevention of Dutch vessels from the free use of English ports. Mun repeats in detail Starkey's analyses; he shows the good examples given by the Italians and the Dutch, who based their success on production, and criticises Spain, who wastes her gold instead of using it to increase production.[10]

Holland adopted a policy similar to England's. Its national spirit was formed through the fierce war of independence from Spain. The struggle for religious liberty gave cohesion to the Dutch community and encouraged a state policy for the support of economic development. It is worth noting that some Italian states did the same, although they were now too small and peripheral. Venice, Genoa and Tuscany maintained relatively prosperous economies, thanks to their good government.

*

On the contrary, Spain represented the negative model depicted by Mun. She was a perfect example of how, despite a huge wealth and good merchants, the lack of good government can drive an economy to ruin. Because of her previous development and the massive imports of American gold, 16th-century Spain was much richer than England and Holland. But in less than a century, she became much poorer for the lack of balance between different social interests.

Once they regained the upper hand, Spanish landlords imposed on the monarchy their freedom to export raw wool (also Spanish wool was high quality, like English wool). They harassed peasants through the magistrates in order to force them to undersell their properties.[11] Because they wanted very low wages, thanks to an excess of labour supply, they impeded the collection of alms and the organisation of beggars in workhouses and boycotted every attempt to create manufactures.[12]

The huge inflation and the lack of production forced the Spanish to employ their gold to buy nearly everything they needed abroad. So, American gold enriched Holland, France and some Italian states.

In conclusion, the mercantilist policy implemented capitalist development thanks to a synthesis between individual autonomy and collective strategies. But such a synthesis was reached only on an empirical level. It was not able to give a general interpretation of the new relationships between the individual and society. Other steps were needed in social analyses to form a theory of modern society.

Materialist individualism

The other approach, materialist individualism, derived from the classical and humanist traditions. In the 15th century, Lorenzo Valla, the Roman circle of Pomponio Leto and other Italian humanists rediscovered Epicurus, who had been marginalised since antiquity.

Epicurus has a fully materialistic approach: Not only the physical realm is made up of atoms but also the soul. Individual behaviour and society are not governed by gods; they are determined by passions, which must be moderate. Scepticism also greatly influenced this attitude. It was rediscovered by Charron and Montaigne in the 16th century. Montaigne distrusts reason and believes that social relationships are based on utility.[13]

Another important step was taken by Descartes. In his dualistic view, social life does not belong to the realm of reason, which is confined to individuals. It belongs to the mechanical world, which regulates not only bodies but also social relationships. Bodies, says Descartes, naturally tend to expand. But they soon meet other bodies that hinder their expansion. So, the smaller bodies are forced to form whirls (*tourbillions*), which all tend to converge in the same direction. Likewise are individuals.

Gassendi, one of Descartes' contemporaries, puts together these different approaches in an explicitly materialist view. He inspired the first circles of *libertines* (the Free Thinkers). Free Thinkers distrusted rational behaviour in the same way as religious asceticism, either Protestant or Jansenist. But they also distrusted traditional values, both those of the Catholic Church and those of the aristocracy. In the 17th century, French aristocracy was rapidly losing its political power to the advantage of the monarchy. The aristocracy struggled against the King's Prime Minister Mazzarino (the *Fronde*, 1648–52) but was defeated. Its values, such as courage and honour, appeared inadequate to the bourgeois society, making room for scepticism.

A decisive addition to these tendencies was given by Hobbes's theory of men's state of nature. Originally, men tend to grasp all they want and assault one another. But soon, they realise that such behaviour is neither the safest nor the most efficient way to reach their selfish goals. So, they accept the loss of some of their original "rights" in order to save others: first of all, their safety (this is the social contract).

In the second half of the century, the Free Thinkers produced many moral analyses, which were imbued with scepticism and were regarding individual behaviour. The most important of these were those of La Rochefoucauld, whose *Maximes* were enormously successful. This author maintains that all human actions, even the most altruistic ones, are dictated by egoism. In fact, one behaves in a certain way because he expects to have the approval of the others or at least to fulfil his own satisfaction.

La Rochefoucauld, who had joined the *Fronde*, shares the crisis of aristocratic values and the scepticism that followed. His attitude reduces all social behaviour to self-interest and dissimulation. He distrusts man, reason and virtue. Moreover, he confines himself to the analysis of the individual. He does not take the step of creating a social theory.[14]

Such a step is taken by Bayle and his follower Mandeville, the last Free Thinkers of the 17th century. Bayle opposes commercial society to the "society of true Christians". The former is based on utility only and will be successful, while the latter is based on renunciation and is bound to fail. Economic progress, Bayle states, is incompatible with virtue, and a dishonest man can be a good citizen.[15]

Mandeville repeated Bayle's thesis and extended it in a detailed social analysis. He started with the very effective metaphor of the two beehives: one virtuous, bound to close down; the other vicious, bound to succeed. His argument became famous, also thanks to the happy subtitle of his work: "private vices, public benefits".[16]

Jansenism: from individualism to the analysis of society

Like Calvinists, Jansenists lived a sober and severe life while having an ardent faith and aiming at a direct relationship between the individual and God.

This movement too was strongly influenced by the Augustinian doctrine. Its origin is explained by the Church's reaction to the Protestant schism. After a period of uncertainty, the Catholic hierarchy chose to fight strenuously against the Reformation. The so-called Counter-Reformation imposed a more severe behaviour of the clergy, developed a great commitment for social assistance to the poor and sick people and called for missionary expeditions to other continents.

A new order, the Society of Jesus, was the leader of the Counter-Reformation. Jesuits were hostile to the Augustinian approach based on predestination. They considered the Church's mediation to be necessary for salvation. Jesuits managed to control the political and economic elites of society through schools for the upper class and by becoming advisers and confessors of the sovereigns and of powerful people. They were welcomed by the latter because of their very tolerant morality, which did not question the immoral customs of the rich. They elaborated on a series of detailed rules (casuistry), which substantially aimed at a very broad indulgence through tortuous arguments.

As to the humble classes, the Jesuits pursued a policy of impressing them through the splendour of ceremonies, altars and statues and the practise of an elementary faith.

Such an attitude gave rise to great discontent in those believers who wanted a deeper and more intimate faith. The Dutch Bishop Cornelis Jansen wrote a little book titled *Augustinus*, posthumously published in 1640, that strongly criticised the Jesuit policy. The book was ardently diffused by the abbot of Saint-Cyran, who made the monastery of Port-Royal the centre of this movement. The leading figure of the Jansenists was Antoine Arnauld, who preached an inflexible rigorousness and asceticism. One of his statements is that every true Christian should treat his own body as an enemy.[17]

An outstanding personality among Jansenists was that of Blaise Pascal. He distinguished himself in the bitter polemics against the Jesuits, for which he wrote the literary masterpiece *Lettres provinciales*. Pascal perfectly expressed the pessimistic vision of the movement: the misery and irremediable weakness of man, predestination, the anguished relationship of the individual with God, the sense of belonging to a spiritual elite, the contempt for solemn ceremonies and formalism, the rejection of the extreme tolerance and authoritarianism of the Jesuits.[18]

Like the Calvinists, Jansenists neglected society as the place of sin and worldliness; although Pascal's observations about various aspects of social relationships, in his unfinished *Pensées*, are extremely insightful and revealing.[19]

However, being Catholic, the Jansenists could not neglect the Church's mediation in the itinerary to salvation. Pierre Nicole, the faithful follower of Arnauld and Pascal, was apparently a minor personality. Yet it was Nicole who provided the most fruitful analysis of modern society. He had the great merit of wanting to learn from the non-religious social thought of his time. His main work, *De la charité e de l'amour-propre*, [20] synthesises what he wrote in many other works.

Nicole tacitly accepts Machiavelli's methodological rule that we should examine men as they really are, not as we would like them to be. He is also much indebted to Montaigne's and La Rochefoucauld's scepticism about reason and passions. However, unlike them, he goes beyond individual behaviour. Nicole's analysis of the latter reveals the psychological motivations that create social and economic relationships.

Nicole also repeats Descartes's theory of whirls and Hobbes's theory of the state of nature. The individual, corrupted by original sin, loves himself beyond any limits. Then, he tends to expand indefinitely and dominate other people in order to get what he wants (ibidem, pp. 382–83). But experience teaches him that a continuous universal struggle is damaging and dangerous. It is much safer to pursue his goals by pretending to be concerned with the well-being of the others (this analysis of pretence and dissimulation is taken from La Rochefoucauld and other Free Thinkers). In the end, man's behaviour becomes very similar to that guided by charity (pp. 385–86).

The attitude that allows performances of this kind is called by Nicole enlightened self-love (*honnêteté*). Enlightened self-love produces the same results as charity. Nicole states that, although society is corrupt, nothing is better organised than it: Nothing is more civil and fair, more pacific, honest and generous (p. 408). In his comment (ibidem, fn), Thirouin appropriately recalls one of Pascal's sentences: "On a fondé et tiré de la concupiscence des règles admirables de police, de morale et de justice".

However, unlike Pascal, Nicole approves this resemblance. He writes that these two systems contrast each other. But they are so similar that it is difficult, even for ourselves, to understand whether our behaviour is driven by charity or by self-love. Moreover, he adds: It is better so because society would not work properly if vicious men could be clearly distinguished from the virtuous (pp. 409–10). Therefore, today, we can conclude that charity is superfluous to a well-functioning society.

Self-love is the guide of commercial economy. Nicole says, "On donne pour obtenir. C'est la source et le fondement de tout le commerce qui se pratique entre les hommes, et qui se diversifie en mille manières" (p. 384). Exchange is not confined to commodities. It also involves work, services and mutual respect. Economic competition derives from natural competition. In fact, all the needs of our life can be satisfied without charity (pp. 384–85).

Thus, Nicole paves the way to a fully secular view of society. His book enjoyed an astonishing success and went through a great number of editions. Evidently, by the end of the century, society was tired of religious wars and moral disputes. It aimed at industrial progress.

Conclusion

Several works have brilliantly shown how in the second part of the 17th century, the various materialist views merged with the religious views. They also stress that both approaches were based on the individual.[21] While being influenced by many authors, Nicole in turn influenced Bayle. But the religious Nicole appears even more secular than the two sceptic Free Thinkers Bayle and Mandeville. The latter maintain the opposition between vice and virtue and argue for a paradoxical praise of vice, while Nicole sees charity and self-love as interchangeable. On the other hand, Bayle and Mandeville show a sense of progress and of economic development that is lacking in Nicole. In the end, these three authors, considered as a whole, provided the general foundation of the new economy.

Notes

1 See Alberti (1432–41); Bracciolini (1428–29). Compare Viner (1957–62, pp. 123–33); Brazzini (1988, pp. 81–82); Gualerni (2001, pp. 15–18).
2 See Ruffini (1926, pp. 29–52).
3 Luther (1520).
4 Weber (1904–05, II.1). See also Ruffini (1926, pp. 52–56). Compare Calvin, *Commentaries*, VIII.3.
5 See, for ex., Robertson (1933); Lessnoff (1994).
6 Tawney (1922, pp. 97–120). Müller-Armack (1959, IV.1). Troeltsch (1912, pp. 75–88; T. 1931, pp. 641–50).

7 See Eden (1797, I, pp. 104, 121–30; III, pp. clxvii–clxxiii). "Proposal to abolish the royal right of purveyance" (1548), in *Tudor Economic Documents* (1924, II, pp. 219–22). Compare Jordan (1959, pp. 91–108).
8 See Appleby (1978, pp. 129–57); Thirsk (1978, pp. 158–61); Solar (1995, ch. 2); Sharpe (1987, pp. 223–34).
9 Starkey (1529–32).
10 Mun (1623).
11 See Vicens Vives (1972, II and III). Sierra Bravo (1975, I, pp. 204–9). Vilar (1964). Viñas y Mey (1970).
12 See documents in Campomanes (1775, pp. 250–67). For the dispute on the poor, see the writings by Domingo de Soto and Juan de Medina in Soto (1545). Compare Sempere y Guarinos (1801, pp. 16–17, 55–64).
13 See the texts collected in Adam (1964) and in Pompeo-Faracovi (1977).
14 See Schneider (1970).
15 Bayle (1704, pp. 359b–61b). See also Schneider (1970, pp. 203–82).
16 Mandeville (1705).
17 Arnauld [1727], vol. VIII, lettre 97, p. 320.
18 Pascal (1656–57). See also, in his *Oeuvres completes, Écrits sur la grace*, pp. 947–1044.
19 *Penseés*, pp. 1081–1345.
20 Nicole (1675).
21 Rothkrug (1965, above all, pp. 36–85). Hirschman (1977, pp. 15–17); Horne (1978, p. 21). Faccarello (1986).

References

Adam, Antoine, ed. (1964) *Les libertins au XVII siècle*, Paris: Buchet/Chastel.

Alberti, Leon Battista (1432–41) *I libri della famiglia*, Torino: Einaudi, 1969.

Appleby, Joyce (1978) *Economic Thought and Ideology in 17th c. England*, Princeton: Princeton U. P.

Arnauld, Antoine [1727] *Lettres*, Nancy: Nicolai, 8 vols.

Bayle, Pierre (1704) *Continuation des pensées diverses*, in B., *Oeuvres diverses*, vol. 3rd, reprint Hildesheim: Olms, 1966.

Bracciolini, Poggio (1428–29) *Avaricia*, in E. Garin, ed., *Prosatori latini del Quattrocento*, Milano-Napoli: Ricciardi, 1952, pp. 248–301.

Brazzini, Gianfranco (1988) *Dall'economia aristotelica all'economia politica*, Pisa: ETS.

Calvin, Jean, *Commentaries*, Library of Christian Classics: vol. 23rd, London: SCM Press.

Campomanes, Pedro (1775) *Apéndice a la Educación popular*, Madrid: Sancha, vol. 2nd, *Introducción*.

Eden, Sir Frederic (1797) *The State of the Poor ...*, London: J.Davies, 3 vols.

Faccarello, Gilbert (1986) *Aux origines de l'économie politique libérale: Pierre de Boisguilbert*, Paris: Anthropos.

Gualerni, Gualberto (2001) *L'altra economia e l'interpretazione di Adam Smith*, Milano: Vita e Pensiero.

Hirschman, Albert (1977) *Le passioni e gli interessi*, Italian trans., Milano: Feltrinelli, 1979.

Horne, Thomas (1978) *The Social Thought of Bernard Mandeville*, London and Basingstoke: Macmillan.

Jordan, Wilbur (1959) *Philanthropy in England, 1480–1660*, London: Greenwood, 1978.

Lessnoff, Michael (1994) *The Spirit of Capitalism and the Protestant Ethic*, Aldershot, Hands.: E. Elgar.
Luther, Martin (1520) *Della libertà del cristiano*, Italian trans., in Lutero, *Scritti politici*, Torino: UTET, 1959, pp. 349–92.
Mandeville, Bernard (1705) *The Grumbling Hive*, in his *The Fable of the Bees*, Oxford: Clarendon, 1924, vol. I, pp. 3–37.
Müller-Armack, Alfred (1959) *Genealogia de los estilos económicos* (trans. of *Religion und Wirtschaft…*), México: FCE, 1967.
Mun, Thomas (1623) *England's Treasure by Forraign Trade*, in McCulloch, 1856a, pp. 115–209.
Nicole, Pierre (1675) *De la charité e de l'amour-propre*, in N., *Essais de morale*, ed. by L. Thirouin, Paris: PUF, 1999.
Pascal, Blaise (1656–57) *Lettres provinciales*, in his *Oeuvres complètes*, Paris: Gallimard, 1954, pp. 659–904.
Pompeo Faracovi, Ornella, ed. (1977) *Il pensiero libertino*, Torino: Loescher.
Robertson, H. M. (1933) *Aspects of the Rise of Economic Individualism*, Cambridge U. P.
Rothkrug, Lionel (1965) *Opposition to Louis XIV. The Political and Social Origins of the French Enlightenment*, Princeton U. P.
Ruffini, Francesco (1926) *Studi sul giansenismo*, Firenze: La Nuova Italia, 1947.
Schneider, Gerhard (1970) *Il libertino* (trans. of *Der Libertin*), Bologna: Il Mulino, 1974.
Sempere y Guarinos, Juan (1801) *Policía de España…*, in his *Biblioteca española económico-política*, Madrid: Sancha, Tomo I, pp. 1–150.
Sharpe, J. A. (1987) *Early Modern England*, London etc.: Arnold, 1997.
Sierra Bravo, Restituto (1975) *El pensamiento social y económico de la Escolastica…*, Madrid: Consejo de Investigaciones Cientificas.
Solar, Peter (1995) "Poor relief and English economic development…", *Economic History Review*, 1995 Febr., pp. 1–22.
Soto, Domingo (1545) *Deliberación en la causa de los pobres*, Madrid, Inst. de Estudios políticos, 1965.
Starkey, Thomas, (1529–32) *A Dialogue between Pole and Lupset*, London: Royal Historical Society - Univ. College, 1989.
Tawney, Richard (1922) *La religione e la genesi del capitalismo*, Italian trans. Milano: Feltrinelli, 1967.
Thirsk, Joan (1978) *Economic Policy and Projects*, Oxford: Clarendon.
Troeltsch, Ernst (1912) *Protestantism and Progress*, English trans. London: Williams & Norgate.
——— (1931) *The Social Teaching of Christian Churches*, English trans., vol II, London: Allen & Unwin.
Tudor Economic Documents (1924) London etc.: Longmans, Green & Co., 3 vols.
Vicens Vives, Jaime (1972) *Historia de España y America social y económica*, Barcelona: Vicens Vives, reprint vol. II, 1988 and III, 1985.
Vilar, Pierre (1964) *Crecimiento y desarrollo*, Barcelona: Ariel.
Viner, Jacob (1957–62) *Religious Thought and Economic Society*, in *History of Political Economy*, vol. 10, Duke U. P., Spring 1978
Viñas y Mey, Carmelo (1970) "Notas sobre primeras materias… siglo XVI", *Anuario de Historia Económica y Social*, Univ. de Madrid.
Weber, Max (1904–05) *L'etica protestante e lo spirito del capitalismo* (trans. of *Die protestantische Ethik …*), Firenze: Sansoni, 1965.

11 A 'Tory outré'? Le Blanc and Forbonnais as readers of Hume

Thierry Demals

1.

David Hume was not well known to the French public before his *Political Discourses* was published. His philosophical works, which appeared before this date, were little reported, and the image that the few commentators circulated about him was that of a sceptical thinker, possibly anti-religious, and a manipulator of paradoxes (Malherbe 2005, 2010). This image is still widespread amongst French readers of the *Political Discourses*. Despite that, the appearance of this work began a decade of almost uninterrupted publicity for Hume (Robel 2012).

Political Discourses was published at the beginning of 1752 and, as a sign of its success, was republished in the same year. It is a collection of twelve essays, eight of which are on economic themes. Previously, Hume had published a first series of non-economic essays, *Essays, Moral and Political* (1741–2), which were scarcely commented on in France.

From the month of January onwards, the *Journal britannique* (1752 VII: 227–31) announced the publication of the book. Then, this journal devoted its March edition (1752 VII: 243–7) to reviewing the first nine essays and its April edition (1752 VII: 387–411) to reviewing the tenth essay, "Of the Populousness of Antient Nations". A few months later, in its July-September issue (XLIX: 229–31), the *Bibliothèque raisonnée des ouvrages des savants de l'Europe* included a short note comprising a résumé of the first two essays and a simple mention of the ten others.

Two years later, benefiting from the publication of the third English edition of the book in 1753, the April-August issue of the *Journal étranger* listed three essays: "Of Commerce" (April, 46–55), "Of Luxury" (May, 219–28) and "Of the Balance of Power" (August, 210–8). The same year, two French translations of the twelve essays were published a few months apart: one by Éléazar Mauvillon and the other by the abbé Jean-Bernard Le Blanc. The editorial success of *Political Discourses* in Great Britain partly explains these two translation initiatives. The translation by Le Blanc was republished in 1755 and that of Mauvillon in 1756 as the first volume of a collection equivocally entitled *Discours politiques*.

L'Année littéraire (1754 V: 73–97) praised Hume's book and its translation by Le Blanc. In contrast, the *Bibliothèque des sciences et des beaux-arts* of October-November 1754 (II: 2, 475) inserted in its pages a short note on the Mauvillon translation. This translation was also listed by the *Nouvelle bibliothèque germanique* of October-November 1754 (xv: 410–35). Finally, in the same year, the *Journal œconomique* proposed a two-part translation of "Of the Balance of Trade" in its September and November issues (1754: 176–84, 167–76).

In the next few years, the translation of Hume's essays took on an unsuspected scale. In 1755–6, the *Journal étranger* published nine translations of non-economic essays that had appeared in the previous decade, then, in 1760, two translations of new essays, "Of the Jealousy of Trade" (August, 85–97) and "Of the Coalitions of Parties" (September, 21–40). Between 1756 and 1758, the *Mercure de France* published the translation of seven of the *Essays, Moral and Political.* Finally, a third translation of *Political Discourses* appeared in 1766–7, now only including seven of the eight original economic essays.

Most of the French language reviews provided a summary that was more or less faithful to *Political Discourses.* In general, they agreed with the ideas developed in "Of Luxury": the distinction between innocent luxury and vicious luxury and the need to trace a moderate path between the lack of pleasure and the excess of pleasure; the consideration that, even if taken too far, luxury was not the worst of vices and was never detrimental. The reviews took as commonplace the assertion that the development of commerce allows the happiness of the subjects and the greatness of the State to be reconciled by releasing, thanks to the productivity, the supernumerary workforce that had until then been occupied in agriculture and manufacturing for the public service or foreign trade. They accepted *grosso modo* the price-specie-flow mechanism. Finally, they clearly conceived the balance of power as an instrument capable of countering any project of universal monarchy.

The most problematic essay was "Of Public Credit". The *Journal britannique* (1752 VII: 262) refused Hume's pessimistic view, by which modern politics had involved nations, particularly England, in the catastrophic spiral of increasing debt to fund new wars. *L'Année littéraire* (1754 V: 89) found Hume "somewhat enthusiast" when he announced "the most dreadful evils in Great Britain". By contrast, the *Nouvelle bibliothèque germanique* (1754 XV–2: 423) clearly agreed with him:

> *England* is overloaded with it [paper-credit]. This whim renders paper equal to metallic money, makes it circulate throughout the State, substitutes it for species, increases or reduces the price of labour and commodities, and by doing so it banishes a large part of these precious metals, or prevents them subsequently from increasing. Mr. Hume victoriously proves the abuse of this way of thinking.

Finally, inspired by the comments of Le Blanc, *L'Année littéraire* (1754 V: 97) concluded its review with a criticism:

> M. *Hume* is indisputably a man of genius, but slightly sceptical. His theory is sometimes more clever than solid, because it is not always based on practice, no more than that of the late M. *Melon*, from whom he has extended some principles, even if together they do not agree on several others.

2.

The Mauvillon translation provides the essays with no introduction or comments; on the contrary, that of Le Blanc accompanies them with an impressive preface and many notes. It is illustrative to examine this critical material. Jean-François Melon is the most quoted author, far ahead of François Véron de Forbonnais, Louis-Joseph Plumard de Dangeul or Nicolas Du Tot. This gives the impression that Le Blanc translated Hume's *Political Discourses* through the prism of Melon's *Essai*.

Melon is omnipresent; however, Le Blanc does not always praise him. Although the abbé easily admits that Melon's approach to commerce is better than those of British writers, even though it owes a lot to them, he readily admits that Hume surpasses it in his turn (Hume 1754 I: xix). One of Melon's faults is indicated in the preface (ibid.: xxj–xxij): this is the spirit of the system. The argument is repeated in the second volume (Hume 1754 II: 35).

The two authors agree on luxury but, Le Blanc adds (Hume 1754 I: xx), this essay by Hume is not at all original, all things considered. The authors are passionate advocates of the trading profession and of foreign trade (ibid.: xxxix, xliv). Finally, they both maintain that an extensive and profitable trade, attracting new merchants and new capital, will yield modest profits for the private merchants whilst continuing to be beneficial for the nation (ibid.: 161–3). But the disagreements between Hume and Melon seem to prevail over the agreements. The two authors, writes Le Blanc (ibid.: xx–xxj), have "diametrically opposed opinions" on the essays "such as State Debts, the usefulness of Paper Credit, Banks, Annuities and other Public Funds, the chapter on Slavery, etc." There are three points of disagreement. The first concerns a passage from "Of the Balance of Trade", in which Hume explains that one way to make metallic money fall below its natural level is to increase paper-credit. This, writes Hume, is the policy of Britain, which is sinking beneath the great abundance of paper-credit, unlike France, which is in want of this. Le Blanc adds in a note a quotation from Melon praising Britain and its circulation of money (ibid.: 211–2) and makes this comment, bringing together the viewpoints of Hume and of Henry St John, Lord Bolingbroke:

> With regard to commerce, that [advantage] of England, which consists of this multitude of circulating paper, is, as we see, still problematic,

> even in England itself. Several wise authors who have written on these matters share Mr Hume's view, even that of those to whom one cannot refuse both the position and the authority of statesmen. I will only name one of these, it is My Lord Bolingbrocke.

The second point of disagreement concerns "Of Public Credit". In this, Hume criticises the argument by which public debts are beneficial to a State on the grounds that they would be transformed into a fund of money that could be passed from hand to hand and stimulate commerce. Le Blanc (ibid.: 289–90), realizing that this criticism is addressed to Melon, reproaches the latter for having based this argument on an English memorandum of 1731, of which he had only read extracts, and which was just a plea to use the sinking fund for the repayment of the public debt to pay current expenditure. Slightly later, Le Blanc (ibid.: 291–2) annotates a passage in which Hume ridicules the systematic use that Melon, Du Tot and John Law made of the word circulation. Adding in a note a quotation by Melon that defines a public credit as a representation of money and a restricted convention that only becomes general "if it is solidly established", Le Blanc (ibid.: 293) concludes with an apparent neutrality:

> This restricted credit is the main danger of using paper, and the biggest difficulty of a question that I would dare not try to decide. I will only say that in these opposite opinions, these two authors each seem to have buckled down and challenged the most received opinions in their different countries. In England we usually think like Mr Melon, in France like Mr Hume.

Careful to avoid taking sides, Le Blanc refers (ibid.: 329) to Forbonnais and Dangeul's recent books but also to that of Bolingbroke, which he translates and adds to his translation, arguing that English authors are precious to the penetration of the public debt issue.

The third disagreement concerns slavery. Le Blanc takes the opportunity of "Of Populouness of Antient Nations" to oppose Melon three times. First, commenting on a passage in which Hume calls for a restraint, even a decline, in servile conditions in the European colonies of America, Le Blanc (Hume 1754 II: 35–6) makes Melon an advocate of the doctrine by which slaves are not as wretched as they seemed, thanks to the Louis XIV's *Code noir*. A few lines later (ibid.: 36–7), he draws Robert Wallace, an opponent of Hume in this essay, closer to the position of Melon concerning slavery and naturally finds that of Hume more solidly built. Further in the essay (ibid.: 57), Le Blanc again agrees with Hume's recommendation of preferring the use of hired servants to slavery and concludes:

> It is easy to realise that in this Discourse, full of so much erudition, Mr Hume had no purpose other than to destroy the principles on which

> Mr Melon took his authority to show the benefits that society in general could draw from slavery.

The final impression left by these notes on *Political Discourses* is that Le Blanc tends, at least on these three crucial subjects, to be more in favour of Hume, Bolingbroke and the Tories than of Melon. This opinion was much less noticeable when reading his earlier writings, in which the abbé confessed to a preference neither for the Whigs nor for the Tories but on the contrary, criticised British party politics. Indeed, he (1745 III: 202–3) assimilated these parties to factions instilling disunity into the country, which was, in his eyes, the demonstration of "a flaw in the Government":

> Since the Reign of James I where, under the odious names of *Whig* and *Tory*, two parties began to divide up the State, one can say that there have always been two nations in one, which external affairs have sometimes reduced to a truce, but who have never been at peace with each other.
>
> Every faction is a new State which rises up in the first: and how could there be an innocent faction, when there is not one whose first step is not to escape the established authority? Indeed, most of the factions' attempts tend more to disrupt a State than to reform it.

In contrast, in his notes, Le Blanc (Hume 1754 II: 409) adopts definitions that he must have read in Bolingbroke and Pierre-André O'Héguerty. In his summary of recent British political history, O'Heguerty (1754: 37–9) endorses the distinction between the Whigs, called the "Court Party", and the Tories, "partisans of the Country":

> It is, one dare say, a misfortune for the English, that it is the *Whigs* who govern them, because they will always prefer war. Masters as they are of money and circulating funds, their personal interest demands this. On the contrary, the *Torys* will constantly be partisans of peace, because the main burden of taxes in time of war falls on them, who are generally landed proprietors.

O'Héguerty not only associates Whiggism with the Glorious Revolution but also with another revolution, economic this time, whose main characteristics are the creation of the Bank of England (1694) and the moneyed companies, growth in the stock market, the rise in public debt, the more widespread use of paper-credit and the payment of interest to receivers of government annuities. As pointed out by Walter Bagehot (1874: 92), the Bank of England was a Whig institution established to pay for the war with France, and it was this war that, from 1692, made Great-Britain's public debt soar. Quickly perceived as a burden and a threat that over time weighed on private property, this increasing debt gave rise amongst a series of authors, from Charles Davenant to Hume, to the image of a Britain caught between two dangers: bankruptcy or conquest by France, which French observers identified as Bolingbroke's Toryism. Thus, Le Blanc's comparing Hume to this Toryism is not surprising: "The Author [Bolingbroke], the abbé writes (Hume 1754 I: 312), has the same principles and maintains precisely the same language as Mr Hume" (see also Monod-Cassidy 1941: 409–10; Greig [1932] 2001 I). Likewise, presenting (Hume 1754 II: 390, 394) the *British Merchant* as a voice of the party of the Court and of war and Joshua Gee, one of its contributors, as an advocate of English commercial domination is also not surprising.

3.

In the *Élémens du commerce*, Forbonnais (1754 II: 238) quotes favourably Hume's essay "Of Luxury", taking from this the theme of the consubstantiality of the progress in luxury, the arts, manners, civility and knowledge. As a reader of Melon, this theme was not unknown to Forbonnais. Indeed, Melon maintained that luxury was a "necessary consequence of any well-policed society" (1736: 106). He then asserted that luxury was not necessarily a particular kind of commodity endowed with particular characteristics, but that it was related to conditions and circumstances.

For Melon, luxury marked the difference separating rich and poor: more exactly, the difference between superfluous expense and necessary expense. In addition, Melon (ibid.: 108) maintained that luxury was virtuous because it was "in a way the destroyer of laziness and idleness". It was a result of the labour and industry of men from which one should draw all the economic consequences: it is preferable that the rich man should spend rather than hoard money as his expense supports the poor man by providing him with an occupation and combats idleness, both the rich man's own and that of the poor man. Therefore, there is no reason to fear luxury, even in excess: "Why expostulate upon this foolish expense? This money, locked up in chests, would lie dead to society" (ibid.: 123). Finally, Melon concluded (ibid.: 4–5, 90–2) that the luxury industry does not divert capital and labour from activities considered to be necessary for the society. However relative they are, the luxury needs are not satisfied until necessary needs are themselves satisfied, namely, when the activities producing necessaries experience productivity gains and release part of labour to other activities. Thus, luxury is an opportunity for an expense that is no longer used up by consumption of necessaries and a source of employment for a supernumerary workforce. What is more, the nation that wins in international competition is that which is the most advanced in developing the arts and in using machines – because the machine allows fewer men to be employed for the same quantity produced, which is a condition for selling this quantity abroad more cheaply – and that which diversifies its production to luxury and fashion.

Compared with Melon, Hume presents luxury as a moral question that he quickly turns into an economic one. He subtly substitutes for it a word with a much wider meaning, "refinement", allowing him to associate industry, the arts, manners, freedom and happiness in a reciprocal development. Luxury then becomes the sign of a society taken to its highest point of prosperity and of a population that is employed and industrious.

It is this latter idea that is taken up by Forbonnais. However, his vision of luxury is not exactly the same. Hume's idea remains moral and political, notably, as to whether, in its quest for luxury, a nation does not lose the martial values that contribute to its greatness. This idea is also found in "Of Commerce". Seeking to go beyond an opposition between Spartan nations and Sybaritic nations, Hume intends to show that it is beneficial to a nation to orientate its superfluous labour towards activities producing comforts and luxuries in peacetime and towards military service in wartime. This problem is not that of Forbonnais.

For him, the question of luxury above all joins that of inequality, which originates in the fact that some men have proved to be more ingenious than others in increasing their resources and have established laws to confirm this inequality. From this moment, mankind irremediably abandons this initial order, characterised by the only consumption that is egalitarian: that of necessaries. "This order has not long been compatible, for the first men, with the weakness and corruption of their nature", writes Forbonnais (1754 II: 225). The poorest among them called superfluity or luxury this "ability to exist comfortably" (ibid. II: 223).

Forbonnais's vision shows that: first, luxury is relative (ibid.: 230) and simply explains the differences in living standards or of ranks in society; second, luxury, whatever it is, has a beneficial effect because it satisfies the rich, provides an occupation for the poor and emulates him; third, the spiral of luxury continues, under the condition of a relentless specialisation of activities in rich nations, of a periodic transfer of men from one activity to another and of an increase in the productivity of their labour[1]. Emulation is a crucial idea here, as it encourages production to reach the "equality of opinion" (ibid.: 231), even if it is a chimera, because the real inequalities persist with the advancement of industry and the arts. For Forbonnais, the growth in luxury is slow, but it should be continual to maintain a proportion between the ranks, with property-owners and traders being satisfied first, then, gradually, the lower ranks.

In his memorandum,[2] written in 1755, Forbonnais presents Hume as a "Tory outré", having gone beyond the limits of reasonableness. Hume has exceeded the right balance for two reasons, mainly: his support for the "system of levels" (1755: 191), namely, his belief in the price-specie-flow mechanism and his fear that an increase in the amount of paper-credit in circulation would amplify inflation.

Forbonnais makes an initial quotation – a compilation of three passages, of which two are drawn from "Of Balance of Trade" and one from

"Of Money" – on the theme of the sudden reflux of money outside Britain, which he accompanies with a second quotation drawn from "Of Balance of Trade", which illustrates the opposite example of an influx of money to this country. Presented as demonstrations of the price-specie-flow mechanism, these two quotations allow Forbonnais to challenge one of Hume's arguments: the proportionality of the effects of this mechanism. If we assume that England experiences a reflux of its money, he writes, the consequence would not be that envisaged by Hume – the proportional decline in the prices of commodities and labour – but rather, the flight abroad of a part of impoverished labour, seeking higher wages. As a result, production would fall, and this country, with nothing left to export, would be at the mercy of foreigners for its necessaries and subject to new masters. On the contrary, if we assume an influx of money into this country, neither would the consequence be that envisaged by Hume in this passage – the proportional increase in the prices of commodities and labour – but another that he envisages in another part of his book, say, a greater rigidity of the prices of commodities and labour or a more moderate increase, deferred over time.

Forbonnais (ibid.: 192–3) makes a third quotation – also a compilation – that, in its first part, repeats the harmful effect of too much money on foreign trade and, in its second part, conversely mentions the possibility for poor countries to sell more cheaply than rich countries on foreign markets. This quotation gives rise to the objection that, as the aim of foreign trade is to attract foreign money, to refuse the abundance of money because of its inflationary effect amounts to refusing this trade on the grounds that it would itself be harmful. Hume and the Tories are obsessed with Britain's public credit, which they find disproportionate, to such an extent that they fear its hyperinflationary effect; the error of their system of levels, continues Forbonnais (ibid.: 191–2), is to be fixed on the narrow idea that money is an instrument and not an object of commerce:

> He [Hume] first establishes that money is not the object, but the instrument of commerce, and he has his reasons for this, that, if it is true that money is the object of commerce... his system of the level of money is overturned. To explain more accurately, he should therefore say that money is both the pledge, the security, the motive and the object of commerce, whose aim is only to win and attract money from Abroad, in exchange for the commodities which he has to pay for.

On the contrary, Hume casts doubt upon the banks and paper-credit. He is suspicious of the circulation of paper-credit on the one hand because it risks adding to inflation and on the other hand because it makes gold and silver fall below its level, even makes it disappear. He does not see, writes Forbonnais, that the circulation of paper is a way of mitigating the disadvantage of an outflow of gold and silver, which, for example, could end an external commercial debt:

> But one sure way, it seems to me, of protecting against the disadvantage of an outflow of money, is to increase its amount through proportional credits; since if the definite effect of credits is to increase and to circulate money, to make it usual, and to reduce interest, to employ a larger number of inhabitants, to increase, therefore, the quantity of our commodities, and to make their prices fall at home through their abundance, the result of this increase in money through moderate credits will unfailingly be a growth in foreign trade which will make Abroad our debtor, and which will force it to give us its money, as long as we are able to supply it with more of our commodities than it supplies us with its own.
>
> (ibid.: 198–9)

Thus, among all the essays composing the *Political Discourses*, those dealing with money, balance of trade or public credit brought about the most important divergences within the very network that introduced the book in France, i.e. Gournay's network. And these divergences turned to be political. Probably inspired by the financial experiences of Walpole's Whig government, Forbonnais rejected Hume's fiduciary doctrine, which he considered similar to some Toryism driven up to unreasonableness, and opposed against it Melon's more relevant doctrine. On the other hand, Le Blanc seemed rather to desert Melon and tend towards Hume, whom he tried to liken to Bolingbroke through depicting him as a country Tory. A few months early, Dangeul (1754: 348, 358, 282), another member of the network, made a criticism of Melon similar to that of Hume and expressed the same fears about excessive paper-credit in England.

Notes

1 See Hont (2008).
2 About this memorandum and its context, see Sonenscher (2007: 181–6), Charles (2008: 192–3) and Hont (2008: 269–70).

References

Bagehot, W. (1874). *Lombard Street*. New York: Scribner, Armstrong and Co.
Charles, L. (2008). 'French 'New politics' and the Dissemination of David Hume's *Political Discourses* on the Continent'. In C. Wennerlind and M. Schabas eds., *David Hume's Political Economy*. London and New York: Routledge, 181–202.
Dangeul, L. Plumard de (1754). *Remarques sur les avantages et les désavantages de la France et de la Grande-Bretagne*. Dresde.

Forbonnais, F. Véron de (1754). *Élémens du commerce*, 2 vols., 1st ed. Leyde: Briasson.
______. (1755). *Réfutation de quelques articles des Discours politiques de M. David Hume traduits de l'Anglois l'année dernière 1754*. Paris: Arsenal, Ms. 4591, 181–205.
Greig, J.Y.T. ([1932] 2001). *The Letters of David Hume*, 2 vols. Oxford: Oxford University Press.
Hont, I. (2008). 'The Rich Country-Poor Country Debate Revisited'. In C. Wennerlind and M. Schabas (eds.), *David Hume's Political Economy*. London and New York: Routledge, 243–323.
Hume, D. (1754). *Discours politiques de Monsieur Hume*. Amsterdam and Paris: Lambert.
Le Blanc, J.-B. (1745). *Lettres d'un François*, 3 vols. La Haye: Jean Neaulme.
Malherbe, M. (2005). 'Hume's Reception in France'. In P. Jones (ed.), *The Reception of David Hume in Europe*. London: Thoemmes Continuum, 2005, 43–98.
______. (2010). 'Hume en France: la traduction des *Political Discourses*'. In A. Thomson, S. Burrows and E. Dziembowski (eds.), *Cultural Transfers: France and Britain in the Long Eighteenth Century*. Oxford: Voltaire Foundation, 243–56.
Melon, J.-F. (1736). *Essai politique sur le commerce*, 3rd ed.
Monod-Cassidy, H. (1941). *Un voyageur-philosophe au* XVIIIe *siècle. L'abbé Jean-Bernard Le Blanc. Cambridge: Harvard University Press.*
O'Héguerty, P.-A. (1754). *Essai sur les intérêts du commerce maritime*. La Haye.
Robel, G. (2012). 'Hume's Political Discourses in France'. In B. Bell, S. Brown, D. Finkelstein, and A. McCleery (eds.), *The Edinburgh History of the Book in Scotland*, vol. 2. Edinburgh: Edinburgh University Press, 221–33.
Sonenscher, M. (2007). *Before the Deluge*. Princeton: Princeton University Press.

12 Genovesi and enlightened political economy

José Luís Cardoso

Introduction

Antonio Genovesi lived at a time of considerable transformation. He was not, for sure, fully aware of the extension and far-reaching consequences of the economic, social and political changes taking place in Enlightened Europe. It might even be the case that he supported certain economic policy measures that could be identified with an old-fashioned mercantilist tradition. However, considered as a whole, Genovesi's view of the science of *economia civile* represented the typical conviction of an eclectic yet enlightened political economist who believed that the economy and society could be improved and that material life would get better if changes were made in the way institutions were established.

The habitual thought categories used to address the development of economic discourse throughout the eighteenth century (mercantilism, cameralism, physiocracy, political economy, etc.) do not always provide a helpful framework for the definition and comprehension of the work produced by authors who seem not to fit into, or cannot be identified with, a single category. The work of Genovesi serves perfectly to illustrate this difficulty in adopting a conventional classification system. It is therefore my aim to discuss here the relevance of Genovesi's notion of *economia civile* in the context of a broad conception of enlightened political economy, based on three main ideas: (1) the defense of the virtues of both private wealth and the opulence of nations as the result of a wish to institute new rules of behavior and new habits of life in society; (2) the belief in the ability to attain increased prosperity levels and (3) the defense of the moral advantages of the commercial society as a model for the organization of collective life.[1]

Genovesi was not alone in defending these ideas. They were also embedded in the texts of many other enlightened authors who wrote on economic and policy issues throughout the eighteenth century. The sharing and circulation of common views on the functioning of economic life is a key feature of the European Enlightenment. By paying attention to the process involved in the circulation, adaptation and appropriation of economic ideas, I shall draw attention to the relevance of both the translation of Genovesi's texts and the texts that he himself translated, thus stressing one of the most interesting features of the Enlightenment as an intellectual movement that cut across national borders and encountered different languages. This aspect is particularly relevant to understanding the role played by Genovesi in establishing political economy as the enlightened science of society.

Genovesi, translated and translator: an approach to knowledge appropriation

The richness and relevance of Genovesi's system of thought cannot simply be assessed through its impact on the Italian Enlightenment for we must also acknowledge the spread of his influence abroad. The Spanish case has been thoroughly discussed and highlighted (Astigarraga 2001, 2004) and certainly deserves special attention, though the dissemination of Genovesi's work was not limited to Southern European countries. Nevertheless, it is apparent that his ideas and proposals were particularly appropriate for countries and regions facing similar challenges in terms of the allocation and development of economic resources.

By giving a new focus to the points of reception and to the historical and institutional circumstances explaining the motives for both the adoption and adaptation of economic ideas and practices, I wish to emphasize the relevance of the institutional milieu in order to explain the conditions under which new forms of economic knowledge emerge and develop and are subsequently applied to particular places and contexts of appropriation. Thus, to understand why, when, how and where Genovesi was translated, we need to understand the historical conditions that made the reading of Genovesi useful and relevant in a given context.[2]

The circulation of scientific knowledge is not only an issue of intellectual curiosity or cultural interchange but also an issue of political trust and appropriation. Therefore, with regard to the particular case of the translation of economic texts, these should be viewed as instruments for the dissemination of knowledge, which gains further meaning when it serves the purposes of communities in different places. Translation thus reveals a heuristic capacity applied to the study of the processes of knowledge transmission and appropriation (cf. Gavroglu et al. 2008).

Throughout the second half of the eighteenth century, there was a great upsurge in the translation of economic literature, which corresponded both to the euphoria of translation as a rewarding and useful endeavor and to the growing relevance of political economy as a subject that had reached and conquered the public domain. In most European countries, by the mid-eighteenth century, translations into Latin were no longer needed for international readership, and Latin had also lost its role in scholarly writing as well as in fiction and poetry. The Enlightenment had offered the opportunity for cosmopolitan conversation without a common or universal language, though French had acquired the status of a *lingua franca*. However, being a *lingua franca* did not mean achieving exclusivity or uniqueness, and the common acceptance of French as a language of universal communication implied a wider process of translation from and into French of texts intended for widespread dissemination.

Political economy was one of the main subjects that contributed to the expansion of the market for translations. The main purpose was to reach a wider audience interested in topics related to public administration, the role of government and the functioning of markets and economic life in general. This new science of the market and of the modern institutions that served the dynamics of the newly emerging industrial capitalism was also a science that was placed at the service of the legislator, with added responsibility in the design and implementation of the new functions granted to the State. It was therefore crucial to spread the good news concerning the interpretation and monitoring of economic life. Translations became an important vehicle for the dissemination and popularization of the new science of political economy and therefore became a means for its appropriation in national contexts (cf. Oz-Salzberger 2006; Forget 2010).

Translators of essays and tracts on political economy were also interested in maintaining a dialogue and critically discussing the claims and arguments put forward by the authors translated. Thus, the process of translation was also a way of increasing public debate and revealing the role of the translator as someone who was entitled to the attributes of authorship.

These general remarks apply to the study of Genovesi's case, both as an author translated and as an author-translator. As far as the appropriation of his ideas in the European sphere is concerned, especially in countries like Spain and Portugal, local national contexts were receptive and responsive to Genovesi's vision of the role of useful knowledge as applied to the study of social and economic problems and as an indispensable element in the education of the ruling elite. His acknowledgement of the maturity of the science of commerce and *economia civile* as a field of intellectual inquiry and practical application in the fostering of economic reforms – political economy as science and art as a theoretical exercise and a practical field of problem-solving – was unconditionally welcomed. The critical stance on the Church's monopoly on cultural and educational matters, on the plea for a new type of lay ethics and on the fight against the primacy of canon law (which was regarded as incompatible with a modern, regalist notion of the State's sovereignty) were also issues that were clearly borrowed from the reading of the author of the *Lezioni*. Indeed, education was given special emphasis:

> The state is a large family. Hence it follows that, as in well governed families we are not merely interested in having a numerous offspring, but also in having the means to provide them with a good upbringing, education, and giving them a comfortable life: similarly it is necessary that in a state, additional to the promotion of population growth, it

> takes care to provide education for their bodies and souls, and in equal measure the means of a comfortable livelihood (…). The exclusive abandonment of these provisions to the private interest is the characteristic of barbarian people.
>
> (Genovesi 1765–67, Parte I, cap. 6, §1, 91–2)[3]

The Iberian readers of Genovesi were also concerned with the physical and moral causes of economic backwardness and were naturally receptive to policy measures driven by the need to enhance the population's skills, leading to the increased wealth and power of their nations. In some regards, there was an acceptance of an extended liberalization of economic mechanisms and institutions, especially as far as the defense of free competition in the internal market was concerned. But the typical Genovesian disclaimers were also present: the submission of private property and individual economic agency to the rules of the common good and public purpose; the constraints upon individual actions determined by the rationale of civil society; and the trust in the role of the State as a factor of progress and development.[4] In his own words,

> Furthermore, it is the ordinary rule of the state for reasons of public utility to regulate the classes of people and their occupations; a different thing is to oppress individuals' talents. Every free talent must not however interfere with the rule of public happiness. Therefore, the regulation of the arts and crafts is not the oppression of the scope of talents, but rather the orientation of them towards the public good (…). All wise people will agree, that the sources of revenues, and the strength of the state must be cultivated and taken care of in proportion to their utility and their public benefit.
>
> (Genovesi 1765–67, Parte I, cap. XII, §12, 173)

What makes this appropriation of Genovesi's ideas particularly interesting is the fact that Genovesi himself had followed a similar path in the assimilation of others' ideas. He was aware of the need to learn from the experience of other European countries and acclaimed the benefits of being eclectic and open to different schools and streams of thought (cf. Fusco 2009). His familiarity with the works of Melon, Montesquieu, Hebert, Forbonnais and other authors from the circle of Vincent de Gournay helps us to understand the plurality of his French influences. However, the most remarkable feature of Genovesi's appropriation of economic ideas was his translation (partly shared with his brother) of John Cary's *Essay on the State of England in relation to its trade*, originally published in 1695 (Genovesi 1757–58).

Sophus Reinert (2011) has reconstructed the amazing history of the successful and successive translations of Cary's book, first into French (in 1755), then from French into Italian – translated with many additions by Genovesi (in 1757–58) – and finally from Italian into German (in 1788). According to

Reinert, this impressive case study serves to illustrate the role of emulation, of learning from others' experience, through the translation of economic texts. Emulation implied prior knowledge of the history of the implementation of successful economic policies in rival nations, which was much more effective than the mere replication of abstract theoretical recipes. The emulation of good decisions on economic issues and policy-making was obviously a serious requirement for countries and places, such as Naples in the mid-eighteenth century, which was a backward European region waiting for an opportunity to catch up.

The main goal of Genovesi's translation of Cary's book was to show how England had reached its supremacy and economic power and to demonstrate the main English achievements in building up a commercial society. This was an approach that implicitly claimed that any other nation could follow the same steps and emulate England on its path to progress and growth. Such a process did not imply the expansion of borders or the conquest of other territories. Commerce was a key element, but it was not the only way to catch up. It was also necessary to create industrial power and to reinforce the means for facing economic competition on an international scale. Political economy was precisely the science that could contribute to understand how institutions could be reformed to create the conditions for mutual benefits. Free trade could not be supported in an abstract fashion but could be supported only if it served the purpose of increasing the wealth of the nation.

The legacy of Genovesi as a major and authoritative reference – an author who translated and deserved to be translated – shows that the translation and publication of economic works in the eighteenth century was not only aimed at reaching an erudite audience and regarded as a means for introducing enlightened ideas. It was also directed at a wider range of social segments that could benefit from doctrinal as well as technical teachings, and thus, it could encourage their active involvement in the public sphere.

From the science of commerce to *economia civile* and enlightened political economy

The Italian translation of Cary's book occurred during a period when Genovesi had already initiated his experience of teaching *Commercio e Meccanica* in Naples under the patronage, and at the request of, Bartolomeu Intieri. In the remaining manuscript corresponding to his classes (*Elementi di Commercio*), during the same period of 1757–58, Genovesi presents a notion of commerce as the matrix embracing all economic activities, with the science of commerce being responsible for providing a normative framework for understanding the functioning of real economic life in its three basic dimensions: (a) consumption goods provided by agriculture, (b) population and skills applied to industry and (c) money and the monetary circuit assisting commercial exchanges (in Genovesi 2005; cf. Pii 1984).

Together with Forbonnais, Cary and others, Genovesi conveyed the notion of a commercial society that could challenge the conventional, reconstructed view of the role of market mechanisms and laissez-faire in fostering economic development. Increased production, innovative entrepreneurship and technological change were seen as key elements for understanding the path to economic growth, but they should by no means be solely considered as the outcome of individual agency in competitive markets. In his own words,

> Every person has a natural and innate obligation to obtain his own happiness: but the body politic is just made of such persons; hence all the body politic, and each of its members have an obligation to do on its part whatever it knows and can do for the prosperity of all; assuming that it is possible to do so without offending the rights of other civil bodies.
>
> (Genovesi 1765–67, Parte I, cap. 1, §39, 45)

Furthermore, economic interaction was not only a consequence of *doux commerce* but also of the jealousy of trade (Hont 2005). Commerce is not always peaceful. Because economic development depends on competitive, value-added export goods, conflict and war may be needed to reach such a goal and to guarantee hegemony. Rivalry is a natural outcome of the relationship between countries looking forward to increased material welfare. Therefore, emulation emerges as the other side of the coin, replacing jealousy as a means of attaining the common good.

This reading of Genovesi favors the adoption of an approach to the history of the emergence of political economy that challenges the reconstruction operated by historiographical traditions, which do not always adequately address the combination of individual action with State responsibility in regulating the natural order of markets and society.

Based on the assumption that individuals know full well how to satisfy their own interests, both as producers and consumers, and on the assumption that such satisfaction corresponds to a defining feature of human nature, enlightened political economy is ready to admit that the participation of individual agents in the market leads to optimal results for the community as a whole. Private interests are seen not as vicious but as virtuous ingredients of the natural order. In this way, self-interest is no longer an end in itself but rather an intelligent mechanism that generates actions and institutions that converge towards the common good and the creation of public happiness.

Yet the private area of personal relations and individual interests does not appear just as a factor for further sociability. In a certain way, its existence is only conceivable in a public context that is related to the world of commercial relations, contract systems, universal rules of administration and justice and, above all, the very existence of moral sentiments that encourage individual action aimed at human improvement. This corresponds to the notion of *economia civile* put forward by Genovesi in the *Lezioni*, i.e. a notion that includes "institutions and sociability, plurality of motives for human action, intrinsic motivations and creativity" (Porta 2011, 522) as well as cooperative forces and institutional interactions aimed at achieving individual utility and understood as a readiness to perform good acts as a means of attaining public happiness (cf. Bruni and Porta 2003).

Therefore, this search for happiness should be the subject of policy decisions under the rule of an enlightened legislator. The adherence to the political program of enlightened despotism, grounded in the philosophy of natural law and in light of a wider conception of the role of the legislator in the promotion of wise civil laws as well as in the demand for State intervention in strategic economic affairs, is not considered to be opposed to the competitive framework of a market economy. On the contrary, these programs serve to argue in favor of the right balance between civil life, human wellbeing, social welfare and public happiness, which are the central elements of Genovesi's notion of *economia civile*:

> The most important ends of the civil economy are twofold in my opinion. Firstly, the nation, the economy of which we wish to direct, should be the most populous, making allowance for its internal forces, atmospheric conditions and geographical location. Secondly it should, as much as possible, be affluent and powerful.
>
> (Genovesi 1765–67, Parte I, Introd., 21)

Hence, the search for self-interest follows a set of norms established by the ruler, which individuals freely accept because they know that in this way, they will be able to better satisfy their objectives. This leads to the conception of the functions of the State, which include the explicit recognition of its role in regulating the commercial society.

The defense of the virtues of both private wealth and the opulence of nations is the result of a desire to institute in society new rules of behavior and new habits of life that will allow for the blossoming of economic life and the attainability of increased prosperity levels. In other words, it is important to defend the moral advantages of the commercial society, and of an ethics responsible for the triumph of the future of capitalism, as a model for the organization of an improved collective life (cf. Cardoso 2014).

The increase in the levels of consumption and the generalized access to goods, which previously had a superfluous connotation, illustrate the construction of a decent society in which social status is determined in accordance with a new standard of public prosperity. Luxury is no longer judged by moral conceptions, now incorporating the virtuous attributes of an instrument for the creation and circulation of wealth. The flourishing of commerce generates the additional trust of individuals in the capacity of governments to provide freedom, equality and justice. And there exists a universal disposition of the human mind to understand and accept the reforms that will speed up the achievement of progress, as Emma Rothschild (2001) pointed out when discussing the essence of the spirit of the Enlightenment.

Concluding remarks

The notion of enlightened political economy presented above may be considered controversial, particularly regarding the claim toward the existence of just one political economy of the Enlightenment instead of there being different varieties or approaches. However, I would like to argue in favor of a coherent and unitary conception of the identity of enlightened political economy.

This discussion replicates the unsolved and endless debate about the nature of the Enlightenment as a single intellectual movement, with defining elements of universal meaning, such as reason, humanity, liberty, tolerance, nature, happiness, etc.[5] The critical contribution contained in different approaches, which stress the existence of a range of distinct "Enlightenments" as a plural phenomenon that emerged through different forms and contents in specific historical and national contexts, is certainly worth considering.[6] However, because of the acceptance of many of the caveats concerning the importance of the historical contextualization of different national expressions of the Enlightenment, one should not conclude that it is not possible to apprehend the existence of common features. In fact, when discussing the process of the appropriation of economic texts through translations above, I clearly stressed the relevance of national contexts, which serve as a motivation for the assimilation of ideas created in different institutional and geographical settings. Nevertheless, the appropriation and emulation processes do not preclude the possibility of tracing elements shared at a global level. As Franco Venturi would put it, the "cosmopolitan" elements concerning the awareness of the international similarities between intellectual interests and goals are not contradicted but instead complemented by the "patriotic" elements related to the improvement of the situation of individual countries considered in their singular, national circumstances (Venturi 1972).

The subject matter of political economy provides the ground upon which the intersection of national peculiarities can be drawn. It helps to unify multiple approaches that share a common diagnosis and have similar concerns about economic and social reforms. And it is indisputable that Genovesi played a unique role in this area, providing new concepts, innovative policy recommendations and a coherent global framework for the development of what is now labeled as enlightened political economy. The way in which he was read, translated and used in other countries and the way in which he read, translated and used authors from other countries embody the process of the appropriation and emulation of ideas and practices that represented one of the main features of the Enlightenment. Political economy, dressed in the language of *economia civile*, was a key instrument in rendering it unique and universal.

Notes

1 For the discussion of these reconstructed features, the inspiration offered by the reading of Gilbert Faccarello's illuminating essays on French enlightened economic literature should be acknowledged. See, in particular, Faccarello (1992, 1994); and Faccarello and Steiner (2008).
2 The vision of a universal science for which national and regional features were totally irrelevant had been gradually replaced by a new approach to the cultural and intellectual history of science that very much took into account the "local manifestations of universal science" (Ophir and Shapin 1991, 5). On this topic, see also Livingstone (2003) and Withers (2007).
3 I am thankful to Lilia Costabile and Antoin Murphy for helping with the English translation of Genovesi's quotations.
4 For a recent overview of Genovesi's main ideas on these issues, cf. Palatano 2012.
5 For a brief presentation of this rich historiographical debate, cf. Robertson 2005, Chapter 1. A short presentation of the main interpretations of the Enlightenment and its distinctive features through a genealogy of how, when and where its concept and narrative were first developed is given by Edelstein (2010).
6 The argument that there is not one Enlightenment, *the* Enlightenment, but a variety of many Enlightenments defined by national contexts, different places and spaces was the central message put forward by Porter and Mikulás (1981). For an updated review and further development of the argument, see Withers (2007).

References

Astigarraga, Jesus, 2001. The light and shade of Italian economic thought in Spain (1750–1850). In P. F. Asso (ed.), *From Economists to Economists. The International Spread of Italian Economic Thought, 1750–1950*. Firenze: Polistampa, 227–253.

Astigarraga, Jesus, 2004. Diálogo económico en la 'outra' Europa. Las traducciones españolas de los economistas de la Ilustración napolitana (A. Genovesi, F. Galiani y G. Filangieri). *Cromohs*, 9, 1–21.

Bruni, Luigino and Porta, Pier Luigi, 2003. Economia civile and pubblica felicità in the Italian Enlightenment. *History of Political Economy*, vol. 35, Supplement, 361–385.

Cardoso, José Luís, 2014. The political economy of rising capitalism. In Larry Neal and Jeffrey Williamson (eds.), *The Cambridge History of Capitalism*, vol. I. Cambridge and New York: Cambridge University Press, 574–599.

Edelstein, Dan, 2010. *The Enlightenment. A Genealogy*. Chicago and London: Chicago University Press, 2010.

Faccarello, Gilbert, 1992. Turgot et l'économie politique sensualiste. In A. Béraud and G. Faccarello (eds.), *Nouvelle histoire de la pensée économique*, vol. I. Paris: La Découverte, 254–288.

Faccarello, Gilbert, 1994. '*Nil Repente*!': Galiani and Necker on economic reforms. *The European Journal of the History of Economic Thought*, 1:3, 519–550.

Faccarello, Gilbert and Steiner, Philippe, 2008. Interest, sensationism and the science of the legislator: French 'philosophie économique', 1695–1830. *The European Journal of the History of Economic Thought*, 15:1, 1–23.

Forget, Evelyn L., 2010. "At best an echo": eighteenth- and nineteenth-century translation strategies in the history of economics. *History of Political Economy*, 42:4, 653–677.

Fusco, Antonio Maria, 2009. *Visite in soffitta. Saggi di storia del pensiero economico.* Napoli: Editoriale Scientifica (Capitolo II – Antonio Genovesi e il suo mercantilismo "rinnovato", 47–68).

Gavroglu, Kostas et al., 2008. Science and technology in the European periphery: some historiographical reflections. *History of Science*, xlvi, 153–175.

Genovesi, Antonio, 1757–58. *Storia del commercio di Gran Bretagna scritta da J. Cary (…).* Napoli: Gessari (3 vols.).

Genovesi, Antonio, 1765–67. *Lezioni di commercio o sia di economia civile.* Napoli: Stamp. Simoniana (2 vols.). New edition: Bassano, 1769.

Genovesi, Antonio, 2005. *Lezioni di commercio o sia di economia civile, con Elementi di commercio.* Napoli: IISF (edited by Maria Luisa Pesante).

Hont, Istvan, 2005. *Jealousy of Trade. International Competition and the Nation-State in Historical Perspective.* Cambridge, MA and London: Harvard University Press.

Livingstone, David N., 2003. *Putting Science in its Place. Geographies of Scientific Knowledge.* Chicago and London: University of Chicago Press.

Ophir, Adi and Steven Shapin, 1991. The place of knowledge: a methodological survey. *Science in Context*, 4: 1, 3–21.

Oz-Salzberger, Fania, 2006. The Enlightenment in translation: regional and European aspects. *European Review of History – Revue européenne d'histoire*, 13: 3, 385–409.

Palatano, Rosario, 2012. *Antonio Genovesi.* Roma: Luiss University Press.

Pii, Eluggero, 1984. *Antonio Genovesi: dalla politica economica alla "politica civile".* Firenze: Leo S. Olschki.

Porta, Pier Luigi, 2011. Lombard Enlightenment and classical political economy. *The European Journal of the History of Economic Thought*, 18: 4, 521–550.

Porter, Roy and Mikulás, Teich (eds.), 1981. *The Enlightenment in National Context.* Cambridge and New York: Cambridge University Press.

Reinert, Sophus A., 2011. *Translating Empire. Emulation and the Origins of Political Economy.* Cambridge, MA and London: Harvard University Press.

Robertson, John, 2005. *The Case for the Enlightenment. Scotland and Naples 1680–1760.* Cambridge and New York: Cambridge University Press.

Rothschild, Emma, 2001. *Economic Sentiments. Adam Smith, Condorcet and the Enlightenment.* Cambridge, MA and London: Harvard University Press.

Venturi, Franco, 1972. *Italy and the Enlightenment: Studies in a Cosmopolitan Century.* London: Longman.

Withers, Charles W. J., 2007. *Placing the Enlightenment. Thinking Geographically about the Age of Reason.* Chicago and London: The University of Chicago Press.

13 Jean-Baptiste Say's footnotes to Ricardo

Keith Tribe

In 1819, a French translation of the first edition of David Ricardo's *On the Principles of Political Economy and Taxation* was published in Paris with notes by Jean-Baptiste Say (Ricardo 1819). When a German edition appeared in 1821, this too carried Say's footnotes from the French edition, and it was also based, like the French translation, on the 1817 edition of Ricardo (Ricardo 1821).[1] The original French translation was republished in 1835 in Paris and Brussels,[2] prefaced by a "notice on the life and writings of Ricardo, published by his family", which was, in fact, a sometimes rather free translation of McCulloch's "Memoir of the Life and Writings of David Ricardo, Esq. M.P.".[3] McCulloch here presented Ricardo's *Principles* as being "With the single exception of the 'Wealth of Nations,' … the most important, as it certainly is the most original and profound, work, that has ever appeared on Political Economy" (Anon. 1825, p. 16), proceeding to an executive summary of the text in three points:

> 1st, That rent is altogether extrinsic to the cost of production; 2d, That capital being the produce of previous labour, and having no value except what it derives from that labour, the fact that the value of the commodities produced by its agency is always determined by the quantities of capital laid out or wasted in their production, shows that it is really determined by the *quantities of labour* bestowed on them; and 3d., That a *rise of wages* occasions a *fall of profits*, and not a rise in the price of commodities, and a *fall* of wages a *rise of profits*, and not a fall of prices.[4]
>
> (1825 pp. 18–19; cf. 1835 Paris edition p. XX)

When Karl Marx first read *Principles* in 1844, working through the writings of Jean-Baptiste Say, Adam Smith, David Ricardo and James Mill, it was in this 1835 translation;[5] the fact that this edition of Ricardo was also prefaced by McCulloch's summary of Ricardo should therefore prompt pause for thought.

However, quite aside from any speculation about the impact of McCulloch's simplifications on Marx's thinking, there is, of course, a further issue here. Marx had begun by reading Say's *Traité* in the third 1817 edition and leafing through the third 1836 edition of his *Cours complet*; then he had made some notes on Fryderyk Skarbek's 1829 *Théorie des richesses sociales*, which chiefly offered a pastiche of Say. Marx then continued on to read Smith's *Wealth of Nations* in the 1802 Garnier translation, then Ricardo's *Principles* in the 1835 Paris version, and he rounded off his introduction to political economy with the 1823 French translation of James Mill's *Elements of Political Economy* and the 1825 French translation of McCulloch's *Discourse on the Rise, Progress, Peculiar Objects and Importance of Political Economy*, which came with a substantial commentary on Ricardo by its translator, Guillaume Prévost. Marx commented here, "It goes without saying here that it is a matter of the doctrines that distinguish D. Ricardo from Smith"[6] (MEGA I/3, p. 553). This would very quickly become the parameter along which Marx would develop his approach to Smith: not the Adam Smith as author of a *Wealth of Nations* with whom we are familiar today, but an Adam Smith, seen from the restricted perspective of the early nineteenth century as the founding theorist of value and price upon whom Malthus, Mill and Ricardo built.[7] This was essentially a Ricardian vision but as we have also seen, a vision buttressed by McCulloch's version of Ricardo's achievements as expressed in his *Memoir*. And added to all this, the edition of Ricardo that Marx read came with a running commentary from Jean-Baptiste Say. And so when Marx read Ricardo for the first time his perspective upon English political economy was not direct; it was mediated by both McCulloch and Say.

Say and Ricardo had first met during Say's visit to England in the autumn and early winter of 1814–1815; they met again in Paris in 1817 and 1822.[8] In August 1815, Say had sent Ricardo a copy of his *Catéchisme d'Economie politique*; Ricardo thanked him for it in a letter of 18 August but in so doing, making a criticism:

> You have I perceive a little modified the definition of the word *value* as far as it is dependent on utility, but with great diffidence, I observe, that I do not think you have mastered the difficulties which attach to the explanation of that difficult word. Utility is certainly the foundation of value, but the degree of utility can never be the measure by which to estimate value. A commodity difficult of production will always be more valuable than one which is easily produced although all men should agree that the latter is more useful than the former. A commodity must be useful to have value but the difficulty of its production is the true measure of its value.
>
> (Letter 107 18 August 1815, *Works and Correspondence* Vol. VI, pp. 247–8)

Ricardo was here objecting to the way in which Say in his *Catéchisme* introduced the idea of value creation and linked it directly to value:

> *Is there anything that can create wealth?*
>
> Yes, for to do that it is enough to create value, or augment the value already present in the things one possesses.
>
> *How does one give value to an object?*
>
> By giving it a utility that it does not have.
>
> *How does one augment the value of things one already has?*
>
> By augmenting the degree of utility that they have when one acquires them...
>
> (Say 1996, pp. 314–5)

Say responded by emphasising that Ricardo was imputing to him the idea that utility was the unique source of value; whereas he had instead maintained that utility is the prime source of value for if there was no use for something, it would not be demanded and there would be no price and no value (Letter 117, Say to Ricardo, 10 September 1815 *Works and Correspondence* Vol. VI, p. 271). Say added that Ricardo and he were in agreement about the costs of production – "what you call *the difficulty of its production*" – as setting the lowest price at which a good could be sold, but he then repeated that this was not "la cause premiere [sic]" of the price set by the producer.

Say continues then to maintain that he and Ricardo were fundamentally in agreement, even if they did not share precisely the same terminology. Later commentators would point to differences in the level of abstraction or to the fact that Say makes no concession to differences in the time period being considered. But the most explicit difference, evident here, was that the prime source of value originates not in the "difficulty of production" of a good but in whether anyone has any use for it.[9]

Say and Ricardo did meet in 1817, but there was no further correspondence between them relating to these issues until Say sent Ricardo the fourth edition of the *Traité* in October 1819, although Ricardo did not receive it until he returned to London (Letter 347, Say to Ricardo, 10 October 1819, in *Works and Correspondence* Vol. VIII, p. 136). In his reply, Ricardo remarks on a gradual convergence of their ideas and comments that the chapter on value in the new edition is greatly improved, but he is also moved to make a clarification:

> In that Chapter [on value] you appear to have misapprehended a position of mine. I do not say that it is the value of labour which regulates the value of all commodities, for that is an opinion I do all in my power to overthrow; but I say that it is the comparative quantity of labour necessary to the production of value, which regulates their relative value.
>
> (Letter 352, Ricardo to Say, 11 January 1820, in *Works and Correspondence* Vol. VIII, p. 149)

Ricardo had in the meantime seen a copy of the French translation of *Principles* for he continues on to correct a misunderstanding on the part of Say, involving the existence of land that pays no rent, which Ricardo had identified in the notes to the French translation of *Principles*, indicating that he had by this time worked through Say's footnoted comments. It seems rather doubtful that he would have found in these notes much evidence of a convergence of opinion. More than a year before, Ricardo had reported to Mill that his publisher had received a copy of the translation but not forwarded it immediately, assuming that Say would have also sent it directly; Ricardo commented to Mill, "I fear that Say is not quite friendly towards me..." (Letter 292, Ricardo to Mill, 12 December 1818, in *Works and Correspondence* Vol. VII, p. 361). Mill was considerably more direct about his attitude to Say, being "full of contempt for these notes of Say" (Letter 297, Mill to Ricardo, 24 December 1818, in *Works and Correspondence* Vol. VII, p. 375). Responding, Ricardo remarked that "Some of them are ingenious, but he does not grapple with the real question in dispute, - he makes a shew of answering it, but he completely evades it" (Letter 298, Ricardo to Mill, 28 December 1818, in *Works and Correspondence* Vol. VII, p. 378).[10]

Say's commentary on Ricardo takes the form of footnotes, and he begins with a long comment appended to the end of the very first paragraph of Ricardo's opening chapter, in which Ricardo had summarised Smith's distinction between "value in use" and "value in exchange" (Vol. I, p. 11). But as Say correctly notes here, while this distinction is fundamental to political economy, Smith devoted his book primarily to exchange value, devoting very little attention to "use value" (1835, p. 2).[11] Whereas Ricardo places this distinction in the first paragraph of his first chapter "On Value", the passage he is referring to in Smith is buried towards the end of the fourth chapter of *Wealth of Nations* (WN I.iv.13), and Smith then passes directly to exchange value, opening the following chapter with the idea that "Labour, therefore, is the real measure of the exchangeable value of all commodities." (WN I.v.1). Ricardo goes on to argue at the start of his following paragraph that "Utility then is not the measure of exchangeable value, although it is absolutely essential to it" and devotes the next two pages to clarifying a distinction he has attributed to Smith but to which Smith had given much less attention. In the course of so doing, Ricardo emphasises that he uses the term "commodity" and talks of the commodity's exchangeable value with respect to "such commodities only as can be increased in quantity by the exertion of human industry, and on the production of which competition operates without restraint" (Vol. I, p. 12). Say, for his part, devotes most of his initial footnote to a rebuttal of the idea that exchange itself can be the source of social wealth for as he argues, it is value itself that became the fixed base of the science of political economy.

Say's next annotation comments on Smith rather than Ricardo, who had quoted from the second paragraph of WN Book I Chapter V that "labour was the first price". Say objects that Smith, like all English writers after him, confounds "travail" and "industrie"; productive labour, he argued, includes all kinds of work, from studying the laws of nature through the work of an entrepreneur to that of a labourer, and so it is more appropriate to call this "industrie" than "travail", a term more fitted to repetitive, physical activity (1835, p. 7).

In the third annotation, Say directly states that Ricardo has erred. He comments on the following passage in Ricardo's first chapter:

> If the quantity of labour realized in commodities, regulate their exchangeable value, every increase of the quantity of labour must augment the value of that commodity on which it is exercised, as every diminution must lower it.
>
> (*Works and Correspondence* Vol. I, p. 13)

This, suggests Say, seems wrong for it is not just the amount of labour applied that regulates the value of things: Ricardo neglects the prime element, utility – it is utility that occasions the demand in the first place. Costs of production affect the scarcity of a good, limiting the amount offered in exchange. The exchange value rises or falls with the demand for it, which reflects utility:

> It is therefore not the cost of production *alone*, which Ricardo, following Smith, calls the *natural price* of a thing, which regulates its exchangeable value, its usual price (*prix courant*), if one wants to express this value in money. When the costs of production increase, for the exchangeable value to likewise increase it would be necessary that the relation of supply and demand remain the same, that the demand also increases; and if it in fact diminishes, it is impossible, other things being equal, that it does not fall. Exchangeable value cannot therefore increase like the cost of production.
>
> (1835, p. 10)

Some conception of elasticities seems to creep in here to muddle the argument slightly, but it is nonetheless clear that Say disputes a premise that he attributes here to Ricardo, and which Ricardo clearly states: that the labour embodied determines the cost of production of one good and the cost of production determines its exchange value. Just like Smith, in fact. As is plain from the comment in the letter of 15 January 1820 to Say, Ricardo later articulated a far more nuanced approach to this issue; but he did not do so, it should be said, in these opening pages of the first edition of *Principles*, and it is this version of Ricardo that Say is commenting upon. We could, of course, read into this statement Ricardo's later clarification; and Ricardo does then go on in his discussion of Smith and an invariable standard to hint at this. But in this first edition of *Principles*, Ricardo fails to state (what later became) his own conception clearly. Consequently, we cannot argue that Say's reading of Ricardo's statement of the relationship between the quantity of labour and the *regulation* of exchange value is mistaken. Say dismisses this idea of an invariable value as a "pure chimera" because one cannot measure values with values, with an essentially variable standard (1835, p. 12). He comments further on Ricardo's discussion of the fact that corn is subject to fluctuations (In quantity? In value? Ricardo does not say), suggesting that it is not clear why Ricardo treats corn and labour as less invariable than anything else (1835, p. 13). When Ricardo postulates that if an invariable value were found, it would be "of considerable use towards attaining a correct theory, to ascertain what the essential qualities of a standard are..." (Vol. I, p. 17 fn. 3), Say simply dismisses the idea (1835, p. 16).

He refrains from further comment until p. 25 where he objects to Ricardo's "adding up" the total quantity of labour necessary to manufacture stockings to arrive at their exchangeable value:

> the aggregate sum of these various kinds of labour, determines the quantities of other things for which these stockings will exchange, while the same consideration of the various quantities of labour which have been bestowed on those other things, will equally govern the portion of them which will be given for the stockings.
>
> (I, pp. 25)

Say comments here that Ricardo has forgotten about profits and interest payments, that there is nothing left in the cost of production to recompense the different amounts of capital used in the production of the stockings. The same goes for the rent of land – this was the note that especially enraged Mill in his letter of 24 December 1818. But at this point, Say relents; he adds no further comments in the remaining thirty pages of this first chapter.

Chapter II is "On Rent", which begins with a discussion of what Smith meant by the word. He had been primarily concerned with why it exists and how it affects the progress of wealth; he had devoted one hundred pages to a somewhat rambling consideration of agricultural production and improvement. Ricardo has in view the much narrower question of "whether the appropriation of land, and the consequent creation of rent, will occasion any variation in the relative value of commodities, independent of the quantity of labour necessary to production." (Vol. I, p. 67). He first devotes a couple of paragraphs to a discussion of Smith before developing his own account of the progress of differential rent.

Say's first note here (1835, p. 59) relates to Smith's discussion of forestry and whether any part of the payment made for timber was a rental payment. He objects to Ricardo's assertion that in a new country, there will be no rent paid – this is not an empirical observation but is merely a property of Ricardo's model (Vol. I, p. 70; 1835, p. 64). Ricardo devoted a long footnote to Say's apparent neglect in his *Principes* of the idea that it is the cost of production that ultimately regulates price (Vol. I, p. 73 fn.*) to which Say simply responds in a footnote by reasserting his view that if something is too expensive to sell, it will just cease being made (1835, p. 70). Say next objects to Ricardo's point that the price of corn is not high because a rent is paid but that a rent is paid because the price of corn is high and that if landlords were to forego their rents, some of their tenants would be able to live like gentlemen (I, pp. 74–5). Say's remarks extend over four pages, arguing that the fruits of nature are special and that supply and demand regulate the price – so he simply does not accept or, perhaps more pertinently, understand the function of Ricardo's account of rent in his general theory of distribution (1835, pp. 73–6). The comment by David Buchanan on Smith, which Ricardo appends to a very long footnote over pp. 76–7, is itself then elaborated on by Say for another three pages (1835, pp. 81–3), making similar points about land and profitability. Say then argues in another note that the productive faculties of the soil are comparable to those of labour because human faculties, such as muscular power and intelligence, are also ultimately gifts of nature (1835, p. 84); the chapter then continues for another ten pages without further comment.

Chapter III, "On the Rent of Mines", is very short; Say appends one note, stretching over six pages, which is probably longer that Ricardo's text, and which returns to the same issue of the supply and demand for goods and the relation of this to human labour and repeats what Say had previously argued with regard to profit and rent (1835, pp. 98–103). Likewise, Chapter IV, on natural and market price, has only one long footnote at the end, forming an appendix to the chapter:

> The distinction between natural price and usual price (*prix courant*) that M. Ricardo allows, following Smith, seems completely chimerical. In political economy there is only the usual price.
>
> (1835, pp. 111–12)

But it seemed that Say's combativeness waned as he got further into the book. Chapter V, on wages, has likewise only one comment, simply supporting Ricardo's view that the poor must be taught the value of independence and not look to charity – this was the view, according to Say, "not just of a philanthropist, but an enlightened philanthropist" (1835, pp. 136–7). The chapter on profits has only one short, explanatory comment on the first page (1835, p. 140), and chapter VII, on foreign trade, has just two (1835, pp. 185–6, 206–7). The density of rebuttal and argument gives way to occasional remarks.

What can be learned by looking at Say's footnotes to the core chapters of Ricardo's *Principles*? At one level, it points up the contrast between Say's simple insistence on supply and demand and Ricardo's more complex, if troubled, analysis of labour and exchange value. But paying attention to Say's own comments forces us to re-examine Ricardo's text through Say's eyes, detached from what we might otherwise know about the book's subsequent editions or Ricardo's clarifications in correspondence and arguments with Malthus. The text that this approach reveals is indeed very ambiguous.

Ricardo begins his argument by referring to a distinction that Smith did make but that he did not consider important. Going back to Smith, one is forcibly struck by how clear and consistent the exposition of Smith is, compared to that of Ricardo. The first chapter of *Principles* teems with "clarifications" that only become clear if one already understands what Ricardo might be construed to mean. What, indeed, can one make of the following?

> If I have to hire a labourer for a week, and instead of ten shillings I pay him eight, no variation having taken place in the value of money, the labourer can probably obtain more food and necessaries, with his eight shillings, than he before obtained for ten: but this is owing, not to a rise in the real value of his wages, as stated by Adam Smith, and more recently by Mr. Malthus, but to a fall in the value of the things on which his wages are expended, things perfectly distinct; and yet for calling this a fall in the real value of wages, I am told that I adopt a new and unusual language, not reconcileable with the true principles of the science. To me it appears that the unusual and, indeed, inconsistent language, is that used by my opponents.
>
> (I, p. 19)

Ricardo's writing conveys a sense of order and logic, but the composition and production of the first edition of the *Principles* was anything but orderly and logical as Piero Sraffa makes clear in his introduction to it. Modern readings tend to Whiggishly indulge Ricardo: What Ricardo "really meant" is read back into his writings from a rational reconstruction of his later ideas so that the first edition of *Principles* is "clarified" in light of this. The *Works and Correspondence* version of the *Principles*, which Sraffa edited with the assistance of Maurice Dobb, is rightly based on the 1821 edition, with variations noted; in the case of the first chapter, an appendix prints the second half of the chapter in its original version rather than that of the 1821 edition. But Say's comments on Ricardo are all directed to the first edition, and by reviewing how Say read this text, we create a perspective upon Ricardo that works forward, not backward.

Notes

1 The French edition corrected the duplication of chapter numbers in the first edition of *Principles* but did not have the subheadings, together with associated rephrasing, that were introduced in Chapter 1 of the second 1819 edition of *Principles*. The 1821 German edition retained the duplicated chapters, marking them as Va & Vb and VIIIa & VIIIb. A new translation was made in the 1830s by Edwin Baumstark and published in 1837 by Engelmann of Leipzig.

2 "Seconde Édition, Revue, corrigée et augmentée d'une notice sur la vie et les écrits de Ricardo, publiée par sa famille", J.-P. Allaud, Paris 1835. The Brussels edition was pirated from the Paris edition and described on the title page as the Third Edition; the text is, however, the same as the Second Paris edition, with some slight variation in pagination.

3 The opening of the translation summarises McCulloch's first two paragraphs. McCulloch at times draws verbatim on the family memoir printed in Works Vol. X pp. 3–15; some passages of the French translation therefore look as though they come directly from this source. See Anon. [J. R. McCulloch] (1825). It is also worth noting that in McCulloch's discussion of the value theories of Smith and Ricardo, the original term "exchangeable value" is consistently translated as *valeur courante* - cf. the 1835 translation p. XIX and the 1825 English original pp. 16–18. Likewise, McCulloch's "rent" (p. 18) in the passage cited here is rendered as *revenu* (p. XX).

4 This passage in the 1825 Memoir repeats verbatim, apart from one minor grammatical revision, the summary that MacCulloch had already given in his *Discourse* (1824, pp. 67–8).

5 See (MEGA I/3, pp. 437–560). When I refer in the following to "the 1835 edition", I mean the Paris version.

6 The attribution in MEGA I/3 is incorrect and also involves a typo regarding the year of publication of the second edition of Mill's *Elements*, leading some commentators to assume that this involves a separate work by Prévost rather than a translator's supplement to the McCulloch text.

7 Piero Sraffa drew attention the way that each of the first six chapters of Ricardo's *Principles*, after which the book becomes entirely diffuse, were organised as a critique of individual chapters from Book I of *Wealth of Nations*: "Introduction" in Ricardo Vol. I p. xxiv.

8 See the summary of their relationship in Sraffa (1952). Terry Peach outlines their differences as regards value, utility and price in his 1993 (pp. 269–74).

9 Say sent Ricardo a copy of the 3rd Edition of the *Traité* on 21 July 1817, in which "my theory of values is better than the one you criticised" - Letter 221 in *Works and Correspondence* Vol. VII p. 166. Ricardo reported to Mill on 12 December 1818 that his publisher had received a copy but had not forwarded in immediately, assuming that Say would send it directly. Ricardo commented, "I fear that Say is not quite friendly towards me..." - Ricardo to Mill, 12 December 1818, Letter 292 in *Works and Correspondence* Vol. VII p. 361.

10 See more generally on this exchange Philippe Steiner (1996, p. 23 fn. 29).

11 Because Say's notes spread over several pages, I will refer here to the page numbers where the passage in question actually appears.

References

Anon. [J. R. McCulloch] (1825) *Memoir of the Life and Writings of David Ricardo, Esq. M.P.* London: Richard Taylor.

McCulloch, J. R. (1824) *Discourse on the Rise, Progress, Peculiar Objects, and Importance, of Political Economy*. Edinburgh: Archibald Constable & Co.

MEGA I/3 (1932) *Marx/Engels Gesamtausgabe* Erste Abteilung Band 3. Berlin: Marx-Engels Verlag, pp. 437–560.

Peach, T. (1993) *Interpreting Ricardo*. Cambridge: Cambridge University Press.

Ricardo, D. (1819) *Des principes de l'économie politique, et de l'impôt*, 2 volumes, trans. F. S. Constancio. Paris: J.-P. Aillaud.

Ricardo, D. (1821) *Die Grundsätze der politischen Oekonomie oder Staatswirthschaft und der Besteuerung*, trans. C. A. Schmidt. Weimar: Landes-Industrie-Comptoir.

Ricardo, D. (1835a) *Des principes de l'économie politique, et de l'impôt*, 2 volumes, trans. F. S. Constancio. Paris: J.-P. Aillaud.

Ricardo, D. (1835b) *Des principes de l'économie politique, et de l'impôt*, 2 volumes, trans. F. S. Constancio. Brussels: H. Dumont.

Ricardo, D. (1951–73) *The Works and Correspondence of David Ricardo*, ed. Piero Sraffa with Maurice Dobb, 11 volumes. London: Cambridge University Press.

Say, J.-B. (1996) *Cours d'économie politique et autres essais*, ed. Philippe Steiner. Paris: Flammarion.

Smith, A. (1976) *An Inquiry into the Nature and Causes of the Wealth of Nations*, ed. R. H. Campbell and A. S. Skinner. Oxford: Oxford University Press (cited as WN).

Sraffa, P. (1951) "Introduction" in *The Works and Correspondence of David Ricardo* Vol. I, pp. Xiii–lxii.

Sraffa, P. (1952) "Introductory Notes", *The Works and Correspondence of David Ricardo* Vol. VI, pp. Xxv–xxvii.

Steiner, P. (1996) "L'économie politique comme science de la modernité", in Say (1996) pp. 9–35.

14 German editions of Adam Smith's *Wealth of Nations*

Harald Hagemann[1]

Gilbert Faccarello is known internationally as one of the finest scholars in the history of economic thought, being a co-founder and co-editor of *The European Journal of the History of Economic Thought* and chairing the Council of the European Society for the History of Economic Thought (ESHET) from 2010 to 2015. He became widely known due to his scholarly contributions in two areas. The first main area embraces economic thought before, during and after the French Revolution as well as the investigation of the works of Pierre Le Pesant de Boisguilbert (1646–1714), Anne-Robert-Jacques Turgot (1727–81), Abbè Ferdinando Galiani (1728–87), or Marie-Jean-Antoine-Nicolas Caritat de Condorcet (1743–94). The second main area comprises classical economics, in particular the works of Adam Smith and David Ricardo as well as Karl Marx's critique of political economics and Piero Sraffa's post-classical theory of production. This holds for the theoretical treatment of analytical problems, such as Sraffa's construction of a "standard commodity" as an invariable measure of value, as well as a more historical investigation of the reception of the works of classical economists, such as Ricardo. A long-time collaborator with Faccarello in these studies is his friend Philippe Steiner. One of the works that stands out is their joint contribution on "The Diffusion of the work of Adam Smith in the French language" (Faccarello and Steiner 2002) to *A Critical Bibliography of Adam Smith*, edited by Keith Tribe.

Tribe himself contributed an erudite essay on "The German Reception of Adam Smith", which also dealt intensively with *The Theory of Moral Sentiments* and the German debate in the late nineteenth century on the "Adam Smith Problem", i.e. on the supposed antithesis between Smith's "altruistic" account of human motivation in his earlier *Theory of Moral Sentiments* and the "selfish" account in the *Wealth of Nations*. Whereas we can agree with Tribe (2002: 121) and the editors of the Glasgow edition of *The Theory of Moral Sentiments* that the Adam Smith Problem has to be considered as a "pseudo-problem based on ignorance and misunderstanding" (Raphael and Macfie 1976: 20), Tribe, on the other hand, elucidates an important difference in the history of the reception of Smithian ideas between France and Germany. Thus, Faccarello and Steiner discuss in detail the key role of Smith's *Wealth of Nations* before, during and after the French Revolution, a role which is also indicated by the many translations in this period. However, they also point out "that Smith's works endured a long eclipse – from the early 1880s to the 1940s" (119). Tribe rightly emphasises that, on the other hand, "in Germany of the 1920s Adam Smith's work was a continuing stimulus to both scholarship and teaching" (Tribe 2002: 122), which came to an abrupt end with the Nazis' rise to power. That the "*Zeitgeist*" was favourable to the reception of Smithian ideas in Weimar Germany is also reflected in the many new editions and reprints of earlier translations of the *Wealth of Nations* that were sold in the 1920s. In the following article, I will focus on the history of German editions of the *Wealth of Nations*, commenting also on the quality and impact. The first German edition of Adam Smith's *Wealth of Nations* was already published as early as 1776/78 in two volumes, Books I-III appearing within the same year as the original and Volume II, with Books IV–V, appearing two years later. The editor and translator of this edition, which was entitled *Untersuchung der Natur und Ursachen von Nationalreichthümern*, was Johann Friedrich Schiller (1737–1814), a godfather of the famous poet Friedrich Schiller. Since 1769, Schiller had worked and lived in London, where he observed the British book market for bestsellers on behalf of German publishers and sometimes translated the works himself as he had done with John Hawkesworth's famous account of the voyages in the Southern Hemisphere. There was no copyright protection for foreign books at the time, and it could happen that a quick translation directly from galley-proofs meant that the translated book was published before the original work. In London, Schiller came to know Smith personally. Smith's book in Schiller's translation got several reviews, the most remarkable being by the philosopher Johann Georg Heinrich Feder (1740–1821), who was teaching at the University of Göttingen since 1768 and in his March review of Volume I, in contrast to some later critics, praised the good quality of Schiller's translation. Feder, as well as other reviewers, such as Friedrich Nicolai and in particular the Swiss physiocrat Isaak Iselin (1728–82), in benign neglect of Smith's critique in Chapter 9 of Book IV, interpreted Smith as supporting physiocratic doctrines. Despite these reviews, however, in contrast to contemporary France, Smith's *Wealth of Nations* had only little impact on German economic discourse, which is also indicated by the fact that the Schiller edition sold only very poorly and did not go into further editions.

After the French Revolution, a new and better German translation by Christian Garve (1742–98), who was Extraordinary Professor of Philosophy in Leipzig from 1768–72, thereafter bookseller in Breslau, Silesia, and an important mediator for the diffusion of the ideas of the Scottish Enlightenment (see Waszek 2006), was published. Garve had already translated works by Adam Ferguson and Edmund Burke and, after becoming ill, was supported in the finalisation by his friend August Dörrien, Postmaster of

Leipzig. With the new Garve edition entitled *Untersuchung über die Natur und die Ursachen des Nationalreichthums* and published in two volumes in 1794/96, the Smithian doctrines were now perceived well and discussed on a much broader scale. This new German edition also became an economic success as indicated by further reprints, a second and third edition published in 1799 and 1810, and pirate editions published in Frankfurt and Leipzig (1796–99) and in Vienna in 1814.

A particular role was played in this process by the two universities of Göttingen and Königsberg (see Treue 1951 and Winkel 1986). As the University in the Kingdom of Hanover, Göttingen had a high number of British students, including Princes, for whom special lectures had to be given. However, among the students, there were also many Germans who later became liberal reformers or well-known economists, such as Johann Heinrich von Thünen (1783–1850) who studied with Georg Sartorius in 1803–04. Sartorius (1765–1828) taught Smithian ideas from 1792 onwards, when he got his habilitation from the University of Göttingen. In two review articles of the third volume of the Schiller edition upon the appearance of the first volume of the new Garve edition in the *Göttinger gelehrten Anzeigen* of 19 October 1793 and 29 November 1794, Sartorius explains the slow diffusion process of Smith's ideas in Germany with the complexities and the great difficulties in understanding the *Wealth of Nations*, even for a native Englishman. He also consoles Schiller's publisher Weidmann, who had complained of his low sales figures, that Smith's work would not remain a shelf-warmer because reason finally is confirmed. Sartorius had been a student of Feder. He became Extraordinary Professor in 1797 and Full Professor in 1802, and taught at the University of Göttingen until his death. He based his *Handbook of the State Economy* for the use at academic lectures explicitly on Adam Smith's principles (Sartorius 1796). In his Preface, Sartorius expresses his conviction "that Smith had found the truth" and that it is therefore his duty to contribute to the diffusion of Smithian ideas because twenty years after its original publication, the *Wealth of Nations* hardly had any influence in Germany, neither in economic policy nor in academic lectures.[2]

A decade later, Sartorius's *Handbook* was published in a second edition under a different title. Whereas this work is faithful to the Smithian principles and can be read as an introduction to the *Wealth of Nations*, Sartorius (1806) published his own textbook in the same year. It is deeply influenced by Smith but also full of constructive criticism. In the first of his four treatises, Sartorius criticises Smith's assumption of labour as a constant objective measure of value, whereas in the final two treatises, he deals with Lauderdale's objections against Smith's treatments of savings and the distinction between private wealth and the wealth of nations. Most important is the second treatise in which Sartorius, although in general also favouring the principle of free competition, makes a number of historical objections against the unlimited validity of this principle. The state could not always be passive but must fight against all attempts to restrict competition and against a too high concentration of power. Great capitalists could crush small ones and thereafter exploit the public. After a bad harvest, merchants might want to export corn to increase their profits to the disadvantage of their compatriots who might starve. It could therefore happen that the pursuit of private interests does not always contribute to the public benefit.

Whereas Göttingen was the opening gate for Smithian ideas and the Scottish Enlightenment in the northwest of Germany, Königsberg played a similar role in the distant northeast. Since the mid-eighteenth century, Königsberg had been an important place for trade and commerce where British industrial products were exchanged against agricultural products from Eastern Prussia and a wider hinterland. In the "city of enlightenment" of Immanuel Kant (1724–1804), it was particularly Christian Jakob Kraus (1753–1807) who taught "practical philosophy" and cameralism and was an important mediator of Smithian doctrines and liberal ideas. Kraus had started to study at the University of Königsberg in April 1771 and became a close student and later friend of Kant, who also strongly supported Kraus's appointment to Professor in 1781. In 1779, Kraus had moved to Göttingen, where he did advanced studies with Feder, Christian Gottlob Heyne, and August Ludwig von Schlözer before making a doctorate in Philosophy at the University in Halle in fall 1780. Kraus was the first professor at a Prussian university who based his lectures and seminars in economics on the liberal principles of Adam Smith, which became the focus of his teaching only after he had been asked by the political authorities to develop a curriculum for modern cameralistic studies in 1794/95. As Wilhelm Roscher (1874: 609) points out, Kraus exerted his impact less by his publications than by his teaching skills. The first four volumes of his main work *Staatswirthschaft* were only published by his friend Hans von Auerswald posthumously (Kraus 1808–11). In the first four volumes, Kraus mainly repeats, sometimes even verbally, Smith's arguments. Volume V, however, contains an applied state economics in which the practical needs of Prussia are addressed. Kraus, here, benefits from his long-term expertise since 1786 in writing reports on practical economic policy issues. The text shows Kraus as a clear supporter of free trade and agricultural reforms, favouring the abolition of bondage and arguing against the interests of reactionary squires.

Kraus's lectures were crowded by students.[3] This development was enhanced when in August 1800, Provincial minister von Schrötter, who was a supporter of Kraus and liberal ideas, decreed "that in Eastern Prussia nobody is permitted to be hired by the Civil Service who could not document the successful attendance of Kraus's lectures"[4]. With the implementation of the Stein-Hardenberg reforms in 1807, after Prussia's defeat against Napoleon, many of his former students who had entered the higher ranks of the civil service became main carriers of the liberal policies. Carl

August von Hardenberg (in 1766–67) and Heinrich Friedrich Karl vom und zum Stein (from 1773–76) themselves had studied at the University of Göttingen, which had been an open-minded place already before 1776, and were later strongly influenced by liberal Smithian ideas in their thinking on economic problems. Therefore, Roscher, in his survey on the reception of Smith in Germany,[5] could state that most Prussian statesmen who clustered around vom Stein economically stood on the shoulders of Smith (see Roscher 1874: 598).

Among the first generation of eminent German economists who became enthusiastic Smithians were also Gottlieb Hufeland (1760–1817), who first used the term *Volkswirthschaftslehre*, and Ludwig Heinrich von Jakob (1759–1827), who coined the expression *Nationalökonomie* (Jakob 1805). It should be pointed out that the use of the terms "Volkswirtschaftslehre" and "Nationalökonomie" had no nationalist connotation; this was an interpretation that entered only later with authors such as Adam Müller (1779–1829) and others who dismissed Smith's approach as "cosmopolitan". Müller also tried unsuccessfully to avoid the appointment of a "Smithian" as Professor of Cameralistic Studies at the newly founded University in Berlin in 1810.[6] Müller, who was a fierce opponent of the Stein-Hardenberg liberal reforms in Prussia and later became a high-ranked civil servant in Metternich's restauration policy, heavily attacked Kraus and the Smithians in the *Berliner Abendblätter* edited by him and Heinrich von Kleist. Kraus had written a memoir on the reform of cameralistic studies on behalf of the Prussian government in 1806 but died in the subsequent year. His successor on the chair for practical philosophy and cameralistic sciences at the University of Königsberg was Johann Gottfried Hoffmann (1765–1847), who now defended his beloved teacher against Müller's attacks. Wilhelm von Humboldt was quite instrumental in the Berlin chair's being first offered to Sartorius and after the attempts failed because of Sartorius's demands for a higher salary and other privileges, its being offered to Hoffmann. At the same time, Hoffmann, who until 1834 was the only Professor of Economics at Berlin University, also became the Director of the Prussian Statistical Bureau. He is hardly remembered for his contributions to economics today rather than for the building-up of Prussian statistics and having been reported to be as good a teacher as his master Kraus. From 1813–21, he was on leave from his duties as Professor and engaged in Prussian politics. Roscher (1874: 732–3) rightly comes to the conclusion that "almost every more important peculiarity of the Prussian state at his time finds in him its eulogist: in particular also those peculiarities which do not correspond to the principles of Adam Smith's system". Thus, it can be argued that Hoffmann could be regarded as a key product of the confusion arising from the mix of an older German cameralistics with the new British political economy stated by Keith Tribe, or as Treue (1951: 132) puts it, "The Smithianism taught and practiced in Germany was more of Göttingen and Königsberg than of Scottish origin."

Tribe explicitly exempted Hoffmann, Jakob and Christian von Schlözer (1774–1831) from this confused mix. However, Jakob emigrated to Russia after Prussia's defeat against Napoleon in 1807, from where he came back to Halle only in 1816, whereas Schlözer had already moved from Göttingen to Russia in 1796, where he became the first academic economist.

The next major step has been the new German translation of Smith's *Wealth of Nations* by Max Stirner, which was published in three volumes in 1846–47. Stirner, or Johann Caspar Schmidt (1806–56), is mainly known as an "anarchistic" philosopher, the author of *The Ego and His Own* (Stirner 1845). Despite being heavily criticised as petty bourgeois and for his "nihilistic" ideas, he exerted a stronger influence on the development of historical materialism by Karl Marx and also influenced Friedrich Nietzsche. Less known is the fact that Stirner was also editor and translator of classical economic works (see also Say 1845), which show him as a profound expert of the contemporary economics literature. In his new, third German edition of Smith's *Wealth of Nations*, Stirner did not write a general introduction. Instead, he added notes to many chapters based on earlier English and also French editions, such as those of John Ramsey McCulloch, Joseph Garnier and Adolphe Jérôme Blanqui. The Stirner translation, in which "*Natur*" in the German title was replaced by "*Wesen*", a term later preferred by Schumpeter in his writings, became the standard for the next century. Thus, the later editions by H. Schmidt (1910), J. Jastrow (1920), and even by Ernst Grünfeld in Heinrich Waentig's renowned and influential "*Sammlung sozialwissenschaftlicher Meister*" were all based explicitly on Stirner's translation[7] despite the fact that three further translations by Asher (1861), Stöpel (1878), and Loewenthal (1879) had been published in the meantime.

Against the background of the bicentennial of the *Wealth of Nations*, two new translations were published in the then-divided Germany:

- *Eine Untersuchung über das Wesen und die Ursachen des Reichtums der Nationen*, translated and introduced by Peter Thal and published by the Akademie Verlag in East Berlin in three volumes in 1963 (^{2}1976), 1975, and 1984, and
- a new West German edition, *Der Wohlstand der Nationen. Eine Untersuchung seiner Natur und seiner Ursachen*, translated and edited by Horst Claus Recktenwald and published by the renowned Beck Verlag in Munich in 1974. Available as a cheap paperback edition since 1978, this version is still dominating the market with regard to sales figures.

Some of the interpretations given by the two respective editors are highly instructive as to how contemporary politics and the "*Zeitgeist*" have influenced the reception of Smithian doctrines ever since their original publications. Thus, Recktenwald points out in his article "Adam Smith today and tomorrow" that the *Wealth of Nations* contains "a *peaceful message* which stands in sharp contradiction to the dialectics and the inhumane class struggle in Karl Marx" (Recktenwald 1975: 7; author's translation). On the other hand, Peter Thal, the editor of the East German edition, not only points out the link from Smith via Ricardo to Marx and "the importance of the doctrines of Adam Smith as the theoretical root of Marxist-Leninist economics" but also goes so far as to state "that Smith's work lives on in the proletarian political economics; yes only here his true scientific elements have found a lasting monument" (Thal 1963: II–III; author's translations).

Despite these and some other reminiscences to the communist regime, Thal's introduction is full of insightful passages. It also has to be said that the Thal translation was a remarkable achievement and is clearly superior to the Recktenwald edition. The Recktenwald translation had been criticised devastatingly by Monika Streissler (1976: 711; author's translation) for "(i) simply bad German, (ii) mistranslations of words and phrases, (iii) errors due to the technique used when preparing the manuscript, and (iv) distortions of whole sentences". Streissler, who gave many illuminating examples of misrepresentations from Book I, came to the conclusion that Recktenwald's "text deviates partly past recognition from the English original" (Ibid: 710; author's translation) and recommended that a group of translators should engage in a new German translation of the *Wealth of Nations*, taking Stirner's useful translation as their point of departure (Ibid: 715).

Twenty-three years later, this new German translation, done by Monika Streissler herself, edited and introduced by her husband Erich W. Streissler, and entitled *Untersuchung über Wesen und Ursachen des Reichtums der Völker*, was published (1999). It is the first German translation of the *Wealth of Nations* that is based on the 1976 Glasgow edition, although the extensive apparatus of notes by Roy Harold Campbell and Andrew S. Skinner has been shortened substantially. Monika Streissler also thanks other colleagues, in particular Heinz Rieter, for checking the manuscript and suggesting several improvements. No doubt, the Streissler translation is excellent as is the production of the book by the publisher. Unfortunately, the pricing policy and Gresham's law have prevented a wider distribution among students and the general public as compared to the Recktenwald edition. However, the pagination is questionable. It is a little bit odd that Smith's original text starts not before page 77 (!). The very useful and knowledgeable introductory essays by the editor Erich Streissler and the translator Monika Streissler should have received separate Roman page numbers. The new title *Reichtum der Völker*, instead of *Wohlstand* (or Reichtum) *der Nationen*, is difficult to get used to. Despite some rationale being given by Monika Streissler (1999: 73), the change of the title is not fully convincing and has not been successful among historians of economic thought in the German language area. On the other hand, the different translations of the title indicate the sometimes insurmountable difficulties even careful and scrupulous translators have to face.

Appendix

German translations of Adam Smith's *Wealth of Nations* (1776) – an overview

The following list is taken from Streissler and Streissler (1999: 898) and supplemented by the author.

- Transl. by J. F. Schiller and C. A. Wichmann (1776–78) as *Untersuchung der Natur und Ursachen von Nationalreichthümern*, 2 vols. Leipzig: Weidmanns Erben und Reich. 3rd vol. published 1792, based on 3rd ed. of 1784.
- Transl. of the 4th ed. 1786 by Christian Garve (1794–96) as *Untersuchung über die Natur und die Ursachen des Nationalreichthums*, 2 vols., Breslau: W. G. Korn.
    - 1796–1799: reprint, 4 vols., Frankfurt & Leipzig.
    - 1799: 2nd ed., 3 vols, ed. by A. Dörrien, Breslau & Leipzig: W. G. Korn.
    - 1810: 3rd ed., 3 vols., ed. by A. Dörrien, Breslau & Leipzig: W. G. Korn.
    - 1814: new edition, 3 vols., ed. by A. Dörrien, Vienna: B. P. Bauer.
- Transl. by Max Stirner (1846–47) as *Untersuchungen über das Wesen und die Ursachen des Nationalreichthums*, 3 vols., Leipzig: Otto Wigand.
    - 1910: ed. by H. Schmidt, 2 vols., Leipzig: A. Kröner.
    - 1920: ed. by J. Jastrow, 2 vols., Berlin & Leipzig: W. de Gruyter.
    - 1924: 2nd ed. by J. Jastrow, 2 vols., Berlin & Leipzig: W. de Gruyter.
    - 1924: 2nd ed. by H. Schmidt, 2 vols., Leipzig: A. Kröner.
- Transl. by C. W. Asher (1861) as *Ueber die Quelle des Volkswohlstandes*, 2 vols., Stuttgart: J. Engelhorn.
- Transl. by Franz Stöpel (1878) as *Untersuchung über das Wesen und die Ursachen des Volkswohlstandes*, 4 vols. in 1 vol., Berlin: Expedition des Merkur.
    - 1905–1907: 2nd ed., 2 vols., ed. by R. Prager, Berlin: R. L. Prager.
- Transl. and ed. by W. Loewenthal (1879) as *Natur und Ursachen des Volkswohlstandes*, 2 vols., Berlin: E. Staude. 2nd ed. 1882, 2 vols.
- Transl. of the 4th ed. 1786 by Ernst Grünfeld, based on the transl. by M. Stirner, ed. by Heinrich Waentig (1908–23), as *Eine Untersuchung*

über Natur und Wesen des Volkswohlstandes, 3 vols., Jena: Gustav Fischer.

- 1920: 2nd ed. vol. 1, 1st ed. vol. 2, Jena: Gustav Fischer.
- 1923: 3rd ed. vol. 1, 2nd ed. vol. 2, 1st ed. vol. 3, 3 vols., Jena: Gustav Fischer.
- 1926: 3rd ed. vol. 2, 3 vols., Jena: Gustav Fischer.

- Transl. and with an introduction by Peter Thal (1963–84) as *Eine Untersuchung über das Wesen und die Ursachen des Reichtums der Nationen*, 3 vols., vol. 2 1975, vol. 3 1984, Berlin (East): Akademie-Verlag.
- Transl. of the 5th ed. 1789 and ed. by Horst Claus Recktenwald (1974) as *Der Wohlstand der Nationen. Eine Untersuchung seiner Natur und seiner Ursachen*, München: C. H. Beck.
  - Revised paperback ed. since 1978, München: dtv.
- Transl. of Adam Smith, *An Inquiry into the Nature and Causes of the Wealth of Nations*, edited by R.H. Campbell and A.S. Skinner, Glasgow Edition of the Works and Correspondence of Adam Smith, Vols. 1 and 2, Oxford 1976: Oxford University Press, by Monika Streissler, ed. and with an introduction by Erich W. Streissler (1999) as *Untersuchung über Wesen und Ursachen des Reichtums der Völker*, 2 vols., Düsseldorf: Verlag Wirtschaft und Finanzen.

Notes

1 This paper has been written within the research project *Economic e-translations into and from European Languages EE-T*, funded within the Lifelong learning program of the European Union.
2 See Sartorius (1796: IV, X). For details on the structure and content of the book, see Tribe (2002: 131–2).
3 Tribe (2002: 134–5) is quite critical of Kraus, Sartorius et al. because of "the confusions arising out of this confrontation of an older German cameralistics with the new English political economy" and because of Kraus's admiration for James Steuart, which was reported by Roscher. However, the impact of Kraus on the carriers of the liberal reforms in Prussia cannot be denied.
4 See Treue (1951: 115).
5 Roscher also characterises the French translation of the *Wealth of Nations* by Germain Garnier as "exemplary" (1874: 597).
6 See Treue (1951: 128–33) and Waszek (1988).
7 See the detailed overview of the earlier German editions, which had been put together meticulously in the new German edition by Erich and Monika Streissler (1999: 71–3, 898).

References

Faccarello, Gilbert and Steiner, Philippe (2002), 'The Diffusion of the Work of Adam Smith in the French Language: An Outline History', in Keith Tribe (ed.), *A Critical Bibliography of Adam Smith*, London: Pickering & Chatto, pp. 61–119.

Feder, Johann Georg Heinrich Feder (1777), Review of Adam Smith, *An Inquiry into the Nature and Causes of the Wealth of Nations, Göttingische Anzeigen von gelehrten Sachen,* 10 March and 5 April.

Hufeland, Gottlieb (1807–13), *Neue Grundlegung der Staatswirthschaftskunst*, 2 vols., Gießen and Wetzlar: Tasche und Müller.

Iselin, Isaak (1777), Review of Volume I of Adam Smith, *An Inquiry into the Nature and Causes of the Wealth of Nations, Ephemeriden der Menschheit*, 5. Stück, pp. 61–101.

Jakob, Ludwig Heinrich von (1805), *Grundsätze der National-Oekonomie oder National-Wirthschaftslehre*, Halle: Ruff.

Kraus, Christian Jakob (1808–11), *Staatswirthschaft*, 5vols., edited posthumously by Hans von Auerswald, Königsberg: Friedrich Nicolovius.

Nicolai, Friedrich (1777–79), Review of Volumes I and II of Adam Smith, *An Inquiry into the Nature and Causes of the Wealth of Nations, Allgemeine deutsche Bibliothek*, vol. 31(2), pp. 586–9 and vol. 38(1), pp. 297–303.

Raphael, D.D. and Macfie, A.L. (1976), 'Introduction' to Adam Smith, *The Theory of Moral Sentiments,* Glasgow Edition of the Works and Correspondence of Adam Smith, vol. 1, Oxford: Oxford University Press.

Recktenwald, Horst Claus (1975), 'Adam Smith heute und morgen', *Kyklos*, 28(1): 5–22.

Roscher, Wilhelm (1874), *Geschichte der National-Oekonomik in Deutschland,* Munich: R. Oldenbourg.

Sartorius, Georg (1796), *Handbuch der Staatswirthschaft, zum Gebrauche bey akademischen Vorlesungen, nach Adam Smith's Grundsätzen ausgearbeitet*, Berlin: Johann Friedrich Unger; 2nd ed. as *Von den Elementen des Nationalreichthums und von der Staatswirthschaft, nach Ad. Smith*, Göttingen 1806, J.F. Römer.

Sartorius, Georg (1806), *Abhandlungen, die Elemente des National-Reichthums und die Staatswirthschaft betreffend*, Göttingen: Johann Friedrich Röwer.

Say, Jean-Baptiste (1845), *Ausführliches Lehrbuch der praktischen politischen Ökonomie*, translated and commented by Max Stirner, 3 vols., Leipzig: Wigand.

Stirner, Max (1845), *Der Einzige und sein Eigentum*, Leipzig: Wigand.

Streissler, Monika (1976), 'Anmerkungen zu H. C. Recktenwalds Ausgabe des "Wohlstands der Nationen"', *Zeitschrift für die gesamte Staatswissenschaft*, 132(4): 710–717.

Treue, Wilhelm (1951), 'Adam Smith in Deutschland. Zum Problem des "Politischen Professors" zwischen 1776 und 1810', in Wilhelm Conze (ed.), *Deutschland und Europa. Festschrift für Hans Rothfels*, Düsseldorf: Droste Verlag, pp. 101–133.

Tribe, Keith (2002), 'The German Reception of Adam Smith', in: Keith Tribe (ed.), *A Critical Bibliography of Adam Smith*, London: Pickering & Chatto, pp. 120–152.

Waszek, Norbert (1988), 'Die Staatswissenschaften an der Universität Berlin im 19. Jahrhundert', in Norbert Waszek (ed.), *Die Institutionalisierung der Nationalökonomie an deutschen Universitäten. In Memoriam Klaus Hinrich Hennings*, St. Katharinen: Scripta Mercaturae, pp. 266–301.

Waszek, Norbert (2006), 'The Scottish Enlightenment in Germany, and Its Translator Christian Garve (1742–98)', in Tom Hubbard and R.D.S Jack (eds.), *Scotland in Europe*, Amsterdam and New York: Rodopi.

Winkel, Harald (1986), 'Adam Smith und die deutsche Nationalökonomie 1776–1820', in Harald Scherf (ed.), *Studien zur Entwicklung der ökonomischen Theorie V*, Schriften des Vereins für Socialpolitik Vol. 115/V, Berlin: Duncker & Humblot, pp. 81–109.

15 John Ruskin in early twentieth-century Japan

Some episodes[1]

Masashi Izumo

Introduction: modern Japan and Ruskin[2]

Modern Japanese society was at a turning point after the Meiji government had built, albeit imperfectly, a modern state by promoting 'fukoku kyōhei' (rich country, strong army) after its 'victory' in the 1904–1905 Russo-Japanese War. At the time, there was an alternative way of proceeding to create a modern society; however, instead, the government continued to push ahead with the expansion of Japanese militarism and led Japan's invasion of countries in Continental Asia, such as Korea and China. At the same time, the government strengthened its oppression of any critics of the Meiji imperial bureaucratic system and formed a sense of solidarity and peer pressure among the people.

As a consequence of Japan's rapid industrialisation, serious social and economic problems, such as poverty, war, and environmental pollution, had emerged by the start of the twentieth century. However, despite the state's repression, various social movements and activities were undertaken by peasants, workers, women, students, socialists, Christians, citizens, and others alongside the distribution of a wide variety of publications through which the government could be criticised by using limited freedom of speech, even under severe censorship, against the authorities.

John Ruskin (1819–1900) was one of Britain's leading thinkers in the Victorian age, but surprisingly, he also played an important role in early twentieth-century Japan, especially so for those involved in promoting the ideas and movements sympathetic to anti-industrialisation. Since his works were introduced in 1888 in the popular journal *Kokumin no Tomo* (Nation's Friend) by Tokutomi Sohō (1863–1957), who was a remarkable journalist, Ruskin came to be recognised in Japan as a well-known Western artist and social thinker in the decades that followed. Why did Japanese intellectuals follow Ruskin? What was the impact of Ruskin on Japan at the time? These are the questions that I attempt to consider. However, to discuss these questions comprehensively is beyond the scope of a brief paper and only a sketch of some selective episodes will be traced in this chapter.

Criticism of literary art: Natsume Sōseki and Iwamura Tōru

An outstanding novelist and critic: Natsume Sōseki[3]

Natsume Sōseki (1867–1916), a great novelist and scholar of English literature, mentioned Ruskin in *Bungakuron* (Literary Criticism) in 1907 and in *Sanshirō* in 1909.[4] Although there is just the phrase 'Have you ever read Ruskin?' in *Sanshirō*, it leaves a deep impression on the reader (Natsume 1907: 610–12, 1909: 42).

Sōseki was sent to Britain by the government from 1900 to 1902 to study English literature. However, he spent unhappy days in London as he witnessed serious social problems in the British Empire and stayed indoors most of the time, devoting himself to books describing various fields of study that were of interest in those days. His landlady and friends feared that he would have a nervous breakdown. Sōseki remembers his days in London with contempt:

> The two years I spent in London were the most unpleasant years in my life. Among British gentlemen, just like a pitiable dog among a pack of wolves, I lived in misery.
>
> (Natsume 1907: 14–15)

Despite his loneliness and lack of living expenses, and because he spent 'the most unpleasant years' of his life in London, Sōseki extended and deepened not only his profound knowledge of English literature but also his critical viewpoint of the modern industrial societies that were characteristic of this period. After returning to Japan in 1903, Sōseki was invited to become a lecturer at the Daiichi Kōtō Gakkō (First Higher School) and Tokyo Imperial University. There, he served as the successor to Koizumi Yakumo (another name for Patrick Lafcadio Hearn), who had lectured on the history of English literature.[5] However, Sōseki began to feel even more strongly that something was out of place in modern Japanese society. He expresses his criticism of a general trend to consider Japan one of the world's first-class powers after its 'victory' in the Russo-Japanese War. In a light and humorous phrasing, Sōseki shows his feeling in his books *Wagahai wa Neko de Aru* (I Am a Cat) and *Sanshirō*, which were published just after the war:

> 'Yamato damashii (Spirit of Japan)' scream the papers, and pickpockets scream it too. […] Admiral Tōgō has the Spirit of Japan. So has the man in the street, fish dealers, swindlers, and murders. […] But if you ask what this Spirit is, they give that cough and say 'The Spirit of Japan is the Japanese Spirit', then they walk away.
>
> (Natsume 1905–07: vol. 2, 50)

> 'We can beat the Russians, we can become a first-class power, but it doesn't make any difference. We still have pinched faces and feeble

> bodies. [...] You've never seen Mount Fuji. [...] It's the finest thing Japan has to be proud of, and the only thing we can boast about. It's nothing but a natural object that has been there for all time. We certainly didn't make it'. [...] Sanshirō had never expected to meet anyone like this man after the Russo-Japanese War. The man doesn't look like a Japanese, he thinks. 'But still', Sanshirō countered, 'Japan will develop more and more from now on'. 'Japan is going to perish', the man replied coolly.
>
> (Natsume 1909: 24–25)[6]

After the Russo-Japanese War, there was a movement toward nationalism and the pursuit of something unique to Japan, which was a nation-state of its own, and consequently, Japanese 'traditional' culture and thought attracted people's attention once again. Under these circumstances, however, Sōseki continued to take a critical stance against Japan's superficial modernity, yet for him, neither Japanese nationalism nor European modernism was adopted. It is not entirely evident whether Sōseki was under the direct influence of the ideas of Ruskin, but it can be said that they shared a critical viewpoint of the modern industrial societies of the time.

A pioneer art critic: Iwamura Tōru

Iwamura Tōru (1870–1917), a pioneer art critic and of the same generation as Sōseki, was greatly influenced by Ruskin.[7] When he was a student at Tokyo Eiwa Gakkō (later Aoyama Gakuin) from 1885 to 1888, Iwamura read the first few pages of Ruskin's *Lectures on Art* delivered at the University of Oxford in 1870. He was 17 or 18 years old when he found the old book, published by Clarendon Press in 1875, at a bookshop in Tokyo. This was his first encounter with Ruskin. He wrote this memorable story in his first biographical article 'John Ruskin' in *Bijutsu Hyōron* (Art Criticism) in 1900 (Iwamura [1900] 1971: 130). Interestingly, he later began translating Ruskin's Oxford lectures, three times in 1902 (Iwamura 1902: 6, 14, 27), but never finished them, and he also wrote 'Ruskin Sensei to Alps Yama' (Mr Ruskin and the Alps) in 1911 (Iwamura 1911: 305–10), both in *Bijutsu Shinpō* (Art News).

Iwamura lived in America and Europe from 1888 to 1892, in order to study painting and art history. Returning to Japan in 1893, he became an English teacher at his old college Tokyo Eiwa Gakkō and in 1899, a part-time lecturer of Western art history at Tokyo Bijutsu Gakkō (Tokyo Fine Arts School). The series of Western art history lectures was given by Okakura Tenshin (1863–1913), the first president of Tokyo Fine Arts School, and Mori Ōgai (1862–1922), an army surgeon and notable novelist alongside Natsume Sōseki, for ten years, until 1899, when Iwamura assumed the post.[8] He became a lecturer in 1901 and a professor the following year and was actively involved in art criticism through his contributions to *Bijutsu Hyōron*, *Bijutsu Shinpō*, and *Bijutsu Shūhō* (Weekly Art News). In these publications, he often featured hard-hitting articles against the old-fashioned art world and the bureaucratic and authoritarian system in Japan, and he also satirised Japanese snobbery in a plainspoken style. In 1902, Iwamura leaped to fame by writing *Pari no Bijutsu Gakusei* (Art Students in Paris), a best seller in its time. His pungent criticism of Japanese society was filled with humour and irony. It is clear that Iwamura saw his reflection in Ruskin's critical mind.[9]

In 1909, Iwamura, along with Masaki Naohiko (1862–1940), who was president of Tokyo Fine Arts School at the time, organised an art circle 'Gorakukai', which aimed to foster the beauty of life created by small-sized works, such as art medals. Bernard Leach (1887–1979) and Tomimoto Kenkichi (1886–1963), both original designers and potters, also joined this circle (Tanabe 2008: 134–37). It is not difficult to find a reflection of William Morris's idea of 'lesser art' in this circle's approach to art, but it is also located on the extended line of the idea and practice in Ruskin's intention for social reform through art. Iwamura's 1915 article 'William Morris to Shumiteki Shakaishugi' (William Morris and Aesthetic Socialism) was written especially for his book *Geijutsu to Shakai* (Art and Society), the title of which clearly conveyed Ruskin's thoughts on art. Iwamura states,

> Morris was an admirer of Ruskin. He avidly read Ruskin's *The Stone of Venice* all his life, and was strongly inspired, particularly by the chapter 'The Nature of Gothic', in the latter half of his life. In fact, Morris's idea of social reform is that of Ruskin's ideal: 'A thing of beauty is a joy forever. However, it must be also a joy for all people'. [...] 'The popularisation of beauty' and consequently 'the promotion of human happiness' Morris dreamed of and endeavoured to achieve had made good progress in the last twenty years.[10]
>
> (Iwamura [1915] 1971: 245, 248)

It is not well known that Iwamura was a keen reader of the *Heimin Shimbun* (Commoner's News), which was first published in 1903 by Kōtoku Shūsui (1871–1911) and Sakai Toshihiko (1871–1933) just three months before the Russo-Japanese War to promote and spread socialist thoughts. It was forced to cease publication in 1905 because it advocated pacifism against the war (Tanabe 2008: 46–49). Kōtoku Shūsui, a famous socialist and anarchist, who had a great influence on the socialism in Japan, was executed along with eleven others in 1911 for his involvement in the 'Taigyaku Jiken' (High Treason Incident) of 1910. However, this was a frame-up by the Meiji state to crack down on anti-government movements. Although the Social Democratic Party — the first socialist party in Japan — was established in 1901, the Heiminsha (Commoners' Society) was founded in 1903, and the Japanese Socialist Party was established in 1906, they were all forced to shut down by the government, and the so-called wintertime of socialism deepened, especially for five years after 1910, when most socialist and democratic movements declined.[11]

Iwamura was expected to continue with his work; however, he was forced to resign from the Tokyo Fine Arts School in 1916 and died one year later after his diabetes worsened.

Criticism of economics and social reform: Kawakami Hajime and Mikimoto Ryūzō

'Japanese Ruskin': Kawakami Hajime[12]

Kawakami Hajime (1879–1946) was one of the most influential economists in early twentieth-century Japan. He began to introduce Ruskin's economic and social ideas in 1917.[13] These ideas were popularised in the country through his articles and books. One of his students, Mikimoto Ryūzō (1894–1971), says about Kawakami:

> The first man that introduced Ruskin as economist to Japan may be said, if I am not wrong, to have been professor Hajime Kawakami; It may be an unexpected fact that the greatest Marxian teacher in Japan has once been so Ruskinian that he was called the Japanese Ruskin by his colleagues.
>
> (Mikimoto 1931: 40 [Mikimoto's English])

Kawakami, who was a professor of political economy at Kyoto Imperial University, first became well known through the publication of *Binbō Monogatari* (Tale of Poverty), which became popular in 1917 and in which he refers to Ruskin in the preface[14]:

> Ruskin famously says, 'There is no wealth, but life'. Wealth is the purpose of life — that is, the only purpose of life is to quest the way, wealth is significant simply as a means of achieving this purpose. Therefore, I hope to eradicate poverty from human society because poverty obstructs the way of life human beings pursue.[15]
>
> (Kawakami [1917] 1982: 4)

Kawakami expressed his deep sympathy with Ruskin's concept of wealth and his criticism of 'individualist economics' in his 1918 article, 'Ruskin no *Kono Saigo no Mono nimo*' (Ruskin's *Unto this Last*) (Kawakami [1918a] 1982: 159). Moreover, in his preface to Ishida Kenji's 1918 translation of *Unto this Last*, Kawakami, probably for the first time, classified economics into three streams: 'individualist economics', which is characterised by selfishness and the pursuit of profits; 'socialist economics', which seeks to reform the economic system; and 'humanitarian economics', which demands the reformation of the human mind. Kawakami typecasts Adam Smith, Jeremy Bentham, James Mill, Thomas Robert Malthus, and David Ricardo as leading economists of 'individualist economics'; Karl Marx as a leader of 'socialist economics'; and 'our John Ruskin' as a great figure of 'humanitarian economics' (Kawakami [1918b] 1982: 509–10). He repeats the same argument in 1919 and again refers to Ruskin as a humanitarian economist in his book *Shihonshugi Keizaigaku no Shiteki Hatten* (Historical Development of the Capitalist Economics) in 1923. In this book, Kawakami redescribed the 'historical development' of the mainstream justification of 'self-interest' and its criticism, from Bernard de Mandeville and Smith via Malthus, Ricardo, Bentham, and J. Mill to Ruskin through John Stuart Mill and Thomas Carlyle, in the history of economic thought.[16]

Ironically, Kawakami ultimately became a Marxist after his view of economics based on 'humanitarianism' was strongly challenged in 1924 by Kushida Tamizō (1885–1934), a noted Marxian economist and pupil of Kawakami. Subsequently, Mikimoto Ryūzō and Ōkuma Nobuyuki (1893–1977) were left to carry on Ruskin studies in place of Kawakami, and many translations of Ruskin's works and books about him were published in Japan from the 1920s to the 1930s.[17]

A disciple of Ruskin: Mikimoto Ryūzō

During the 1910s and 1920s, parallel to the rise of Christian socialism and the labour movements, the Christian socialist Mikimoto Ryūzō, along with Kagawa Toyohiko (1888–1960), a Christian social movement activist, became leading Ruskinians and published numerous translations, articles, and books on Ruskin in the 1920s and the 1930s.[18]

Although Mikimoto Ryūzō was the only son of Mikimoto Kōkichi (1858–1954), who established the Mikimoto Pearl Company, Ryūzō criticised his father's business for being run by 'a small capitalist' and did not succeed him in running the pearl company. Mikimoto became interested in Ruskin when he was a student of First Higher School, probably in 1913, as a result of reading Ada Earland's *Ruskin and His Circle*, published in 1911. He was deeply influenced by Kawakami Hajime at Kyoto Imperial University and decided to devote his life to Ruskin studies, following Kawakami's advice. In 1920, leaving the university before graduation, Mikimoto went to Britain and gathered Ruskin's books, letters, original manuscripts, drawings, and paintings.[19] Hence, he became the foremost Ruskinian and Ruskin scholar in Japan as a successor to Kawakami (Honma 1985: 2; Watanabe and Kikuchi 1997: 91; Washi 2000: 120).

Mikimoto often published his works through Shimeisha (the Mission Publisher), which was based on Christian socialism and was originally established in 1915 by Yusa Toshihiko (1888–1973), who was a reliable cooperator with Kagawa Toyohiko and who later became head of the central office for employment placement. Shimeisha suspended its business in 1917; however, under Mikimoto and along with Yusa and others, it resumed operations to help unemployed Mikimoto workers after the Mikimoto factories closed down due to the Great Kantō Earthquake in 1923.[20]

Saitō Shinkichi, Ryūzō's uncle and later head of the Mikimoto precious metal factory, also had a close connection with the Christian socialist movement. He visited America in 1905 and Europe in 1909 in order to attend exhibitions and open the overseas branches of Mikimoto Pearl Company in New York and London. During these trips, Saitō was deeply impressed by the education and enlightenment evident in managers' support for their workers' moral culture and welfare, particularly in Britain. He established a Workers' Church inside the factory and tried to foster a spirit of mutual support and Christian love for humanity among his workers. As might have been supposed, it is highly probable that Mikimoto was strongly influenced by the ideas and practices of his uncle Saitō (Miyoshi 1962: 4–9, Watanabe and Kikuchi 1997: 91, 306, Kusamitsu 2001: 118–20).

Mikimoto established the Tokyo Ruskin Kyōkai (Tokyo Ruskin Society) in 1931 and published the journal *Tokyo Ruskin Kyōkai Zasshi* (Tokyo Ruskin Society Journal). In 1934, he also built the Ruskin Bunko (Ruskin Library), which was a Ruskin cultural centre with a library and a tea room.[21] Moreover, Mikimoto opened 'the Ruskin Hall' and 'the Ruskin Cottage', which is a kind of handicrafts guild, and tried to establish cultural places where ordinary people could learn about the beauty of life in Ginza — the centre of Tokyo — during this period. In 1937, regrettably, he went bankrupt prior to achieving these goals (Watanabe and Kikuchi 1997: 91–92; Kusamitsu 2001: 122–24). However, his attempts and projects should be greatly appreciated despite their failures, not only because of his ideas for social reform but also because he put Ruskin's ideas into practice in Japan.[22]

Concluding remarks

The early twentieth century was a transitional time in Japan's history. The social and economic system that had existed was beginning to break down with the infiltration of rapid industrialisation and environmental devastation proceeding in both the material and spiritual sense. Under these circumstances, a strong interest in the thoughts and practices of John Ruskin arose among Japanese intellectuals. Yet it was not until the 1920s that Marxism came to be widely known in Japan, and the notion of anti-capitalism and anti-industrialisation, such as that advocated by Ruskin and Morris, became an intellectual viewpoint for criticising the system that was predominant at that time. Various social movements also emerged, including the Christian socialist movements, before Marxism assumed leadership over these movements, which were influenced by the 'Taishō Democracy'— and also the period of humanitarianism—during the 1910s and the 1920s and encouraged by the Russian Revolution.[23]

It was not surprising that many of those who were involved in the movements were Christians. Through Christianity, the Japanese could acquire fundamental knowledge of various fields, and this system of thought was also particularly significant in helping intellectuals assess the existing systems in

Japan in comparison with those used in the West.[24] Moreover, it should be emphasised that some intellectuals attempted to practice Ruskin's ideas in their own ways in Japan. Although most of them were unsuccessful, their experiences of failures and defeats offer the key to an understanding of serious problems that modern Japan, which is at a turning point again, is still facing today.

Notes

1 This chapter first appeared, in an earlier form, in Izumo (2016).
2 In this chapter, Japanese names are given in the customary order, i.e. surname first.
3 He is known by his common name, Natsume Sōseki, which comes from his haiku pen name and which was given to him by his best friend Masaoka Shiki (1867–1902), a distinguished haiku poet, but his real name is Natsume Kinnosuke. He is customarily called 'Sōseki'.
4 *Sanshirō* originally appeared serially in the *Asahi Shimbun* from September 1 to December 29 of 1908. At the beginning of the previous year, 1907, Sōseki resigned from all his faculty positions at universities and joined the Aasahi Shimbun Company.
5 Patrick Lafcadio Hearn (1850–1904), who is known also by the Japanese name Koizumi Yakumo, taught the history of English literature at Tokyo Imperial University from 1896 to 1903, and his lectures remain in his book, titled *A history of English literature: in a series of lectures*. According to the prefatory note, 'these lectures are word for word as they were taken down by his students at the time of their delivery [from September 1900 to March 1903], and appear here without any revision by Hearn himself, who indeed never dreamed of their publication'. In this book, he gives an enlightening lecture on Ruskin (Koizumi 1927: vol. 2, 826–841).
6 These English sentences are based on the translation by Ito and Wilson (2002) and Rubin (1977), but some of them are modified.
7 Only a few studies have examined Iwamura's role. However, Tanabe (2008) is an exception. This is the first critical biography of Iwamura.
8 The first professor of art history at Tokyo Fine Arts School was Ernest Fenollosa (1853–1908), who was also the first professor of economics at Tokyo Imperial University and is still famous today as an eminent American art historian of Japanese art.
9 According to his son, Iwamura 'was a Christian, without concern for rules or formality, and loved reading the Bible to the end of his life', but further details are unknown (Iwamura 1933: 116).
10 See Ruskin ([1853] 1903–12: vol. 10, 194) and Morris ([1892] 1936: vol. 1, 292).
11 It is, of course, no accident that the High Treason Incident coincided with the unification of Korea with Japan in 1910.
12 This section is based on part of my previous papers (Izumo and Sato 2014 and Izumo 2015).
13 This is the same year that Iwamura died and one year after Sōseki passed away. In the next year, 1918, the Rice Riots broke out at the instigation of housewives in the small fishing village of Toyama and subsequently spread across Japan, just a year after the start of the Russian Revolution.
14 This story originally appeared serially in the *Osaka Asahi Shimbun* from September 11 to December 26 of 1916. The preface to *Binbō Monogatari* was added when it was published as a book in 1917.

15 These English sentences are based on the translation by Watanabe and Kikuchi (1997: 305), but some of them are modified.

16 The reason Marx is seldom mentioned is thought to be that Kawakami planned to publish another book, *Shakaishugi Keizaigaku no Shiteki Hatten* (Historical development of the socialist economics); however, this plan was never realised (Kawakami [1923] 1982: ch.5).

17 Ōkuma Nobuyuki (1893–1977), under the direction of Fukuda Tokuzō (1874–1930), who was a prominent economist and professor of the Tokyo Higher Commercial School (later, Hitotsubashi University), wrote three articles on Ruskin and Morris. He published *Shakai Shisōka toshiteno Ruskin to Morris* (Ruskin and Morris as social thinkers), including these articles with others in 1927 (Ōkuma 1920, 1921). As already indicated in my previous papers, the contrast studies of Ricardo between Fukuda and Kawakami, both from the Marshallian and Marxian points of view, were introduced into Japan in the 1910s and then passed on, through a complicated process, to later generations of scholars, such as Koizumi Shinzō (1888–1966), Hori Tsuneo (1896–1981), and others (Izumo and Sato 2014: 218–220; Izumo 2015: 146–149). In another paper, I would like to go on to consider the contrast between Kawakami or Mikimoto and Ōkuma in their Ruskin studies.

18 Mikimoto translated twelve works by Ruskin from 1930 to 1936 and wrote over twenty essays on Ruskin during the 1920s and 1930s (Watanabe and Kikuchi 1997: 93).

19 Mikimoto visited Britain six times, in 1920, 1925, 1927, 1928, 1929, and 1930, and collected a lot of material regarding Ruskin (Washi 2000: 120).

20 Ōsugi Sakae (1885–1923), a great anarchist, was murdered, along with his partner Itō Noe (1895–1923) and his nephew Tachibana Sōichi (1917–23), by the military amidst the chaos after the Great Kantō Earthquake in 1923. Ōsugi began the publication of the monthly Journal *Kindai Shisō* (Modern Thoughts) in 1912 and translated both Romain Rolland's *People's Theatre* and Kropotkin's *Mutual Aid* in 1917. The publications *Heimin Shimbun* and *Kindai Shisō* played an important role in introducing and popularising the ideas of 'humanitarianism' during this period.

21 Both the Tokyo Ruskin Society and the Ruskin Library were re-established in 1984, and they continue to support Ruskin studies.

22 From 1938 to 1945, there was only one book that Mikimoto published (Washi 2000: 146). Kimura points out 'during the militarist period 1937–1945 there was a curiously deviant phase of Ruskin analysis. A few sincere students of Ruskin continued their work along the religious-humanitarian line [...] and Ruskin was now generally deliberately hailed as a totalitarian social reformer, and some of his doctrines and assertions were picked up and specifically made use of to support the imperialist war by the right-wing nationalists' (Kimura 1982: 236–237).

23 Marx's *Manifest der Kommunistischen Partei* was translated by Kōtoku Shūsui and Sakai Toshihiko in 1904, and *Das Kapital* was completely translated for the first time by Takabatake Motoyuki (1886–1928) in 1924.

24 In the late eighteenth to mid-nineteenth centuries, before Christianity had a great impact on Japanese society, Dutch Learning, as a systematised field of enquiry dedicated to the Western sciences, had a huge draw for Japanese intellectuals (Izumo 2015: 136–137).

References

Honma, Sachiko (1985) Mikimoto Ryūzō to Ruskin (Mikimoto Ryūzō and Ruskin), *Ruskin Bunko Tayori* (Ruskin Library newsletter), 2, 2–3. Tokyo: Ruskin Bunko.

Ito, Aiko and Graeme Wilson (tr.) (2002) *I Am a Cat*. Boston, MA: Tuttle Publisher.

Iwamura, Hiroshi (1933) Chichi wo omou (Remembering my father). In Issō, Muraji (ed.) *Iwamura Tōru Tsuiokushū* (Remembering Iwamura Tōru). Kochi: Iwamura Hiroshi (self-published).

Iwamura, Tōru ([1900] 1971) John Ruskin, *Bijutsu Hyōron* (Art criticism), 25. In Miyagawa, Torao (ed.) *Geien Zakkō hoka* (Essays on Art and others). Tokyo: Heibonsha.

——— (1902) Rashi bijutsu kōgi (Ruskin's lectures on art), *Bijutsu Shinpō* (Art news), 1 (1, 2, 4), 6, 14, 27. Tokyo: Tozai Bijutsu Shuppansha.

——— (1911) Ruskin Sensei to Alps Yama (Mr Ruskin and the Alps), *Bijutsu Shinpō*, 10 (10), 305–310. Tokyo: Tozai Bijutsu Shuppansha.

——— ([1915] 1971) William Morris to shumiteki shakaishugi (William Morris and aesthetic socialism), *Bijutsu to Shakai* (Art and Society). In Miyagawa, Torao (ed.) *Geien Zakkō hoka*. Tokyo: Heibonsha.

Izumo, Masashi (2015) Senzen nihon no Ricardo kenkyū: 1869–1929 nen shiron (Ricardo studies in Japan 1869–1929). *The Annual Bulletin of the Institute for Economic Studies*, 28, 133–162. Tokyo: Seijo University.

——— (2016) John Ruskin in early 20th century Japan: some episodes, *Shōkei Ronsō*, 51 (4), 13–23. Yokohama: Kanagawa University.

Izumo, Masashi and Shigemasa Sato (2014) The reception of Ricardo in Japan. In Faccarello, Gilbert and Masashi Izumo (eds.) *The Reception of David Ricardo in Continental Europe and Japan*. London: Routledge.

Kawakami, Hajime ([1917] 1982) Jo (Preface to *Binbō Monogatari*). *Kawakami Hajime Zenshū* (The complete works of Kawakami Hajime), vol. 9. Tokyo: Iwanami Shoten.

——— ([1918a] 1982) Ruskin no Kono Saigo no Mono nimo (Ruskin's *Unto this Last*). *Kawakami Hajime Zenshū*, vol. 9. Tokyo: Iwanami Shoten.

——— ([1918b] 1982) Jo (Preface to Ishida Kenji's translation of *Unto this Last*). *Kawakami Hajime Zenshū*, vol. 9. Tokyo: Iwanami Shoten.

——— ([1923] 1982) *Shihonshugi Keizaigaku no Shiteki Hatten* (Historical development of the capitalist economics). *Kawakami Hajime Zenshū*, vol. 13. Tokyo: Iwanami Shoten.

Kimura, Masami (1982) Japanese interest in Ruskin: some historical trends. In Rhodes, Robert and Del Ivan Janik (eds.) *Studies in Ruskin: Essays in Honor of Van Akin Burd*. Athens: Ohio University Press.

Koizumi, Yakumo (1927) *A History of English Literature: in a series of lectures*, vol. 2. Tokyo: Hokuseido Shoten.

Kusamitsu, Toshio (2001) Ruskin no shito: Mikimoto Ryūzō (A disciple of Ruskin: Mikimoto Ryūzō). In Tsuzuki, Chūshichi, Gordon Daniels and Toshio Kusamitsu (eds.) *Nichi-Ei Kōryūshi 1600-2000, vol. 5, Shakai Bunka* (The history of Anglo-Japanese relations, 1600-2000, vol. 5, Social and cultural perspectives). Tokyo: University of Tokyo Press.

Mikimoto, Ryūzō (1931) *What is Ruskin in Japan*. Tokyo: Shimeisha.

Miyoshi, Akira (1962) Rōdōkyōkaishi josetsu (Introduction to the history of workers' church), *Hokusei Ronshū*, 1, 1–19. Sapporo: Hokusei Gakuen University.

Morris, William ([1892] 1936) Preface to *The Nature of Gothic: A Chapter of the Stones of Venice*. In Morris, May (ed.) *William Morris: Artist, Writer, Socialist*, vol. 1. Oxford: B. Blackwell.

Natsume, Sōseki (1905–07) *Wagahai wa Neko de Aru* (I Am a Cat), vol. 2. Tokyo: Okura Shoten.

——— (1907) *Bungakuron* (Theory of literature). Tokyo: Okura Shoten.

——— (1909) *Sanshirō*. Tokyo: Shunyodo.

Ōkuma, Nobuyuki ([1920] 1927) Ruskin no *Munera Pulveris* (Ruskin's *Munera Pulveris*), *Kokumin Keizai Zasshi*, 29 (1-2). In *Shakai Shisōka toshiteno Ruskin to Morris* (Ruskin and Morris as social thinkers), [Republished by Ronsosha in 2004]. Tokyo: Shinchosha.

——— ([1921] 1927) Shakai shisōka toshiteno Ruskin to Morris (Ruskin and Morris as social thinkers), *Shōgaku Kenkyū*, 1 (2). In *Shakai Shisōka toshiteno Ruskin to Morris*, [Republished by Ronsosha in 2004]. Tokyo: Shinchosha.

Rubin, Jay (tr.) (1977) *Sanshiro: A Novel*. Tokyo: University of Tokyo Press.

Ruskin, John ([1853] 1903–12) *The Stones of Venice*, vol. 2. In Cook, Edward T. and Alexander Wedderburn (eds.) *The Complete Works of John Ruskin*, vol. 10. London: George Allen.

Tanabe, Tōru (2008) *Bijutsu Hihyō no Senkusha Iwamura Tōru: Ruskin kara Morris made* (A pioneer art critic Iwamura Tōru: from Ruskin to Morris). Tokyo: Fujiwara Shoten.

Washi, Naohito (2000) Ruskin tono deai (Encounter with Ruskin). *John Ruskin: A Thinker's Vision through Mikimoto Ryuzo Collection: Centenary Exhibition* (Catalogue). Tokyo: Ruskin Bunko.

Watanabe, Toshio and Yūko Kikuchi (1997) Ruskin in Japan 1890-1940: Nature for Art, Art for Life. In Mizusawa, Tsutomu and Takiko Nagayama (eds.) *Ruskin in Japan 1890–1940: Nature for Art, Art for Life* (Catalogue). Tokyo: 'Ruskin in Japan 1890–1940' Exhibition Committee.

16 Translation and the circulation of economic ideas across nations

Marco E.L. Guidi[1]

Prologue

In the summer of 1990, a group composed of Massimo Augello, Marco Bianchini, and myself visited the *École Normale Supérieure de Fontenay – St. Cloud* (ÉNS) to meet Gilbert Faccarello and a team of researchers, including Philippe Steiner and Jean-Jacques Gislain, to plan the collaboration between the *Seminario permanente sulla storia del pensiero economico italiano* and the *Centre Alexandre Vandermonde pour l'Histoire de la pensée économique*. The Italian research network was established in 1988 as an offspring of the *Società Italiana per la Storia dell'Economia* and was the foundation of a series of conferences and publications, which have promoted the comparative analysis of national cases on institutionalisation and dissemination of political economy.[2] The *Centre Vandermonde* organised important workshops and conferences, and its members have since then produced seminal contributions on the French tradition of political economy and sociology.

The following spring, on behalf of Gilbert's invitation, I spent a semester at ÉNS, where I had the opportunity to present a paper in which I discussed the notion of 'styles of economic reasoning' and applied it to the national traditions of economic thought. The paper defended the efficacy of studying the phenomena of institutionalisation and dissemination of political economy. As intimated by Bob Coats (1969), there was much to know beyond the contributions of the 'great economists' encompassed by the canonical reconstructions of the history of economic thought

This paper is connected with the ideas illustrated in that paper and even more so with the research projects above mentioned. It owes a great deal to discussions with Gilbert and the other above-mentioned scholars, which span over last 25 years.

Introduction

This paper aims to analyse the phenomenon of translations of economic texts, these texts' being considered as an aspect of the international circulation of economic ideas. It is based on the results of the European project entitled 'EE-T. Economic e-Translations from and into European Languages'.[3]

In most cases, the translation of economic works is the product of individuals and intellectual circles that play key roles in institutions, economic activities, and politics. Those actors promote social changes, reforms of educational systems, reorientations of economic policies, political movements, political propaganda, publishing strategies, and other projects related to the ways in which societies organise themselves and evolve through divisions, conflicts, and further reconstructions.

Political economy and governmentality

The intuition that underpinned the research project on economic translations is that, for some areas of thought, translations have historically played a peculiar role, closely connected to their nature and social functions (see Reinert 2011). This is most seemingly the case with political economy. The Weberian approach propounded by Philippe Steiner (1998) highlights the idea that, in the new science of political economy, which originates with the physiocrats and Adam Smith, the economic discourse is characterised by two intertwined dimensions: a scientific and a 'performative' one. These two dimensions are connected to different types of rationalisation of economic knowledge: The 'scientific' dimension of political economy develops as a formal rationalisation, i.e. a systematisation of economic knowledge within an internally consistent and rational framework of universal principles and structured methods. The naturalistic umbrella under which both the physiocrats and the Smithians place their analysis directs their efforts towards the discovery of the natural laws that regulate the phenomena of production, exchange, and distribution of wealth.

On the other hand, the performative dimension of political economy is connected with another type of rationalisation of economic knowledge called material rationalisation. With its typical normative approach, such a rationalisation aims to direct private and public behaviour in the light of those elements of objective knowledge that are required to give them consistency and sustainability over time. Its subject is not the nature of norms but rather the consistency between ends and means. However, as argued by Steiner, the scope of material rationalisation undergoes a substantive turn with the rise of classical economics. In pre-physiocratic political economy, the study of economic phenomena, though rational and rigorous, proceeds by segments, focusing only on those subjects that are relevant to the discussion of the normative problems at stake (an example is Gresham's Law). Conversely, in classical political economy, norms and rules of behaviour are a necessary consequence of a consistent system of natural laws. In the private sphere, such norms consist of some forms of enlightened interest[4]; in the public sphere, political economy recommends laissez-faire policies.

In his lectures at *Collège de France* of the mid-1970s, Michel Foucault (2004a, b) found in this normative message a crucial political meaning. The natural laws of exchange and population have become the pillars of a new political paradigm that Foucault called 'governmentality'. Such public goods as social order; the provision of means of subsistence; the wealth, well-being, and populousness of nations; internal and external security; and the 'politeness' of nations were no longer attributed to the paternal care of the sovereign. They now appeared as the result of the natural laws of political economy, and the responsibility of 'governing' nations switched from the visible hand of rulers to the invisible hand of economic laws.

Nevertheless, classical economists understood that the governmentality of market laws does not enjoy the necessitous character of physical events. Human actions may be inconsistent with these laws when partisan interests and short-sighted goals mislead them. In the private domain, with the help of a 'deontologist', individuals must adopt rules consistent with the public interest (Bentham 1983). In the public domain, legislators must be guided by an enlightened opinion in order to avoid counterproductive distributions of punishment and reward. Therefore, political economy tended to produce representations and rules that were consistent with a market-based political order. This was conceived as an ideological and pedagogical tool and aimed at influencing the social construction of the market.

For this reason, since the beginning, political economy possessed a marked institutional dimension. We can distinguish at least four converging processes of institutionalisation. The first is academic institutionalisation: In the 18th and 19th centuries, political economy becomes a subject of teaching in universities, schools of commerce, and secondary, popular, and even primary schools, being employed as a source of indoctrination for educational and disciplinary goals, a background for a wider political and legal training, or a subject for the creation of technical expertise. In every case, the process is characterised by strict political control.

The second process is institutionalisation of political economy in the public sphere through academies, cultural and publishing ventures, associations, and political movements. In the 19th century, associations, journals, and publishing houses were established to propagate the tenets of laissez-faire and later, of a paternalist, 'Christian' or Socialist political economy. The story of these organisations sometimes runs parallel to academic institutionalisation; in other circumstances, like in France during the early decades of the 19th century, 'social' institutionalisation was a substitute for academic institutionalisation (Levan-Lemesle 2004). The promoters of these ventures aimed at animating the public sphere or organising political movements, either by enlightening people on their supposedly 'true' interests or by fuelling their critical regard on governments.

Thirdly, there is a political institutionalisation of economics. Very often, on the initiative of the same groups that animate associations, economists became MPs, ministers, top bureaucrats, and party leaders. They considered political economy as *expertise* at the service of political institutions or the background for direct involvement in legislative and governmental activity.

Finally, these three processes of institutionalisation jointly contribute to the most important process of all, which may be called 'cognitive institutionalisation'. This occurs when the principles of political economy become *common sense*, mental frames, or socially constructed representations and models of economic behaviour (Lebaron 2009), which in turn contribute to the social construction of reality, specifically the reality of market order.

The role of textbooks

A by-product of the institutionalisation of political economy is the proliferation of textbooks. As recent research revealed, there are thousands of textbooks on economics published in Europe and in the rest of the world in the 19th century and in the early 20th century (Augello and Guidi 2012). Such a macroscopic phenomenon requires an explanation.

The wide range of readers, to which they were addressed, can explain the success of these texts. Post-Smithian textbooks were the medium through which political economy became a cognitive framework to interpret the phenomena of the market society, contributing to its social construction. They provided representations and behavioural models that were consistent with the governmentality of political economy. Specifically, they offered to relatively untrained minds a systematic vision of economic principles, explaining their logical connections. These texts conveyed the idea of a natural order regulating the reproduction of society and guaranteeing beneficial results. Finally, they translated economic truths into norms for the private and public activity.

The Sayian-Millian textbook, divided into four parts (production, circulation, distribution, and consumption), was perfectly adapted to these aims. This explains why, for a long time, it became the standard. The last part on the theory of consumption was of special interest and was generally divided into two distinct sub-parts: the first sub-part discussed public consumption, examining the areas in which State expenditure was necessary (security, education, infrastructures) and those in which it was superfluous or harmful; the second sub-part examined 'correct' private consumption, extolling the virtues of exchange, industry, saving, providence, marriage, and responsible generation. This part reveals that during the 19th century, textbooks became powerful devices for pedagogical and normative aims. Interiorising certain norms of behaviour was indispensable for, and preliminary to, the functioning of the market society. In the last resort, market norms revealed their nature of conditions of possibility of market laws.

From teaching to transnational circulation of economic ideas

The rise of a modern publishing industry, favoured by significant technological innovations and by the organisational and commercial model of large-scale and -scope industry (Barbier 2012, Ch. 3), made literary works available to a large public and generated the phenomenon of scientific and technological popularisation. The publication of popular manuals also involved economics. Differently from natural sciences and technology, however, popularisation was an organic element of political economy as it was essential to its performative function. In a sense, political economy *was* dissemination and popularisation because it was conceived as a truth revealed in order to dictate unambiguous and consistent rules of behaviour.

This may explain why the dissemination of economics – already a significant phenomenon in the 18th century – had in the 19th century an intense viral expansion, crossing national borders and affirming itself in different national contexts. This viral expansion was not merely an intellectual process: First and foremost, it called for action, transformation, and institutional innovation. Its messages fascinated an ever-increasing number of individuals and groups. This is because they spoke of a form of governmentality that, more than the great political revolutions that had marked the passage from the 18th to the 19th century, seemed to solve all the contradictions, inefficiencies, and corruptions of the Old Regime, generating an age of reason, efficiency, and rapid improvement.

It was perhaps at this transnational level that the practical side of political economy appeared more evident: the circulation of political economy was a phenomenon of importation, adaptation, and implementation, not only of theories, policy strategies, and recipes for national success but also of institutions and models of social organisation. Furthermore, the creation of replicas of the institutional models imported from abroad was rarely the fruit of isolated initiatives, clustering around easily recognisable 'institutional packages' that aimed to reorganise society at a general level. For the sake of the present analysis, an institutional package can be defined as a coherent system of 'devices' or institutional and discursive arrangements (*agencements*) that has been successful in a certain area in promoting a new form of governmentality and is imported in another area by individual or collective key actors in order to replicate their success.

In a way, economic books, journals, encyclopaedias, dictionaries, and – with their specific doctrinal function – textbooks circulate, are translated, or are imitated as tools to promote or support the imitation of these 'packages', and conversely, these institutional settings are responsible for circulating and translating economic texts and ideas. The promoters of such a circulation are actor-networks (Callon 1988; Latour 1987) connected with the government and the public sphere. According to the actor-network theory, actors may be either human or non-human. The first type is represented, in our case, by *emigrés*, exporters and importers, leaders of movements, intellectuals, students, and scholars. 'Devices' or *angencements* makes up the second type, such as educational institutions, charities, associations, textbooks, periodicals, etc. (Callon, Muniesa and Millo 2007).

An example is an institutional package that circulates across various countries in the 19th century, taking its origin in the systematic activities of the *école libérale française*. Following in their turn some British examples, the French liberals took a coordinated series of initiatives in the 1840s and 1850s to create a set of institutions that functioned as 'devices' in the sense above clarified: a debating society (*Société d'économie politique*); a mouthpiece (*Journal des économistes*); a propaganda society (*Association pour la liberté des échanges*) and a connected journal (*Le libre échange*); a successful campaign for sending to the Parliament (1848) their members; 'public lectures' (by Adolphe Blanqui, Pellegrino Rossi, Michel Chevalier, and Joseph Garnier) and textbooks based on these lectures; and lastly, the Guillaumin publishing house, which issued the *Collection des principaux économistes* and the *Dictionnaire de l'économie politique*. It was the coordination among these initiatives that made the French liberal school a powerful and irresistible movement that favoured important policy changes and a long-lasting turn in the public opinion on economic matters.

But the most interesting fact is that many contemporaries in various European countries understood this success. Classical political economy was disseminated in Europe, not only through the circulation of ideas and theories but also through the replication of the institutional package connected to them. The French model was imitated in Belgium, Spain, Portugal, Germany, Italy, Greece, and possibly elsewhere. Similar sets of associations, journals, publishing initiatives, and political activities were undertaken by cohesive groups of laissez-faire economists in all these countries. And this also occurred in other circumstances: For example, in the 1870s, various replicas of the *Verein für Sozialpolitik* decreed the success of the German 'Socialists of the Chair' not only in Europe but also in other countries as Japan testifies (Kumagai 2001; Nishizawa 2012).

Translations and translators

The actor-network theory has highlighted the ubiquity and complexity of the processes of 'translation' (Callon 1986). Translation is the precise activity that generates an actor-network, i.e. the process through which key or focal actors in an organisation ally to themselves other actors by 'translating' their goals into the representation, interests, and visions of potential adepts. As explained by Callon, such a process of translation includes three steps: problematisation, involvement, and enrolment. Problematisation consists of the focal actor's definition or redefinition of the identities and interests of other actors in order to become a critical standard for them. Involvement is the process through which other actors are persuaded to accept the definitions of the focal actor. Lastly, co-optation or enrolment occurs when involved actors accept what the focal actor recommends as their own interests.

Actors, especially those emerging as focal actors, are translators along the process of construction and growth of a network. Again, there are human and non-human actors. Among 'actors' there are the institutional packages that combine in significant ways the human and non-human actors.

Therefore, the translation of identities, representations, interests, ideologies, and practices precedes and shapes the translation as a 'linguistic act' and as a 'text'. However, the process of textual translation is far from being unrelated to translation in a broader sense. This case perfectly applies itself to economic texts, the content of which is closely connected to projects of social and institutional innovation, which require in their turn problematisation, involvement, and enrolment. Translations play the role of non-human actors intervening at the crucial moment in which national borders are crossed towards the creation of international networks or towards the replication of institutional packages. Equally, translators, editors, and sponsors of translations are very often focal actors in these processes.

In the cases studied by Monica Lupetti and myself, this characteristic is quite evident. The Portuguese translator of Véron de Forbonnais' *Élémens du commerce* (Forbonnais 1766, original 1754), José Manuel Ribeiro Pereira, was a graduate in law who was soon to become secretary of the Managing Board of the *Companhia Geral do Grão Pará, e Maranhão*, one of the chartered trade companies created by the future Marquis of Pombal to foster the commercial interest of Portugal (Lupetti and Guidi 2014). The translator of Smith's *Considerations Concerning the First Formation of Languages* (Smith 1816, original version 1761, Francisco Xavier Ribeiro de Sampaio, was a magistrate who, under Pombal's government, was appointed to various offices in the *capitanias* of Pará and Rio Negro, and he wrote interesting reports about his explorations of these areas. Jeremy Bentham's *Théorie des peines et des récompenses* was translated in Lisbon in 1822 (original 1811), following a decree of the revolutionary *Cortes*, and Bentham himself actively networked to promote his projects on constitution, penal code, and Panopticon with various leaders of the Portuguese liberal movement. His *Traité des sophismes politiques* was translated in the Brazilian province of Santa Catarina (Bentham 1838, original 1816) by António José Falcão da Frota, who became an active member of the newly elected Provincial Assembly soon after the reforms that had transformed the Brazilian Empire into a constitutional monarchy. The Portuguese translation of Otto Hübner's *Der kleine Volkswirth* (Hübner 1877, original 1852) was made by Francisco Augusto de Almeida, a publicist who had, at the beginning of the 1860s, emigrated to Argentina, where he founded the newspaper *El Diario de Buenos Ayres*. Back to Lisbon, Almeida attempted a career as polymath and reformer of primary education. The text was prefaced by Augusto José da Cunha, who had been member of various government councils and during that time, Commissioner of Education. Finally, the Brazilian translation of Luigi Cossa's *Primi elementi di economia politica* (1888, original 1875) was sponsored by Joaquim José Vieira de Carvalho, professor of political economy at the University of São Paulo, who adopted this textbook for his course. After the creation of the Republic in 1889, Carvalho became a leading founder of the Monarchical Party and was elected to Parliament (Guidi and Lupetti 2014).

These translations, like many similar works, performed the three functions of problematisation, involvement, and enrolment by adapting the original texts to the horizons of expectations of their new readers.[5] Paratextual additions pointed out the utility of these books to defend national policies, to supply national institutions with new and updated materials, and to provide a theoretical background to those fellow countrymen who were engaged in political or social battles. They highlighted the differences between what the original author intended to propagate and the national culture or the national conjuncture, often omitting passages that appeared problematic or conversely adding sections, chapters, and even entire parts to adapt the book to the new context. Nevertheless, translations were also tools for the creation of new networks and new initiatives because they were themselves actors. Once they were brought out, they lived, as it were, their own lives and 'acted' as propagators of projects and aggregators of people.

On the other hand, a prerequisite for the translation of economic texts was the linguistic competence of translators. The availability of such competence was not obvious, especially in 'new' countries, such as the ex-colonies of Latin America or countries opening their frontiers to the West like Japan. Translating from English, French, Italian, or German in a Spanish, Portuguese, or Japanese-speaking country requires human actors who are able to translate from these languages and other actors who make available grammars, methods, conversation manuals, and dictionaries or teach languages in schools and universities. These actors can be political *emigrés*, like the German economists who flew to America in the 1930s (Hagemann 2011); graduate students and young scholars sent to Europe to refine their studies (Borokh 2012; Nishizawa 2012); foreign intellectuals and publishers who maintain contacts with their original communities and promote the translation of their own national literature; or finally, grammarians, lexicographers, and language teachers. Sometimes, grammarians engage themselves in translations as the Portuguese case demonstrates. Manuel de Sousa, an engineer of the Portuguese Royal Army, translated Fénelon from French and Campomanes from Spanish and was probably the author of one of the earliest French-Portuguese dictionaries (Sousa 1769). Before him, Antonio José de Miranda e Silveira translated some issues of *L'observateur hollandez*, a ferociously anti-British periodical publication on colonial trade and treaties of commerce, edited by Jacob-Nicolas Moreau between 1755 and 1759. Some years later, Silveira was involved in an unfortunate attempt to publish the translation of a French treatise on grammar, *Le mécanique des langues et l'art de les enseigner* by Antoine-Noël Pluche (1751) (Lupetti 2016). In the 19th century, João Félix Pereira, the translator of William Ellis's *Outlines of Social Economy* (1846), was the author of Portuguese (1863), English (1875), and Italian grammars (1890). Finally,

Francisco de Almeida, the translator of Hübner's *Der kleine Volkswirth*, published various grammars and dictionaries, such as *Le dictionnaire des six langues* (1902), which was presented at the Paris Universal Exhibition of 1900.

Conclusions: a tentative hypothesis

It is evident that once linguistic competence is created, it becomes available for any kind of activity. However, is economic translation just one among these activities or does it entertain a special relationship with the dissemination of linguistic competence?

A fascinating hypothesis is provided by the notion of 'market for political economy', coined by Claeys et al. (1993) with regard to the institutionalisation of political economy. There is a parallel 'market for foreign languages', connected to flows of human migration and trade relationships. Proof of the connections between these 'markets' is the fact that the institutionalisation of foreign languages in Italy, France, and Germany is rooted in the Schools of Commerce and in technical schools. The reason is that language teaching, linguistic competence, and economic training are equally crucial elements in the social construction of the market. The teaching of foreign languages responds first to economic and social needs and only later becomes a scholarly discipline. There is a demand for foreign languages to both facilitate the circulation of labourers and commodities and grant access to relevant information on other countries and their resources.

The latter aspect is relevant also for economic translations: These are important also as sources of information about the ideas and institutions of other countries. Accordingly, the market for political economy and the market for foreign languages become two aspects of the more extensive process of the migration of institutional packages. Both the knowledge of languages and that of economic notions and realities serve to *categorise* the information that actors require to participate in the market and in its surrounding institutional context. They both play a cognitive function because they contribute to socially constructing what they categorise.

Significantly, the research on economic translations has revealed the global dimension of this phenomenon. The Ottoman Empire, Japan, Russia, and, massively, Northern and Latin America participated in economic translation, often in connection with original practical initiatives. However, it would be wrong to read such a global dimension as an early phenomenon of globalisation. The plurality of source languages and source texts reveals that what was looked for was not the international standard but what best described and interpreted the institutional and social models of other countries with a view to their replication in the target context. The dimension that dominated was trans-regional rather than global. Globalisation would eventually occur but only much later, after a selection process that led to the domination of the Anglo-American model.

Notes

1 An early version of this paper was used as an introduction to the Conference on 'Translations of economic texts into and from European languages', Pisa, Sept. 2013. I owe thanks to Tiffany Tirado for improving the English of the paper, making it sound much better than it was.
2 See latest Augello and Guidi (2012).
3 LLP – Sub-Programme Erasmus – Multilateral Projects 2011–2013 (http://eet.pixel-online.org).
4 This aim is evident in the works of Jean-Baptiste Say, especially those aiming at popularisation, like the *Cathéchisme d'économie politique* or the *Petit volume* (Say 1848). The *Essai sur le principe d'utilité* (Say 2003, 130–54), which was published as an appendix to the *Cours d'économie politique pratique*, well illustrates this connection between economic laws and enlightened interest. See Steiner (1989).
5 Recent trends in translation theory have highlighted the notion of translation as transaction between texts and languages (Bassnet 2002) and as adaptation (Raw 2012).

References

Augello, M.M. and Guidi, M.E.L. (eds.). 2012. *The Economic Reader*. London: Routledge.
Barbier, F. 2012. *Histoire du livre en Occident*. Paris: Colin.
Bassnet, S. 2002. *Translation Studies*. London and New York: Routledge.
Bentham, J. 1822. *Traducção das Obras Politicas do Sabio Jurisconsulto Jeremias Bentham*. Lisboa: Imprensa Nacional.
Bentham, J. 1838. *Tratado dos Sofismas Politicos*. Santa Catarina: Typ. Provincial.
Bentham, J. 1983. *Deontology*. A. Goldworth ed. Oxford: Clarendon Press.
Borokh, O. 2012. Adam Smith in Imperial China: Translation and Cultural Adaptation. *Oeconomia*, 2(4): 411–41.
Callon, M. 1986. Some Elements of a Sociology of Translation: Domestication of the Scallops and the Fishermen of St Brieuc Bay. In J. Law (ed.), *Power, Action and Belief*. London: Routledge & Kegan Paul, pp. 196–233.
Callon, M. (ed.). 1988. *La science et ses réseaux. Genèse et circulation des faits scientifiques*. Paris: La Découverte.
Callon, M., Muniesa, F. and Millo Y. 2007. An Introduction to Market Devices. In M. Callon, Y. Millo and F. Muniesa (eds.), *Market Devices*. Oxford: Blackwell, pp. 1–12.
Claeys, G., Hont, I., Kadish, A. and Tribe, K. 1993. Introduction. The Supply and Demand for Economics in Late Victorian Britain. In A. Kadish and K. Tribe (eds.), *The Market for Political Economy*. London: Routledge, pp. 1–19.
Coats, A.W. Bob. 1969. Research Priorities in the History of Economics. *History of Political Economy*, 1(1): 9–18.
Cossa, L. 1888. *Primeiros Elementos de Economia Política*. Rio de Janeiro: Laemmert & C.
[Forbonnais, F.] 1766. *Elementos do Comercio*. Lisboa: Antonio Rodrigues Galhardo.
Foucault, M. 2004a. *Sécurité, territoire, population*. Paris: Gallimard-Seuil.
Foucault, M. 2004b. *Naissance de la biopolitique*. Paris: Gallimard-Seuil.
Guidi, M.E.L. and Lupetti, M. 2014. Markets for Knowledge. The Institutionalisation of Economics, the Rationalisation of Language Learning and the Brazilian

Translation of Luigi Cossa's *Primi elementi di economia politica*. In E. Carpi and M.E.L. Guidi (eds.), *Languages of Political Economy*. Pisa: Pisa University Press, pp. 135–83.

Hagemann, H. 2011. European Émigrés and the 'Americanization' of Economics. *The European Journal of the History of Economic Thought*, 19(5): 643–71.

Hübner, O. 1877. *A Economia Politica Posta ao Alcance das Crianças*. Lisboa: Mattos Moreira & Ca.

Kumagai, J. 2001. Orchestrating Economic Ideas: The Formation and Development of Economic Societies in Modern Japan. In M.M. Augello and M.E.L. Guidi (eds.), *The Spread of Political Economy and the Professionalisation of Economists*. London: Routledge, pp. 200–15.

Latour, B. 1987. *Science in Action*. Cambridge, MA: Harvard University Press.

Lebaron, F. 2009. La formation des économistes et l'ordre symbolique marchand. In Ph. Steiner and F. Vatin (eds.), *Traité de sociologie économique*. Paris: Puf, pp. 249–88.

Levan Lemesle, L. 2004. *Le Juste ou le Riche*. Paris: Comité pour l'histoire économique et financière de la France.

Lupetti, M. 2016. "António José de Miranda e Silveira and the Portuguese Manuscript Translation of Noël-Antoine Pluche's *Mécanique des Langues* (1766)", paper presented at the LSA Annual Meeting, Washington, DC, 7–10 January 2016.

Lupetti, M. and Guidi, M.E.L. 2014. Translation as Import Substitution: The Portuguese Version of Véron de Forbonnais's *Elémens du Commerce. History of European Ideas*, 40(8): 1151–88.

Nishizawa, T. 2012. The Emergence of the Economic Science in Japan and the Evolution of Textbooks. In M.M. Augello and M.E.L. Guidi (eds.), *The Economic Reader*. London: Routledge., pp. 305–23.

Raw, L. (ed.). 2012. *Translation, Adaptation, and Transformation*. London and New York: Continuum.

Reinert, S.A. 2011. *Translating Empire*. Cambridge, MA and London: Harvard University Press.

Say, J.-B. 1848. *Oeuvres diverses de J.-B. Say*. Paris: Guillaumin.

Say, J.-B. 2003. *Leçons d'économie politique*, G. Jacoud et Ph. Steiner eds. Paris: Economica.

Smith, A. 1816. *Observações sobre a Primera Formação das Linguas e do Differente Genio das Originaes e Compostas*. Lisboa: Impressão Regia.

[Sousa, M. de]. 1769. *Dictionnaire françois, et portugais*. Lisbonne: Georges Rey, & Cie.

Steiner, Ph. 1989. Intérêts, intérêts sinistres et intérêts éclairés: problèmes du libéralisme chez J.-B. Say. *Cahiers d'économie politique*, 16–17: 21–41.

Steiner, Ph. 1998. *Sociologie de la connaissance économique*. Paris: Puf.

Part 4

Theoretical developments

Public economics, money and international trade

17 Individual choice and the public economy

Musgrave vs. Pigou

Richard Sturn

Public economics and Whig history

The price system, market exchange and decentralized allocation mechanisms came to be the main focus of neoclassical economics in the first period of its development, a development that overlapped with the development of economics as an academic discipline transcending national boundaries. Moreover, "modern economics developed more or less as the rationalisation of the laissez-faire economy, hence its preoccupation with the private sector and the operation of the market" (Arrow and Scitovsky 1969, 2).

Public economics, by contrast, is concerned with the working of economic principles in decision contexts in which non-market mechanisms and centralised decision-making play an important role. Moreover, public decision mechanisms are embedded in historically specific modes of governance. Policy issues of public economics are framed by political agendas, which, at least in part, are contextualised by the histories of communities and collectives. They are likely to be related to national specificities and traditions. To be sure, throughout the history of capitalism, neither the organisation of private sector institutions nor labour and capital markets were entirely free from national and cultural specificities. However, there are good reasons to assume that the mechanisms of the public sector were related to national traditions in a specifically profound way. This seems to be particularly relevant in the formative period of the discipline in the 19th century when the nation state as *the* model of modern statehood was anchored in mental models all over Europe.

All those aspects considered, public economics can be expected to be influenced by at least three kinds of developments: *first*, developments in the discipline of economics; *second*, developments concerning the most salient practical problems and tasks of the public sector *as they are perceived in a given historical setting* and *third*, pertinent backgrounds and normative concepts created by dominant theories in political philosophy as well as by folk views on the purpose, the role and the drawbacks of the state.

Consequently, differences between traditions in public economics may be caused by different framings, occasioned by the particular historical mix of practical problems of the public sector and politico-philosophical horizons as well as by differences regarding dominant schools in economic thought. With more or less explicit emphasis, these aspects come to the fore in contributions such as Richard Musgrave's (1997a) "*Public Finance and* Finanzwissenschaft: *Traditions Compared*" or Serge Kolm (2012).

Public economics may be perceived as a showcase in which the importance of the diversity of conceptual developments, of combinatorial progress and of heterogeneous national traditions is more relevant than elsewhere in economics, and it sometimes reappears and becomes visible in surprising ways. It is not a story of linear progress. In order to support this claim, I wish to sketch some differences between two foundational perspectives in public economics associated with the names of two key figures in its early development: Richard Abel Musgrave and Arthur Cecil Pigou. It will be shown that the differences affect not only meta-level issues, such as the architecture of public economics, or foundational, conceptual developments, such as Musgrave's theorisation of public goods and merit goods. Those different perspectives affect technical issues such as the marginal costs of public funds (MCF). "Meta-level" differences may be conducive to different modelling traditions with specific practical implications: The calculations based on those different frameworks may (on efficiency grounds) come to different conclusions when addressing the question of whether a certain public project should be undertaken or not.

The two traditions under consideration share a broadly neoclassical background as far as their theoretical and methodological foundations are concerned and a broadly reformist perspective, according to which the invisible hand sometimes needs help. Yet I will argue that there are significant differences regarding two aspects:

1 the overall architecture of public economics
2 the conceptualisation and explanation of non-market institutions and mechanisms.

These differences are understandable in terms of differences in framing conditions, such as basic understanding of statehood and its challenges and philosophical ideas concerning state, community, and society as well as practical problem settings and normative frameworks. I try to work out the characteristic differences and parallels concerning foundational issues in Public Economics by considering three types of questions:

1 How is Public Economics located within the larger edifice of Political Economy/economics?
2 How is the subject of Public Economics organised and subdivided: according to the distinction between revenue and expenditure or according to a differentiation based on various functions of the public sector?
3 Which are the most important *non-individualist* features of the respective explanation of collective institutions?

Here is a summary concerning some of the main differences to be highlighted: (1) with regard to the basic architecture of the theory of public institutions, a genuine *market failure* approach (Pigou) can be distinguished from a perspective ultimately envisaging market and state as *complementary institutions* (Musgrave). For Musgrave, the overarching concern is the functional structure of the public sector, which in particular includes an integrated analysis of the expenditure and the revenue side. The public budget process is conceptualised as a revenue-expenditure mechanism. The core function of the public sector is the provision of public goods, which are seen as a basic, non-contingent ingredient of a mixed economy – not the occasional malfunctioning of conceptually pre-existing markets. (2) Unlike Pigou, Musgrave emphasises the foundational importance of subdivisions and branches of the public sector in his theoretical architecture: Musgrave's three branches of the public economy (allocation, stabilisation and distribution) are not officially motivated by first principles of political philosophy; they are problem-oriented and pragmatic, with respect both to research strategies and to public decision-making. However, Musgrave's theoretical architecture is in a certain sense more pluralistic. The functional branches allow for a greater scope of reasonable disagreement: Each of them is related to a specific set of principles of judgments. Disagreement, moreover, may occur regarding the appropriate choice of theoretical models for a certain real-world problem setting at hand. From a Musgravian perspective, "models may become prisons", as Sir Anthony Atkinson put it in his Graz Schumpeter Lectures 2012. While Musgrave is certainly not a public choice theorist, his architecture as a whole allows for a more important role of democratic decision-making and discourse. It is less technocratic and in addition may serve as a heuristic for the institutional structures of the public sector. Put another way, Musgrave's theoretical architecture is compatible with the view that the public is the main addressee of economists' expert advice, while for Pigou, the main addressee is the government or the ministerial bureaucracy. To be sure, both (Musgrave in particular) would argue that the two are not mutually exclusive, and one ought to enhance the usefulness of economics in both respects. But the theoretical design has implications for the way in which economics may be thought of as a conceptual infrastructure for reasonable public discussions.

The rest of the paper is organised as follows: A schematic general comparison between the different approaches is provided in Sections (2–4). More specifically, in Section 3, the contrast between Musgrave's function-related branches (allocation, distribution and stabilisation) and Pigou's more conventional organisation of the subject (revenues and expenditures) is dealt with. In Section 4, I will show how those differences may affect the way in which a specific issue is dealt with (such as the marginal cost of public funds). Section 5 discusses the conception of merit wants, comparing it to Pigou's distinction between desires and satisfaction, which also implies a critical view regarding the universal applicability of consumer sovereignty.

Section 6 concludes with some more general observations on the implications of conceptual differences within modern public economics.

The market and the state: a case for unified theory?

The development of neoclassical economics culminated in the idea of *pure economics*, focusing on the logic of exchange (catallactics). Economists such as Emil Sax (1887, 1924), Knut Wicksell (1896) and Erik Lindahl (1919) saw the public sector as a challenge in that context. Broadly speaking, it was not obvious whether and how emphasis on private-decentralised decision-making, individual rationality and price-guided coordination could be related to a sphere where none of those principles appears to play a major role. Several alternative strategies emerged to deal with this seemingly incongruous situation:

1 *The public economy "as if it were exchange"*. The public sector is conceptualised as a cluster of quasi-markets; put another way, political mechanisms are treated as if they were markets. After the Second World War, this research strategy was inaugurated by James M. Buchanan, who was inspired by the Italian public finance literature, and Wicksell, who Buchanan read as a positive theorist of public sector decision-making.
2 *Finanzwissenschaft and fiscal sociology.* The public sector is treated as a cluster of non-market institutions and mechanisms that are analysed and explained by a specific discipline. In a German tradition remaining influential well into the 20th century, pertinent phenomena and problems were covered by *Finanzwissenschaft*, which had developed a strong identity with Lorenz von Stein, Albert Schäffle and Adolph Wagner: "the triad of German *Finanzwissenschaft* in its Golden Age", as Musgrave (1997a) put it. Dealing with issues such as taxation, public expenditures and the mechanisms of the public budget, *Finanzwissenschaft* was widely regarded as a discipline of its own. But German *Finanzwissenschaft* is not the only example of this kind of strategy. There is a second important current of thought that is somewhat similar in that the study of the public sector is relegated to a discipline outside economics: In the first decades of the 20th century, research programs of fiscal sociology were advocated by theorists such as Rudolf Goldscheid and Vilfredo Pareto. This move was explicitly motivated by the search for a methodology that is not constrained by the logic of markets and voluntary exchange, thus making available a superior framework for analysing core phenomena of the realm of politics, such as political power or the mechanisms suitable to give effect to communal preferences. More recently, Wagner (2007, esp. Ch. 2) summarises the core tenets of fiscal sociology by emphasising a "two-forum societal architecture" and the concomitant criticism of the foundational idea of dominant public economics traditions, according to which the *state*

intervenes in a pre-existing market order. The basic architecture of the distinction between the private and the public economy is seen as related to the *borderline between individual choice and social decision-making.* The state itself is *not* justified and explained in terms of its usefulness in dealing with certain types of coordination problems, with respect to which the state is arguably more efficient than alternative institutional arrangements or spontaneous, uncoordinated private decision-making. In fiscal sociology, society, polity and "the state" are considered as *natural facts* at the same level as markets.

3 *Market failure.* In a tradition forcefully developed by Pigou, the market system remains the conceptual point of reference. It is taken as logically pre-existing, as it were. Partial equilibrium analysis of market interactions is supplemented by a systematic study of market failures. Market failures are diagnosed by a comparison with a benchmark afforded by some ideally operating markets. The function of the government (and/or the legal system) is to mimic the market as allocation mechanism, e.g. by imposing corrective Pigovian taxes and subsidies to internalise otherwise non-priced effects on others, i.e. Pareto relevant externalities. Put another way, the analytical focus remains on decentralised decision-making and individual rationality, while emphasis is put on a double transformation: (i) the art of transforming the mechanisms of decentralised decision-making such that public concerns are efficiently accommodated; (ii) the art of transforming political problems (e.g. environmental problems) into market-like transactions. This implies two levels of argument: At a practical level, taxation must be studied in order to make available public funds in a way that does not distort the social efficiency of decentralised decision-making – or perhaps even enhances the efficiency of decentralised decision-making, as in the case of Pigovian taxes. At the level of principles of social reform, the Pigovian approach emphasises the view that market-mediated decentralised decision-making need not be considered as a natural fact but as an artificial mechanism, i.e. as a mechanism based on transformations occasioned by artificial rule systems. Such rule systems may be envisaged as mechanisms subject to (re)design by a utilitarian planner. Put another way, the door is open for a problem-oriented redesign of the rule system: It may be transformed in such a way that decentralised decision-making is no longer a mode of decision leading to the specific pattern of outcomes actually observed, e.g. to environmental destruction or huge inequalities of income and wealth. The market is no longer associated with possessive individualism implicitly privileging the status quo distribution.[1] Markets or market-like decentralised mechanisms may be transformed into an instrument addressing market failure, aiming at the maximisation of a utilitarian Social Welfare Function.

4 *Public Economics.* Economics explicitly transcends the boundaries of the catallactic sphere: In traditions in which public goods or collective

> wants are of pivotal importance (specifically the Sax-Wicksell-Lindahl-Musgrave tradition, as summarised by Musgrave 1939), the scope of economics is widened to include non-market institutions in general and the public sector in particular. Paul Samuelson swiftly recognised that the conceptualisation of public goods is *good news* for the discipline: It allows for exploiting the power of formal analysis at a more fundamental level of the public sector – one that is conceptually independent of a sphere of perfect markets (cf. Pickhard 2005, 2006, 450–1). Samuelson's (1954) paper suggesting the seminal formal representation of efficient allocation in a world including public goods is entitled *The Pure Theory of Public Expenditure* and not without reason. In modern theories, which model public good-problems in a game-theoretic way, the level of pure theory is even more clearly based on a conceptual framework within which public institutions/mechanisms may be introduced as solutions to problems (e.g. the avoidance of bad equilibria) occurring in a world of abstract strategic interdependences. Put another way, this presupposes a level of analysis in which it becomes possible to discuss relevant problems of coordination and incentives at a pre-institutional level. Markets are not considered as pre-existing, i.e. as "more natural" (i.e. as historically/conceptually/logically prior) form of economic phenomena.

The specific process of public decision-making related to the revenue-expenditure process is of relatively little analytical interest for approach (3), whereas it takes (albeit in very different forms) a much more important place in approaches (1) and (2) and also in approach (4). While in his earlier writings, Musgrave did not emphasise the differences between his own type 4-perspective in comparison to type 3 Anglo-Saxon public finance and market failure theory, he (1997a) stresses the lack of focus on public expenditures in the Pigovian tradition, implying a lack of interest in an integrated view of revenues and expenditures.

Analytical interest in public decision-making processes is closely related to the introduction of public goods as a key concept of the "allocation branch". Wicksell (1896) is an early text in which this becomes quite obvious. By way of the conceptualisation of public goods, the power and scope of micro-based economic reasoning is *extended* to a more fundamental level of public activity as compared to Pigovian, externality-based market failure. The conceptual basis of Musgrave's vision of public decision-making is more encompassing than Pigou's more technocratic vision. The latter is based on an understanding of market failure as (at least in principle) unambiguously diagnosable coordination gaps with unambiguous remedies. Externalities are conceptualised as singular "coordination gaps" within the market mechanism. Solutions to such problems call for appropriate models and correct calculations.

Last but not least, here are a few remarks on the choice of (political) institutions in a Pigovian framework. It might be argued that the transaction cost perspective on politics[2] and institutions (whether political or not) is somehow congenial to that framework: Coase (1960) refers in a critical way to the Pigovian approach to externalities and is, in some obvious sense, anti-Pigovian. But his transaction cost approach amounts to a kind of institutional analysis in which a price system (required for specifying "costs") is conceptually pre-existing and can be assumed as given, even in the case of fundamental institutional choices. Political procedures are dealt with in a framework in which drawbacks and frictions are expressed in terms of costs, conceptually presupposing a price system.

To sum up, for a Musgrave-type 4 approach, the scope of positive economic theory is neither confined to the logic of competitive exchange nor to the measuring rod of money. A type-4 research agenda must systematically include *problems of a positive theory of the working of the public sector* itself. At a foundational level, the theory of public goods is not just an appendix to the theory of market exchange. This is the heritage of a continental tradition in public economics, represented by names such as Emil Sax, Friedrich Wieser, Knut Wicksell and Erik Lindahl, with 19th century roots in the more theoretically oriented German currents of economic thought (see Sturn 2006 and Musgrave and Peacock 1958).

By way of conclusion of this section, a few remarks are in order here: It is noteworthy that Pigou and many authors in the Pigovian tradition (including Coase 1960, for whom Pigou is the central target of criticism) almost completely failed to take notice of this tradition. By contrast, in Baumol (1965) and especially in Mancur Olson's (1965) monograph on collective action, we find apt remarks regarding this aspect of the history of economic thought. Olson (1965, 102) observes that "... many of the best-known British economists enumerated the functions they thought the state should perform. ... But these economists did not point out what the various activities appropriate to the state had in common ... Even in this century Pigou ... gave collective goods for the most part only implicit treatment".

In the Wicksell-Lindahl-Musgrave-Samuelson tradition (including its pertinent exchanges with the Buchanan tradition), it took decades to disambiguate issues related to the distinction between (non-)rivalry and (non-) excludability and the fact that they may occur in different combinations, degrees and scopes (i.e. local-global) and to disambiguate issues related to the status of free rider problems and coercion in the context of Wicksell-Lindahl mechanisms of public good provision based on individual preferences. For instance, it was recognised that collecting decentralised information on individual preferences for determining the correct amount of public goods and dealing with funding problems pose different problems regarding the roles of coercion and incentives. Of course, pertinent work did not immediately come up with the right answers, but it identified the problems in a more precise way. Just to give an example: In the search for a unanimously preferred pattern of public good provision and tax prices sufficient for funding those public goods, an important step was the "voluntary exchange mechanism" à la Lindahl. As is well known now, those mechanisms tend to reproduce the incentives occasioned by the free-rider problem, preventing an efficient solution. The properties and drawbacks of such mechanisms (notably including voting mechanisms) presuppose the conceptual clarification of the foundations of public economics, as put forward by public good theory. It would not have been possible to discuss pertinent problems in the conceptual framework of Pigovian market failure.

Public economics and its branches

The above-mentioned contributions by William Baumol (1965) on differences in foundational traditions did not make their way into textbooks on Public Economics. Musgrave suggested that the well-known architecture of the branches of the public sector were "three naves of the cathedral", as he (1986) retrospectively put it: *allocation, distribution and stabilisation.* The three naves made their way into textbooks, partly complementing and partly superseding the traditional distinction of the revenue and expenditure side of the public budget. However, Musgrave's three naves approach was not an unambiguous success. Not only are these sometimes misunderstood (or even ridiculed) as the result of a typical German taste for classificatory schemes. More importantly, the subcategories for public economics within the Journal of Economic Literature-classification are still organised along the more traditional subdivisions of revenue and expenditure.

For Musgrave, the "three naves" are *not just a didactic or expository device.* In the Continental tradition that is important for Musgrave, function-related interdependences of the revenue and expenditure sides are indispensable for analytical reasons. In this respect, Musgrave's move was a partial success. Indeed, the integrated view of revenue and expenditure that goes along with this approach became the starting point for quite important model-based reasoning. As Musgrave makes clear when defending this structure against criticism, the functional subdivision of the subject is related to a *politico-economic dimension*: comprehensive problems must be factorised into tractable aspects, thereby not only allowing for sufficiently clear alternatives for public choices but also for thinking about functionally specialised institutions and mechanisms.

It has been observed that Pigou's oeuvre (esp. 1928, 1932) lacks a systematic approach to public expenditures. Moreover, his main pertinent contributions were written well before Abba Lerner's (1944, 301–22) conceptualisation of functional finance and Keynesian approaches to stabilisation policy. Pigou's quite conventional approach to the subdivision of Public Economics is merely *expository*. This is reflected by his choice to skip the revenue-related parts of *Economics of Welfare* in the later editions and publish them as a separate book (*A Study in Public Finance*, Pigou 1932). Subdivisions along Musgrave's lines are foreign to Pigou's (1928, 1932) understanding of the subject, in which the revenue side not only receives more attention than the expenditure side but is also treated more or less separately.

In various specific problem settings, there are good reasons for analysing the revenue side and the expenditure side of the public budget separately. But Musgrave's function-related branches are setting the stage for a deeper understanding of the role of the public sector in a market economy. The integrated view of revenues and expenditures that accompanied the function-related architecture primarily can be seen as a necessary foundation of the systematic analysis of the choice mechanisms of the public sector. Moreover, in the next section, I will discuss a more technical issue, illustrating the advantages of an integrated analysis of revenues and expenditures.

Musgrave's three branches also offer pragmatic advantages: Issues of allocation can be discussed without being committed to normative standards regarding distributional concerns. Similarly, the issue of macroeconomic stability looms large in Musgrave (1959), but the edifice as a whole is consistent with shifts of emphasis between the three naves. Allocation, distribution and stabilisation each provide distinct policy rationales whose premises can be discussed separately, i.e. abstracting from disputes concerning the two other branches. To be sure, this does not imply that a design in which public policies are primarily guided by the criteria of one particular branch (e.g. allocation efficiency) is necessarily neutral with respect to the other branches. In a Musgravian view, the three branches can also function as a kind of heuristic device, reconciling the specialisation of modelling discourses with the agenda for a balanced public policy mix: It surely makes sense to rigorously think through the adjustments required for an efficiency-enhancing reform of the tax system, abstracting from impacts on stabilisation and distribution. However, Musgrave's architecture makes us aware that a policy reform solely geared to issues of efficient allocation *may* make the system worse with respect to stabilisation properties or reasonable criteria of distribution.

Taxes, public goods, incidence and efficiency: the marginal cost of public funds

In various specific problem settings, there are good reasons for analysing the revenue side and the expenditure side of the public budget separately. In other cases, it may be important to have available a perspective emphasising an integrated analysis of revenues and expenditures. Here is an example showing that this may be true, not only at the level of foundational politico-economic considerations.

Dealing with the marginal cost of public funds in the presence of distortive taxation, Charles Ballard (1990) refers to a conceptual distinction introduced by Musgrave (1959) in the context of *tax incidence*. Musgrave (1959) distinguished between *"differential analysis"* (focusing the differential effect of *different kinds of taxes*) and *"balanced budget analysis"* (focusing on the effect of a *tax-financed public expenditure*). Applying this distinction to the issue of the cost of public funds occasioned by distortionary taxation, Ballard showed its usefulness in disambiguating some pertinent puzzles occasioned by different approaches. More specifically, Ballard stresses that what he calls the Pigou-Harberger-Browning approach is based on *differential analysis*: A distortionary tax is compared to another tax of equal revenue yield. (The obvious relevant comparison in that context is between the distortionary tax and a non-distortive lump-sum tax.)

Unfortunately, the lump sum tax is a hypothetical alternative that need not be relevant for the actual effects of a tax-financed increase in government spending. As is succinctly expressed by Charles Ballard and Don Fullerton (1992, 124),

> To be relevant for cost-benefit analysis, the Pigou-Harberger-Browning approach must assume that the public good itself essentially compensates the consumer so that income effects wash out and only substitution effects remain. This assumption is often left unstated, but it is a strong one: the public good must be just like cash in its effects on consumption of goods and leisure. That is, the tax and rebate must lead to a decrease in labor supply.

Now, there is a different approach invoking what Musgrave introduced as *"balanced-budget analysis"* based on the effect of a tax-financed increase in government spending. Ballard and Fullerton call this the Stiglitz-Dasgupta-Atkinson-Stern approach. Ballard and Fullerton (1992, 125) explain the difference by way of a thought experiment, considering a small lump sum tax, which is imposed on top of a pre-existing wage tax. Users of the Pigou-Harberger-Browning approach would say that this lump sum tax has no excess burden (relative to a lump sum tax). Thus, the marginal cost of public funds would be one. Users of the Stiglitz-Dasgupta-Atkinson-Stern approach would note that the additional lump sum tax has income effects that discourage leisure and encourage labour supply (with the assumption that the public good itself has no effect on labour supply). *Thus, the additional lump sum tax also increases the revenue from the pre-existing wage tax.* The combined increase in revenue exceeds the loss in utility so that the "revenue effect" makes the marginal cost of public funds less than one". In the context of the present article, I am not interested in discussing the circumstances and problem settings rendering either the balanced-budget approach or the differential approach superior. To conclude, the conceptual integration of the revenue and expenditure sides of the public budget may be important for seemingly technical problems, not "only" as a foundation of the systematic analysis of the choice mechanisms and institutions of the public sector.

Merit wants, wantings and likings

There is a tradition in British social theory that deals with cases in which instrumental rationality or consumer sovereignty fail in a certain sense, mainly stressing problems of overly narrow-minded or "myopic" choices occasioned by behaviour such as hyperbolic discounting. Given such behaviour, choice patterns may be expected that systematically lead to outcomes incompatible with enlightened self-interest. In David Hume's treatise (1739 Bk III, section VII "Of the origin of government") we read,

> What strikes with … a strong and lively idea commonly prevails above what lies in a more obscure light …. Now as everything, that is contiguous to us, either in space or time, strikes upon us with such an idea, …, and commonly operates with more force than any object, that lies in a more distant and more obscure light … This is the reason why men so often act in contradiction to their known interest; and in particular why they prefer any trivial advantage, that is present, to the maintenance of order in society.

Hume continues by explaining collective institutions and norms of justice as devices that are useful in the presence of those distortive imperfections of the human individuals that lead to strategic social dilemma situations, if not coped with by those public institutions. While the latter part of this argument is more congenial to a Musgravian view of public sector institutions (see Musgrave 1997a), the way in which agency-related imperfections and deficiencies are emphasised by Hume is similar to Pigou's pertinent distinctions. Both Musgrave and Pigou endorse a strongly individualistic stance. Both acknowledge some limits to consumer sovereignty but endorse different strategies for dealing with its limits. Those different approaches tend to support different methodological approaches of dealing with some drawbacks of social theory based on individual rational choices.

Pigou's approach of dealing with the limits of consumer sovereignty remains at the level of individual rationality and its limitations. It introduces some theoretical complications that may practically motivate some form of liberal paternalism. But there is *no tendency to explicitly move on to the level of collective choices*. In that sense, it is perfectly in keeping with the kind of normative individualism that is a foundational part of orthodox normative economics. More specifically, his approach stresses the possible difference between desires and satisfactions. It implies what I call here a "broadly" individualist perspective. "Broad individualism" simply amounts to rejecting the equation of individualism with claims according to which (in cases not covered by traditional market failure) market-mediated individual choices are the only possible sources of normative authority. While "broad" individualism requires moving beyond the just-indicated narrow versions of consumer sovereignty, it does not entail more philosophically demanding conceptions of reflective individual autonomy. Notice in particular that "broad" individualism does not imply the kind of "broad" rationality (a notion suggested by Munro 2009, 5–6) that includes the theoretical option in favour of a reflective stance with regard to goals (addressing the question of whether goals are reasonable in terms of "true interest") along with instrumental rationality (vis-à-vis consistency either in choices or in preferences). While that kind of "broad" rationality no doubt prepares the ground for interesting interpretations (notably those hinging on higher order preferences and multiple selves), this is certainly *not implied* by stressing discrepancies between "desires" and "satisfactions" along the lines of Pigou (1932). That is, the problems he raises do not presuppose a fully fledged reflective stance with regard to goals but may be discussed at the level of "mistakes" of instrumental rationality. One of the causes of such mistakes is what he calls the (lack of) *telescopic faculties* of individuals.

Notice that the distinction between desires and satisfactions is also playing a role in discussions on merit wants (see e.g. Head 1991, 232) and more recent discourses on libertarian paternalism where it is known as the wantings-likings distinction. Musgrave (1957, 1959) introduced the concept of merit wants, which is typically seen as a somehow problematic move in the context of individualist public economics. Beyond Pigou's argument, according to which desire fulfilment may fail to produce sustainable satisfaction or to be in the true interest of an agent, Musgrave's approach to the pertinent complex of problems has a *tendency to explicitly move on to the level of collective choices.* This is sometimes obscured by the fact that talk about merit goods often was and is linked to the issue of paternalism, implicitly assuming that purported defects of individual rationality are the sole source of problems. A superficial reading of Musgrave (which is reflected in the discussion of merit goods in much of the textbook literature published in the wake of Musgrave 1959) tends to overemphasise the aspect of paternalism in the sense of quasi-custodial choices. Yet for Musgrave, quasi-custodial choices, which are associated with paternalism, are not the most important issue when it comes to the discussion of merit wants.

Musgrave introduces and uses the concept of *merit goods* (or merit wants[3]) with great caution. Sometimes, these indeed appear as an *appendix or a footnote* to an otherwise individualist account of the public sector – rather than a *cornerstone* on which the explanations of the most fundamental part of the public sector appears to be based, as is the case in the related approach suggested by Gerhard Colm (1927, 1936, 1956). Colm's conceptions put emphasis on the idea that certain valuations (which may or may not be valuations actually articulated by individuals) can only be understood if *individuals are considered as members of communities.*[4] In Musgrave's *Theory of Public Finance*, the concept of merit goods or (cf. Musgrave 1959, footnote 5) merit wants are introduced *after* the discussion of pure public goods. In Musgrave's writings, three separate but related dimensions of the argument from merit wants come to the fore: *First*, a merit wants argument may be put forward in favour of collective provision, eventually including coercive elements, if the collective choices triggered by merit wants can be thought of as *representing the informed meta-preferences of a person acting according to her "true" interests* (educational choices of the uneducated are presented as cases in point). Notice that the argument is not necessarily limited to a lack of information or lack of telescopic faculties. It may also go beyond weakness of will. Moreover, the idea that the "consumption" of the good itself would change the wants/preferences/valuations/identities of the consumers (endogenous preferences) may play a role in this context. *Second,* Musgrave is conversant with the idea that it may be reasonable to distinguish between *personal wants* of the consumer and merit wants of the voter whose political preferences are articulated in a public election. He discusses this topic in reaction to Colm's criticism of the public good concept. It is (says Musgrave, commenting on Colm) reasonable to assume that the latter may depend on the fact that she is a member of a political community with certain politico-ethical views on what a good society and state should be. But for Musgrave (1986, 38), the force of this argument is explicitly limited to social choices concerning "great issues of state", such as *defence* or the *education* system. With respect to such issues, more abstract reasoning about "the good education system" (informing one's political choice in a democratic election) may substantially *and reasonably* differ from contingent situation-specific reasoning, as *revealed* in the factual educational choices for one's kids under given constraints. *Third,* there may be a merit want aspect implicit in some distributional norms, entailing a pluralist metric of "basic goods". Under certain conditions, the government may reasonably choose to arrange distribution of these basic goods "in kind" – much in the same way that individuals may sometimes choose to give their charitable donations in kind rather than in cash.

The conceptual clarification of Musgravian merit wants brings to the fore their collective choice dimension. In some of the most interesting work, the roots of the merit wants concept (owing much to German Public Finance and Colm in particular) are made explicit. Geoff Brennan and Loren Lomasky (1983) were among the first to contribute to the conceptual development of the communal wants dimension of merit wants beyond Colm (1965). They explicitly referred to Colm's distinction between homo oeconomicus and homo politicus (and his corresponding distinction between market and politico-fiscal processes), developing those ideas in the context of a democratic institutional perspective with an explanatory agenda. Colm emphasised the conceptualisation of the judgments of homo politicus as referring to overarching "national goals" in a specific way. In an analogous way, Kenneth Arrow's individual *"values"* (contrasting the individual *"tastes"* of consumer theory) refer to aspects of social states other than individually consumed quantities of goods. Brennan and Lomasky (1983) introduced distinctions, such as the one between m-preferences (typically related to outcomes in a market environment), reflective preferences (which are not immediately outcome-oriented in the way that m-preferences are) and p-preferences, which are "intimately related" to reflective preferences as political choice processes typically allow for the expression of preferences with small expected costs. While the analytical difference between the three kinds of distinctions would require some further discussion, their main thrust is somewhat similar. All three conceptualisations illustrate the scope and power of integrating the level of collective choice.

Concluding remarks

Concepts such as social wants and public goods are suitable ingredients for a view emphasising the connections between revenue and expenditures and, above all, the institutions and mechanisms of the public sector as a subject of inquiry. By contrast, Pigou's core rationale for public intervention is the concept of externalities, by definition capturing cases of suboptimality within the working of markets. Externalities are a kind of conceptual device that are primarily used (i) for critical discussions of the premises applying to competitive markets; (ii) as a diagnostic tool for shortcomings of the status quo characterised by private decentralised decision-making.[5] The state is an organisation providing corrective instruments for proper adjustments in which markets fail to yield a coincidence of private and social interest (Pigou 1937, 87).

For Musgrave, the state is not merely a collection of corrective devices intervening when actual markets happen to work in a suboptimal manner. Musgrave (1959, 8) carefully distinguishes between "situations where the market mechanism fails altogether" (described as "the case of *social wants* proper"; Musgrave's italics) on one side and externalities and lack of competition on the other, with respect to which "corrective action may be desirable and feasible; but such action as is taken remains more or less marginal".

Pigovian market failure theory primarily addresses this last-mentioned category of cases. The possible *malfunctioning* of public institutions *is included* in the conceptual framework of Musgravian analysis. Pigou (1937, 89) discusses some problems of political decision-making and bureaucratic implementation mechanisms, emphasising that the degree to which public action is to be recommended also depends on the quality and ability of the institutions of public governance and its employees. But Pigou was not interested in discussing political mechanisms and their shortcomings *at an analytical level.*

Musgrave (e.g. in the preface to his collected papers 1986) emphasised the synthetic character of his oeuvre, bringing together continental traditions in micro-based public economics, such as Wicksell, Sax and Lindahl, with the Pigovian strand. Moreover, Musgrave is influenced by more communal traditions in German public economics and writers such as Colm, at least with regard to some conceptual issues. Regarding the "institutional complementarity perspective", fiscal sociology and Musgrave are closer to each other than either of the two to Pigou. The public sector is not regarded as a set of measures correcting market outcomes when markets "fail". Rather, both fiscal sociology and Musgrave (e.g. 1999, 37) conceive of it as a set of institutions *complementary* to the market system. Some fiscal sociologists (cf. Wagner 2007) may have in mind a stronger version of complementarity than Musgrave, who is inclined to treat the question of how to deal with the implications of this complementarity itself as an *economic* problem in which efficiency considerations play a major role. Nonetheless, there is a second parallel between Musgrave and fiscal sociology: The idea of a co-evolution of market and state in the modern era can be most conveniently elaborated on in either the Musgrave framework or the framework of fiscal sociology. Notice though that with respect to important aspects of the conceptual framework, the Musgrave tradition is closer to the Buchanan tradition. This is not surprising, given the common ancestry in continental marginalist public finance à la Wicksell (see Musgrave 1939 and Buchanan 1952): Concepts such as public goods are important as they allow for modelling mechanisms of collective choice in the public sector.

Commonalities between Musgrave and Buchanan (and between Musgrave and fiscal sociology) notwithstanding, it should be emphasised once more that Musgrave and Pigou are, in important respects, particularly close to each other: Both of them are advocating a basically individualist explanation of phenomena characteristic of a mixed economy and are putting forward a foundation for reformist public sector policies based on individual valuations. That is, we are dealing here with theories *sharing*

1 a basically individualistic stance in terms of method and in terms of their normative background, including an emphasis on the virtues of decentralised decision-making;
2 some sort of enlightenment stance of rational reform as a basic perspective concerning the role of economics in guiding the overall design and specific policies of the public sector;
3 the (if partly implicit) rejection of a voluntary exchange theory of the state or of political processes and of an entirely pessimistic stance regarding the possibility of a well-ordered public sector developing a strong tradition of expedient civil service and
4 the view of public economics as a part of economics as opposed to the view that the public budget and public choice belong to a sphere regulated by altogether different principles.

In terms of pre-analytic political visions, both traditions endorse a liberal stance, connoting decentralisation and individualism. Both do not end up with the conclusion that the state is a necessary evil that should be kept as small as possible. Nonetheless, their different conceptualisations of the public sector have strengths and weaknesses whose discussion may be useful for thinking about the appropriate role of the public sector in a market economy. Indeed, it may be more useful than the type of discussions that became popular in the wake of Nozick (1974), focusing on the question of whether and how the (minimal) state can be justified at all.

Let me conclude with a more general observation. The case for the dehomogenisation of various currents within neoclassical economics is to be contrasted with stories implying over-homogenisation, which are often favoured both by critics and protagonists of the mainstream. Moreover, this case can be seen in relation to the image of unidirectional progress, deeply rooted in the self-understanding of the discipline, not only since the triumph of the marginalist revolution. The specific case for de-homogenisation made here applies to authors concerned with questions of the public economy. The economic theory of the public sector is sometimes specifically close to some big issues transcending the scope of disciplinary economic reasoning and modelling – reaching out to the grand controversies between individualism and collectivism, conservatism and enlightenment reformism and contractarian views of politics and its various critics. Having these issues in mind is helpful in terms of a demarcation of common ground vs. distinguishing specificities, motivating in one case the view of the "government" as an enlightened technocratic institution, regulating an imperfectly operating market system (Pigou), and in the other case the public sector as a set of institutions complementing the market system on the basis of a democratic policy (Musgrave).

Notes

1 Inter alia, the discourse on externalities opens up the following perspective: A new negative externality, which is admissible under the current system of property rights has redistributive effects. While the pollutee is worse off, the polluter is better off as a result of the profitable use of some non-priced scarce environmental services, other things remaining equal. Of course, a corrective tax addressing that externality (which is not compensated by some lump sum transfer) implicitly alters the system of property rights and also has distributive effects.

2 For a comprehensive exposition of the "transaction cost politics perspective", see Dixit (1996). It is not the place here to deal with the merits and drawbacks of such a perspective in comparison to approaches modelling more explicitly genuine "political" features of decision processes and mechanisms.

3 In keeping with the German-language Public Finance tradition, in his early contributions, Musgrave used the notion of merit wants as well as social wants (for public goods). As he was eager to get rid of terminological heritage that might hinder the development of a unified micro-based theory of market failure, he soon adopted the now common terminology. This terminological shift included merit goods, even though the latter are mostly explained in terms of properties of individual values or preferences, whereas rivalry and excludability are properties of goods rather than of wants.

4 Colm distinguishes between four levels of state activities: (i) maintenance of the existence and power of the state itself; (ii) the state as a factor of production for the market economy; (iii) services in specific areas, such as education and transport infrastructure and (iv) corrective interventions due to (temporary or permanent) malfunctioning of existing markets, including macroeconomic instabilities. Colm's (1927, 19–21) arguments with respect to (i) show that (i) constitutes one type of Musgrave's merit wants. They also show the system-theoretic foundations of his approach: His *starting points* are not some pre-institutional individual preferences, scarcities and technologies, but state and market as two complementary *systems*. "The fundamental differences between these economies must be explained before their interrelationship in modern economy can be understood" (1936, 4).

5 Seen from a perspective immanent to a general equilibrium model of a private-ownership economy with a complete set of perfect markets, it is quite logical that the Walrasian tradition (as is sometimes critically remarked, cf. Baumol 1965, 60/1) failed to come up with "externalities" as an analytical tool designed for the diagnosis of a case of divergence between private and social net products. Given a model in which a private-ownership economy with a complete set of markets is the theoretical ideal, missing markets and missing property rights are the appropriate way to describe the problem. It is the task of the other levels of economic reasoning to state conditions (related to these other levels) that are necessary and sufficient for a *framework of a private-ownership economy complemented by a public economy*, in which distortions, such as externality problems, do not occur. Translated into the Pigovian language, "unsolved" problems may manifest themselves as "externalities" in the market sphere. The question of the extent to which increasing returns in certain industries lead to incompatibilities with perfectly competitive conditions (natural monopolies) is subject matter of applied economics, and as far as such incompatibilities are diagnosed, they need to be dealt with by the state.

References

Andel, N. (1984). Zum Konzept der meritorischen Güter. *Finanzarchiv*, 42, 630–648.

Arrow, K. and Scitovsky, T., eds. (1969). *Readings in welfare economics*. London: Allen and Unwin.

Ballard, Ch. (1990). Marginal welfare cost calculations: differential analysis vs. balanced-budget analysis. *Journal of Public Economics*, 41, 263–276.

Ballard, Ch. L. and Fullerton, D. (1992). Distortionary taxes and the provision of public goods. *Journal of Economic Perspectives*, 6, 117–131.

Baumol, W. (1965). *Welfare economics and the theory of the state*. London: Bell.

Brennan, G. and Lomasky, L. (1983). Institutional aspects of "merit goods" analysis. *Finanzarchiv*, 41, 183–206.

Buchanan, J. M. (1952). Wicksell on fiscal reform. *American Economic Review*, 42, 599–602.

Cassel, M. (1924). Die Gemeinwirtschaft oder Die Gründe einer öffentlichen Haushaltung. Inaugural-Dissertation. Leipzig: A. Deichertsche Verlagsbuchhandlung Dr. Werner Scholl.

Coase, R. (1960). The problem of social cost. *Journal of Law and Economics*, 3, 1–44.

Colm, G. (1927). *Volkswirtschaftliche Theorie der Staatsausgaben*. Ein Beitrag zur Finanztheorie. Tübingen: Mohr.

Colm, G. (1936). The theory of public expenditure. *Annals of the American Academy of Political and Social Sciences*, 183, 1–11.

Colm, G. (1956). Comments on Samuelson's theory of public finance. *Review of Economics and Statistics*, 38, 408–412.

Colm, G. (1965). National goal analysis and marginal utility economics. *Finanzarchiv NF*, 24, 209–224.

Dixit, A. (1996). *The making of economic policy: a transaction cost politics perspective*. Cambridge: Cambridge University Press.

Dumont, L. (1977). *From Mandeville to Marx*. Chicago: University of Chicago Press.

Faccarello, G. and Sturn, R. (2010). The challenge of the history of public economics. *The European Journal of the History of Economic Thought*, 17, 537–542.

Faccarello, G. and Sturn, R., eds. (2012). *Studies in the history of public economics*. London and New York: Routledge.

Head, J. 1991. Merit wants: analysis and taxonomy. In: Eden, L. (ed.). *Retrospectives on public finance*. Durham: Duke University Press, 229–252.
Hegel, G.W.F. (1821). *Naturrecht und Staatswissenschaft im Grundbegriffe* sowie *Grundlinien der Philosophie des Rechts*. Berlin: Nicolaische Buchhandlung.
Hermann, F.B.W. (1832). *Staatswirtschaftliche Untersuchungen*. Munich: Anton Weber'sche Buchhandlung.
Hermann, F.B.W. (1870). *Staatswirtschaftliche Untersuchungen. Zweite nach dem Tod des Verfassers erschienene, vermehrte und verbesserte Auflage. Über Vermögen, Wirtschaft, Productivität der Arbeiten, Kapital, Preis, Gewinn, Einkommen und Verbrauch*. Munich: Fleischmann's Buchhandlung.
Hume, D. (1739/40). *Treatise of human nature*. London: John Noon.
Kolm, S. Ch. (2012). *History of public economics: the historical French school*. In: Faccarello, G. and Sturn, R. (eds.), *Studies in the history of public economics*. London and New York: Routledge.
Lerner, A. (1944). *The economics of control*. New York: Macmillan.
Lindahl, E. (1919). *Die Gerechtigkeit der Besteuerung*. Lund: Gleerupska Universitets-Bokhandeln.
Little, I.M.D. (1950). *A critique of welfare economics*. Oxford: Oxford University Press.
Munro, A. (2009). *Bounded rationality and public policy. a perspective from behavioural economics*. The Economics of Non-Market Goods and Resources, vol. 12. Heidelberg: Springer.
Musgrave, R.A. (1939). The voluntary exchange theory of public economy. *Quarterly Journal of Economics*, LIII(February), 213–217.
Musgrave, R.A. (1957). A multiple theory of budget determination. *Finanzarchiv N.F.*, 25, 333–343.
Musgrave, R.A. (1959). *The theory of public finance*. New York et al.: McGraw-Hill.
Musgrave, R.A. (1986). *Public finance in a democratic society*. Vol. I: social goods, taxation and fiscal policy. Collected Papers of R.A. Musgrave. Wheatsheaf Books, distributed by Harvester Press.
Musgrave, R.A. (1987). Merit goods. *The new Palgrave: a dictionary of economics, vol. 3*. London: Macmillan, 452–453.
Musgrave, R.A. (1997a). Public finance and Finanzwissenschaft: traditions compared. *Finanzarchiv N.F.*, 53, 145–193.
Musgrave, R.A. (1997b). Crossing traditions. In: H. Hagemann (ed.), *Zur deutschsprachigen wirtschaftswissenschaftlichen Emigration nach 1933*. Marburg: Metropolis, 63–79.
Musgrave, R.A. and Peacock, A.T., eds. (1958). *Classics in the theory of public finance*. London and New York: Macmillan.
Nozick, R. (1974). *Anarchy, state, and utopia*. Oxford: Basil Blackwell.
Olson, M. (1965). *The logic of collective action*. Cambridge, MA: Harvard University Press.
Pickhard, M. (2005). Some remarks on self-interest, the historical schools and the evolution of the theory of public goods. *Journal of Economic Studies*, 32, 275–293.
Pickhard, M. (2006). Fifty years after Samuelson's "the pure theory of public expenditure". *Journal of the History of Economic Thought*, 28, 439–460.
Pigou, A.C. (1928, 1929). *Economics of welfare*, 4th ed. London: Macmillan.
Pigou, A.C. (1932). *Theory of public finance*. London: Macmillan.

Pigou, A.C. (1937, 1935). *Praktische Fragen der Volkswirtschaft.* Jena: Gustav Fischer. (Transl. of *Economics in practice.* London: Macmillan, 1935.)

Rawls, J. (2000). *Lectures on the history of moral philosophy.* Cambridge, MA: Harvard University Press.

Samuelson, P.A. (1954). The pure theory of public expenditure. *The Review of Economics and Statistics*, 36(November), 387–389.

Sax, E. (1887). *Grundlegung der theoretischen Staatswirthschaft.* Wien: Alfred Hölder.

Sax, E. (1924). Die Wertungstheorie der Steuer. *Zeitschrift für Volkswirtschaft und Sozialpolitik*, N.F., 4, 191–240.

Sturn, R. (2006). Subjectivism, joint consumption and the state: public goods in *Staatswirthschaftslehre. The European Journal of the History of Economic Thought*, 13, 39–68.

Wagner, R. (2007). *Fiscal sociology and the theory of public finance.* Cheltenham: Edward Elgar.

Weber, M. (1968). *Gesammelte Aufsätze zur Wissenschaftslehre.* 3rd ed. Tübingen: J.C.B. Mohr (Paul Siebeck).

Wicksell, K. (1896). *Finanztheoretische Untersuchungen.* Jena: Gustav Fischer.

18 Competition in Public Finance

From De Viti de Marco's lectures to his *Principles*

Manuela Mosca

Introduction[1]

For his course in *Scienza delle Finanze* between 1886 and 1926, the Italian economist Antonio de Viti de Marco (1858–1943) provided his students with continuously updated lithographed lecture notes, which he reworked almost every new academic year.[2] The work of revision continued even after 1928, when the book based on those lectures was first published, through to the book's last edition in 1939. The book was intended for teaching, but it was also very much the foundation for Public Finance.

The basic facts of De Viti de Marco's life are well known[3]; we will mention here those most relevant to our subject. The first lecture notes (1886–87) are from the course he taught at the University of Pavia, where he worked for just one year before moving to Rome. In these early years, the young university teacher published very little, and as evidence of the originality of his theories, he would cite the Pavia lectures on many occasions.[4] No copies of the lithographed lecture notes from this first course are to be found apart from a later typescript[5] with a shortened text, which nevertheless already contained the theoretical framework for the phenomena of Public Finance that would eventually earn him so much recognition. The versions from the years that follow are basically notes taken in dictation or in shorthand by his students.

De Viti would quite soon emerge as the leader of Italy's free traders[6]. From the pages of the daily press, from the benches of parliament, from anti-protectionist public speeches, he fought a strenuous battle for customs reform. The ambition of this radical member of parliament was to dismantle the concealed links between a corrupt state and parasitic industrial groups, the dramatic effects of which fell heavily on consumers and taxpayers. In this context of political militancy, most of his theoretical thinking converges year after year in his lectures on *Scienza delle Finanze*.[7]

De Viti's teaching activities were suspended because of the Great War, a war he believed Italy had to fight in defence of European democracy, but the production of lecture notes was resumed in the academic year 1918–19 and continued until 1921–22. In 1921, after twenty years of parliamentary activity, overwhelmed by the tumultuous post-war events, he didn't stand for re-election and withdrew from the political scene. He was thus in a position to rearrange his lecture notes and at last, authorised the printing of a limited number of copies in the academic year 1922–23; but this was still not the official publication. The frontispiece repeats the words of previous years, "Lectures summarised under the direction of the professor"[8], and the title is still the same. However, comparison of the content demonstrates that this may be considered the first edition of the *Principles* because the more synthetic written style marks a difference from previous versions. After one more printed edition for the academic year 1925–26, the first publication proper arrived in 1928.

The *Principles* then went through many new editions, the most important of which was published in 1934 with the appendix that had first appeared in the German translation of 1932.[9] De Viti further revised his text for the English translation in 1936, whereas his last revision was for the second Italian edition of 1939. He worked on the text almost to the exclusion of other work[10]. We should remember that after abandoning politics, in 1931, De Viti also retired from teaching, refusing to take the oath of allegiance to fascism.

There is much evidence for the undoubted authenticity of the lecture notes. Its definitive demonstration, however, can be found in the first printed edition, in which he ironically thanks those colleagues who had "done me the great honour in their illustrious works of taking my lithographed lectures into account, even though they have forgotten to record their existence" (1922–23: 3).[11] All the material referred to makes up the primary source on which this study is based,[12] concerning the theory of competition in Public Finance.[13]

Competition, in the lectures and in the *Principles*

Because De Viti taught *Scienza delle Finanze*, he used the concept of competition in the context of his subject's teaching objectives. This explains why he didn't deal with it directly but attributed it to the course in Political Economy, as still happens in university programs. After the marginalist revolution, he was living through the phase of consolidation of neoclassical orthodoxy, during which the concept of competition underwent a radical transformation, passing from the classic dynamic vision to the rigorous notion of perfect competition. The Italian economists, of course, who were very close to De Viti, played a significant part in shaping this story.[14] We will therefore review the points of his course in *Scienza delle Finanze* that led De Viti to deal with competition, bringing out the way he responded to the developments in the subject. As will be seen, the use of this concept allows us to illustrate certain important aspects of his thinking.

Patrimonial goods

Twice during his treatment of patrimonial goods, De Viti reveals his concept of competition. Its meaning on the first occasion is very broad indeed because it is used in Smith's sense as the simple freedom of trade,[15] and we find it implicit in the statement that voluntary exchanges are always reciprocally advantageous. In the editions from 1912–13 to 1920–21, his confidence in the market is stated with greater energy:

> The economic condition for the exchange is that each of the contracting parties obtains a benefit or utility. This is a fundamental principle, and the idea that with the exchange there is always a deceiver and a deceived, and that only one of the contracting parties benefits, is both false and threadbare ... on the contrary, given the adequacy on both sides of their knowledge and their freedom to act, the exchange cannot reasonably be imagined without reciprocal gain.
>
> (1912–13: 33–34)

From 1922–23, this generalisation disappears, and De Viti goes back to using just the specific case of the sale of patrimonial goods.

The second occasion concerns his criticism of the idea that the state, insofar as it is the owner of patrimonial goods in a private capacity, must necessarily be subject to the "law of competition [according to which] the private owners, in producing goods from their property, find themselves in competition with all other owners, and they are not in a privileged economic position with respect to them" (1907–08: 18). Competition for De Viti here means the absence of privilege, which allows free entry to the market. His criticism of the traditional theory is based on the fact that in the market, in addition to the competing firms, there are also monopolists. The approach to competition is entirely lacking in the first printed edition of 1922–23 because of a rethink, but it reappears in the edition of 1928 – and remains subsequently – in the following terms: "the state 'patrimony' is subject ... to general economic law, which controls the formation of the price of private goods" (1936: 56–57).

Movable property

De Viti deals with the subject of the tax on incomes from movable property right from the first edition of the lecture notes, but from 1892–93, he sets out the "theoretical premise" that lies in the "theory of interest, wage and profit." And it is in fact the theory of profit that contains a statement on the subject of competition in its meaning of innovation. He writes, "Profit ... disappears in those firms which no longer need the specific labour of the entrepreneur either to organise them, since they are already well established, or to run risks, and so the entrepreneurs abandon these industries to launch themselves into new enterprises" (1907–08: 285). From 1913–14, this phrase disappears, and from the printed editions, the treatment of the income shares are entirely excluded.

Customs duties

We know that for De Viti, the dominant political issue is the struggle against protectionism. His position in favour of free trade is at once evident: "One can arrive at the case for free trade in two ways: 1. by demonstrating mathematically and economically that free trade favours the general economy of consumers, whereas protectionism favours class interests; 2. by demonstrating through experience that protectionism favours class interests" (1886–87: 80). The economic demonstration is based on the theory of comparative costs; in some years (1892–93), De Viti dealt with the subject in a more political way, while in others, he confined himself to explaining that the "general effect of the division of labour and trade is an increase in the mass of utility" (1920–21: 238). From the printed edition onwards, he avoids any reference to politics, but the message is very clear: "Under the system of free trade, two or more countries, by trading freely with each other, become virtually a single market, in which the available capital and labour are distributed in such a way as to give the maximum economic return" (1936: 335). The points of contact with the theory of competition here are the mobility factor and allocative efficiency that free trade achieves. Obviously, the bigger the market, the better the action or effects of competition.[16]

The theory of shifting

Over the years, De Viti radically modifies his theory of shifting of taxes, but the description of the competition process does not alter. Because, following on from tax,

> in the regime of free competition, capital and labour may pass freely from one industry to another, a struggle will take place, with an economic shift between the various industrialists, capitalists and workers, to re-establish the equality of profits, interest and wages in every industry, making capital and labour migrate from the industries affected to those not affected.
>
> (1892–93: 165–166)

In brief, for De Viti, the shift occurs in competition only if tax is not general and demand is inelastic. After a good many years in which his argument sounds more or less the same, in 1922–23, he thinks again, "tax always provokes phenomena of shifting, whether it is imposed equally on everyone, or only on some people" (1922–23: 66). In 1928, this new theory is set out in greater detail, and De Viti, breaking new ground with respect to the consolidated theory up until then,[17] now states, "The *immediate* and *necessary* effect of tax, then, is that it changes the previously prevailing demand curves for private goods" (1936: 154). He then once again describes the operation of competition:

> On the abstract hypothesis of free competition the following results will be found: first, the producers who, as a result of increased demand, have shifted the tax will tend to increase production; second, the producers who, as a result of decreased demand, have borne the tax burden will tend to decrease their own production, transferring their activities to industries of the first group; third, new savings and new labour-power, as they become available, will strengthen the two-fold movement of the first and second groups. To be sure, this process of readjusting supply to demand may take time, and meet obstacles of various sorts and resistant forces of varying strength. There are a number of frictional forces which it would take a very detailed analysis to examine; much depends, for example, upon whether in the enterprise which feels the burden of tax there is more fixed capital, which is difficult to disinvest, or circulating capital, which may be disinvested rapidly; whether the enterprise operates under increasing or decreasing costs; whether the goods involved are subject to an elastic or inelastic demand; whether the incomes involved are fixed or variable, and so forth. Nevertheless, the general framework of the theory permits us to say that in the case of free competition there will be the return to an equilibrium in which the phenomena of temporary shifting and of temporary incidence will neutralize each other in the future, leaving intact, however, the gain that will have been made in the meantime by one group and the loss that will have been suffered by another.
>
> (1936: 155)[18]

Proportional taxation

The equivalence principle is criticised by De Viti as the theoretical foundation of proportional taxation in that the same price is not always paid for every unit of goods consumed. He explains that the single price is a feature of competition, whereas monopoly allows the practice of price discrimination, and that the state, in its relation to taxpayers, finds itself in the position of a monopoly not in competition. This idea was already there in the early lecture notes,[19] and then in the later ones (from 1896–97 to 1920–21), he describes in detail the process in competition leading to the single price, which may be summed up in five points: (1) the single price does not depend on a "constant utilitarian appreciation" of the consumers (2) but on two forces: "the impersonality of the exchange" and the "free competition of the purchasers among themselves, and of the sellers among themselves"; these two forces together determine Jevons' law of indifference[20]; (3) in the market, there are many producers competing with each other; (4) the purchaser, through "the law of personal advantage", chooses the product offered at the minimum price, which becomes the single price and (5) the state, on the other hand, which is monopolistic, can price discriminate (1896–97: 193–197). In the printed editions, the five points are amalgamated into one complex sentence in which De Viti concludes that economic theory is not able to justify the choice between progressive and proportional tax.

The theory of the fee

For De Viti, the fee is the price of public services. To the question of whether it is a price of competition or of monopoly, he replies in different ways as the lecture notes proceed. While initially, he argues that it is of monopoly (1886–87: 21), further on, he specifies that nevertheless, it is a cost-price, as in competition, in that "in modern states … all [the] taxpayers [are] the producers and at the same time the consumers of public services" (1892–93: 65–66). This does not happen "through the power of competition, but through the character of cooperation that the modern state has taken on" (1896–97: 87). He adds that in cooperative societies, even if monopolistic, the price is equal to cost because the producers are at the same time consumers (1907–08: 59). From the first printed edition, he takes up the subject in these terms: the fee is equal to the "*co-operative* price", which is equal to the "*minimum* cost", like the "price which would prevail under conditions of free competition" (1936: 82). Further on, he states, "The price of least cost becomes the point of reference for an appraisal, criticism, or approval of the productive capacity of the State, quite apart from the fact that the State may come to occupy a monopolistic position" (1936: 82).

Theory of the state

The link between competition and theory of the state in De Viti's thinking, and in particular in the various editions of the lecture notes, is complex. He limits his theory to the state as the producer of public goods. Following a logical-historical method, he distinguishes the absolute state "in which the dominant caste has exclusive power and uses it under conditions of monopoly" from the democratic state in which there is no conflict of interest between the rulers and the ruled[21]; this identity of interest means that the democratic state coincides with the cooperative one.

In the lecture notes dealing with the theory of the state, competition is never mentioned. Only with the printed edition does De Viti argue that the democratic state acts as in competition because

> the characteristic element of free competition consists of this – viz., that … one may *substitute* for a producing group another group which comes from the mass of consumers … Now, in the democratic state … [the] alternation … brings to power the group … that is judged … to be better fitted for the production of public services.
>
> (1936: 42–43)

He thus establishes an analogy between the functioning of democracy and that of competition,[22] but this time, it is competition *for* the market, not *in* the market. So, the democratic state, although in a monopoly position, is subject to the threat of new political classes entering. Just as in competition the consumers may become producers, so in the democratic state, the governed may become the governing.

And cooperation? De Viti writes,

> we merely have to imagine that the alternation of the groups in control of the government takes place with sufficient rapidity, and we finally come to regard as practically identical the groups that are in turn governing and governed. This brings out exactly the concept of co-operative society, the essential characteristic of which lies in the *personal identity of producers and consumers.*
>
> (1936: 43)

So, if in a democracy it is possible to obtain similar results to those of a cooperative firm, it is precisely because politics functions with the same logic as competition.

Which competition?

To sum up the conception of competition that De Viti used in his courses of *Scienza delle Finanze*, it is well worth making comparisons with the rest of his work, both scientific and political, on the lookout for references (even implicit ones) to the developments in the literature of the subject. We shall employ the categories of dynamics and statics, drawn from mechanics, given that he himself uses them, as well as other metaphors from physics like "frictional forces"[23].

As for many economists of his generation, for De Viti, too, dynamics consists of the study of the adjustment towards equilibrium[24] (1885: 121). We know that in the lecture notes, he often describes the path towards competitive equilibrium, and we have seen that from 1928, he refers to "very detailed analysis", which he is clearly very much aware of. If we then include innovation in the dynamics, even though this was not done at that time, his praise both for free trade (of which it is the most precious effect) and for the entrepreneurs who "launch themselves into new enterprises" becomes significant; in effect, innovation is the force he has great hopes of, also at the social and political level.[25] We have also noticed other expressions of his that allude to competition as a race, referring, for example, to the "forces" acting within it or describing the "struggle" among the various economic protagonists. In his political writings, this even becomes "open warfare, which the older rival firms normally wage against the new ones" (De Viti de Marco 1914: 184). Finally, his new idea of competition for the market, applied to the cooperative state, looks very much like the one he developed in 1890, concerning the telephone industry (De Viti de Marco 1890).[26]

When we come to the static notion of competition, the main condition for its realisation, according to De Viti, is the absence of privileges; this may be gathered also from his political writings: "the industrialists ... demand customs privileges and premiums because they are unfit to struggle through their own efforts" (De Viti de Marco 1904: 121). As far as input mobility goes, it will have been noticed that he frequently uses the expression of "free competition", according to the classical usage still in vogue in his time, as synonymous with free entry or else to indicate the exit of less efficient firms. Another important condition that we have encountered is information.[27] Among the outcomes of competition, the one mentioned most often is the single price, for which, between 1892–93 and 1921–22, he turns again to Jevons, as indicated above. Finally, the equality between price and cost of production is recalled, which, as emphasised, becomes *minimum* from 1922–23, according to the then most recent supply theory. These static features are not in the foreground in his political writings but give solidity to the ideal aim inspiring the anti-protectionist struggle. De Viti is clearly convinced that competition achieves the optimal allocation of resources and the best possible outcome for consumers.

Despite the fact that as a rule, he doesn't cite his sources,[28] we have thus managed to trace in his writings the reflections or effects of the theoretical advances in his conception of competition, as well as its multiple meanings, characteristic of that era.[29]

Conclusions

We have seen that many references to competition disappear from the lecture notes of 1922–23. The main reason for this lies in De Viti's desire to make the content leaner for the printed edition, and for this purpose he eliminates in the first place the topics that do not strictly belong to *Scienza delle Finanze*. However, the radical new direction produced by Knight (1921) in the history of competition theory may also have played a role. There is, nonetheless, a very significant exception going in the opposite direction. As will have been noticed, in 1922–23, competition *appears* in his theory of the democratic state, and at that time in Italy, under the fascist regime, this can only be interpreted as the courageous assertion of an impenitent liberal. When Joan Robinson (1934) definitively clarified just what perfect competition was, De Viti's book had already been published, but he was not to take any notice of it in the later editions of 1936 and 1939. It is clear that for him, the political value of competition was more important than its analytical aspect because he considered it, just like democracy, a key instrument in the struggle against privilege.

Notes

1 A previous version of this essay was presented to the workshop "The Italian economists: formation, theory and economic policy. New perspectives from the archives", Milan, 25 February 2011; another version was presented at the

conference "The Italian Economists", Rome, 25–26 September 2013, published in Mosca (2015).

2 In Cardini's bibliography (1995), 15 editions of *Lezioni di Scienza delle Finanze* are indicated. Our study has brought to light nine more editions.

3 Biographical information in English on De Viti de Marco can be found in Einaudi (1934, ed. 1936), Kayaalp (1998) Mosca (2011, ed. 2016) and in the documentary at https://vimeo.com/29599475.

4 This was because of a problem of priority with the Austrian economist Emil Sax; see Mosca (2010).

5 On the frontispiece of the typescript, a handwritten note says that the original was at the Istituto di Finanza of the University of Pavia, but in the libraries of Pavia University, it is not to be found.

6 On De Viti's political activities, see Cardini (1985) and Mosca (2016).

7 The other theoretical subject De Viti worked on in these years is banking (De Viti de Marco 1898).

8 In this chapter, the translations are ours, where they are not already available.

9 The German edition of 1934 was used for the Spanish translation. On the diffusion of the *Principles* abroad, see Fausto (1995).

10 Ernesto Rossi recalls, "In 1925, when I met him, he was revising his university lectures" (Rossi 1948: 10). De Viti's other theoretical interest was once again in banking for the new edition in 1934 of De Viti de Marco (1898).

11 In the preface *To the reader*, De Viti regards the 1928 edition as the "third edition", after those of 1923 and 1926, showing the continuous, gradual passage from the lecture notes to the textbook (1928: 7).

12 We have consulted 13 volumes of lecture notes, for 1886–87, 1892–93, 1896–97, 1900–01, 1902–03, 1907–08, 1909–10, 1912–13, 1913–14, 1920–21 and 1922–23; the lithographs were compared with two editions of the *Principles*, the first (1928) and the last (1939). For the parts concerning the subject of this study, the lectures of 1900–01, 1909–10 and 1920–21 do not differ from the texts of the years immediately before them.

13 We are encouraged by Einaudi's opinion on writing about the lectures: "it would have been interesting to study the different variations from one draft to another" (1934, ed. 1936: 29).

14 We refer in particular to Barone, Pantaleoni and Pareto. See Mosca (2018).

15 Blaug (1997: 67) argues that for Smith, competition was simply the system of natural liberties.

16 As Stigler remarks, "Free trade is a sort of international antimonopoly program in itself" (1957: 5).

17 De Viti cites Seligman but also refers back to Ricardo, J.B. Say and others (1928: 137–138).

18 The innovative character of this process is appreciated by D. Black (1939).

19 In the final edition of the *Principles*, De Viti recalls that he had already completely formulated this theory of proportional taxation in his 1887 lectures (1936: 172).

20 Also for Jevons, among the conditions from which the law of indifference stems, there is "perfectly free" competition (Jevons 1871, IV.16).

21 We should remember that for De Viti, the precursor of Public Choice, this form of the state exists juridically but not in practice because the interest of one class always prevails.

22 In the versions after 1922–23, the argument is strengthened: In the "popular state … every class can attain power, and, having attained it, must remain under the continuing control of the community. Thus are realized, at least in *pure theory*, the typical conditions of free competition" (1936: 42).

23 "The forces of friction ... are ... a factor of great theoretical and practical importance, from which we cannot abstract in the study of problems in taxation" (1936: 164).

24 Among the economists in De Viti's time who dealt with the subject of dynamics, there were Barone, Pantaleoni and Pareto (Tusset 2004).

25 These are his sorrowful words: "Every innovation collides with consolidated rights, interests and traditions favouring dynasties, castes, groups, centuries old institutions, all rooted in the lively awareness of those possessing them, who usually have the wherewithal to defend them" (De Viti de Marco 1917: 125).

26 This is one of the methods of regulation that makes natural monopoly contestable, put forward by E. Chadwick in 1859 and rediscovered by H. Demsetz in 1968.

27 This is another of the conditions stressed by Jevons in his definition of the perfect market.

28 These are his arguments in defence of such a drastic choice: "the authors, living and dead, whose thought is set out and interpreted and challenged, are not present to defend themselves" (1928: 7).

29 On the various conceptions of competition, see Morgan (1993). In Italy, too, the research on the frontiers of this subject ranged from Barone's equilibrium to Pantaleoni's selectionism.

References

Baldassarri, M. and Ciocca P. (eds.) 2001 *Roots of the Italian School of Economics and Finance: From Ferrara (1857) to Einaudi (1944)* New York: Palgrave, 3 vols.

Black, D. (1939). *The incidence of income Taxes*. London: Macmillan.

Blaug, M. (1997). *Competition as an end-state and competition as a process*. In *Not only an economist*. Cheltenham and Brookfield: Edward Elgar, pp. 66–86.

Cardini, A. (1985). *Antonio de Viti de Marco. La Democrazia Incompiuta*. Roma-Bari: Laterza.

Cardini, A. (1995). *Guida bibliografica agli scritti di Antonio de Viti de Marco*, in Pedone (1995: 237–308).

De Viti de Marco, A. (1885). *Moneta e Prezzi*. Città di Castello: Lapi.

De Viti de Marco, A. (1890). 'L'industria dei telefoni e l'esercizio di stato,' *Giornale degli Economisti*, s. II, vol. I: 279–306. Engl. transl. *The Telephone Industry and State Exercise of Said*. In Baldassarri and Ciocca (2001, vol. III: 505-529).

De Viti de Marco, A. (1898). 'La funzione della banca,' *Rendiconti della R. Accademia dei Lincei. Classe di scienze morali*, s.V, vol. VIII, n. 1: 7–38; revised version Torino: Einaudi, 1934.

De Viti de Marco, A. (1904). *La politica commerciale e gl'interessi dei lavoratori*, in De Viti de Marco (1930: 79–131).

De Viti de Marco, A. (1914). *Il problema doganale e l'attuale momento politico*, in De Viti de Marco (1930: 165–198).

De Viti de Marco, A. (1918 [1917]). *Un discorso di propaganda pacifista*, in *La Guerra Europea*. Roma: Edizioni dell'Unità, pp. 123–127.

De Viti de Marco, A. (1936 [1928]). *First principles of public finance*. London: Jonathan Cape. Translation of *I Primi Principi dell'Economia Finanziaria*. Roma: Sampaolesi.

De Viti de Marco, A. (1930). *Un Trentennio di Lotte Politiche (1894–1922)*. Roma: Collezione meridionale.

De Viti de Marco, A. (1934). *Principi di Economia Finanziaria*. Torino: Einaudi. Revised edition 1939, reprint 1953 and 1961.

Einaudi, L. (1934). *Introduction* in De Viti de Marco (1936: 19–30).

Fausto, D. (1995). *I "Principii di economia finanziaria" nella letteratura straniera*, in Pedone (1995: 80–102).

Jevons, W. S. (1871). *The theory of political economy*. London: Macmillan.

Kayaalp, O. (1998). *Antonio de Viti de Marco*, in F. Meacci (ed.) *Italian Economists of the 20th Century*. Cheltenham and Northampton: Elgar, pp. 95–113.

Knight F. H. (1921). *Risk, uncertainty and profit*. Boston, NY: Hart, Schaffner and Marx.

Morgan, M. (1993). 'Competing notions of "competition."' *History of Political Economy*, 25, n. 4: 563–604.

Mosca, M. (2010). 'Emil Sax and Italy.' *Storia del Pensiero Economico*, n.s., VII, n. 2: 47–62.

Mosca, M. (2011). *Antonio de Viti de Marco. Una storia degna di memoria*. Milano: Bruno Mondadori. English transl. *Antonio de Viti de Marco. A Story Worth Remembering*. New York: Palgrave Macmillan.

Mosca, M. (2015). 'La concorrenza nella Scienza delle Finanze: dalle *Lezioni* ai *Principi* di A. de Viti de Marco', *Atti dei Convegni Lincei*, 290: 209–225.

Mosca, M. (2016). 'Antonio de Viti de Marco as a political commentator in the daily press.' *History of Economic Thought and Policy*, 5, n. 1: 43–63.

Mosca M. (2018) Monopoly Power and Competition. The Italian Marginalist Perspective. Cheltenham: Edward Elgar, forthcoming.

Pedone, A. (1995). (a cura di), *Antonio de Viti de Marco: Tra Liberismo Economico e Democrazia Liberale*. Roma-Bari: Laterza.

Robinson, J. (1934). 'What is perfect competition.' *Quarterly Journal of Economics*, XLIX, November: 104–120.

Rossi, E. (1948). *A. de Viti de Marco. Uomo Civile*. Bari: Laterza.

Stigler, G. J. (1957). 'Perfect competition, historically contemplated.' *Journal of Political Economy*, 65, n. 1: 1–17.

Tusset, G. (2004). *La Teoria Dinamica nel Pensiero Economico Italiano*. Firenze: Polistampa.

19 The missing equation in E.W. Kemmerer (1903) and I. Fisher (1892, 1911)

Jérôme de Boyer des Roches

Introduction

At the beginning of the twentieth century, German theorists of both quantity and anti-quantity persuasions, emphasising that the utility of money is dependent on its value, concluded that the law of supply and demand should not be applied to money. By contrast, Edwin Kemmerer (1875–1945) and Irving Fisher (1867–1947) emphasised this law and applied it to money in order to determine equilibrium prices in goods markets. First, Kemmerer in his 1903 dissertation "Money and credit instruments in their relation to general prices", followed by Fisher in his 1911 *The Purchasing Power of Money*, argued that the market process cannot determine the equilibrium market price of goods without simultaneously determining the general price level, i.e. the inverse of the purchasing power of money. They argued that the set of markets for n goods equilibrium equations does not contain n unknowns, but (n + 1): n prices of goods plus the purchasing power of money. We are short of one equation. Therefore, an additional equation that would determine the value of money must be added and integrated into the set of n equations for n goods.

We discuss here Kemmerer's analysis of the missing equation necessary to determine the market price of goods, using Don Patinkin's 1965 distinction between money and accounting prices, and also in the light of Fisher's 1892 article "Mathematical Investigations in the Theory and Value of Prices". Then we consider the missing equations underlying Fisher's 1911 quantity theory and compensated dollar plan. Our analysis completes Patinkin's (1965: 598–602) supplementary note on "Newcomb, Fisher, and the Transaction Approach to the Quantity Theory", in which Patinkin first showed that Fisher did not distinguish accounting prices from money prices. We also complete the arguments presented in Boyer des Roches & Gomez Betancourt's (2013a) article "American Quantity Theorists prior to Irving Fisher's Purchasing Power of Money", which had first emphasised the influence of Kemmerer on Fisher on this topic.

Section 2 presents the contrasting views of Karl Helfferich (1903), Georg Friedrich Knapp (1905) and Knut Wicksell (1906) on one side and Kemmerer (1903) on the other. Section 3 presents Kemmerer's introduction of an equilibrium condition between monetary supply and monetary demand – i.e. the equation of exchange - in order to determine the market price of goods. Section 4 questions Kemmerer's analysis: first, we show that although there is indeterminacy of the price level, equilibrium quantities and relative prices are determined, and second, we show that Kemmerer confused the money price level and the accounting price level. Section 5 then discusses how in 1911, Fisher, somewhat surprisingly, once more adopted Kemmerer's theory and proposed two equations for one price. It appears that Fisher, like Kemmerer, did not clearly distinguish money prices from accounting prices, leading him to propose a compensated dollar plan that contradicts his quantity theory.

Two opposing views on money and the law of supply and demand

In 1903, both Helfferich in his book *Money* and Kemmerer in his dissertation "Money and Credit Instruments in their Relation to General Prices" investigated the integration of the theory of the value of money into the general theory of supply and demand. Both employed the marginal utility principle, but they reached two different conclusions.

According to Helfferich, the exchange ratio between goods and money cannot be determined by the marginal utility principle because, contrary to the utility of goods, the degree of utility of money to individuals is dependent on its value:

> The marginal or final utility of money to a given individual is, therefore, the smallest utility which he can derive from the goods which he can procure for the available money, or must give for the requisite money, and this marginal utility is already conditioned by a definite exchange value of money, so that the latter cannot be deduced from the former. (...)
>
> We thus see that in an individual household, as in the national economy as a whole, the utilities of money – in contrast to those of all other goods – are not limited by its quantity, but are conditioned by its exchange value, and that its exchange value itself cannot therefore be derived from the limitation of its utilities by a limitation of supply. In the case of money, therefore, we must, even more than in the case of other goods, refrain from attempting to compute the amount of the value directly from the factors which condition value.
>
> (Helfferich, [1903], 1927: 527–8)

In the same vein, and as noted by Charles Rist (1938), Knapp explained in his *Staatliche Theorie des Geldes* (1905) that money does not, properly speaking, have a value:

> The question of the value of money is secondary; what is important is its validity (*Geltung*) (as opposed to its value), that is to say the power to discharge debt given to it by the State, that to which, in virtue of the law, money gives a right.
>
> (Rist, [1938: 362],[1] 1994: 354)

Hence,

> Money is a creation of law; it appears in the course of history under the most diverse forms. A theory of money must therefore at the same time be a theory of the history of law.
>
> (Rist, [1938: 362],[2] 1994: 353–4)

Wicksell, who did not belong to the German Institutional School but who nevertheless quoted Helfferich and Knapp, wrote in his *Lectures on Political Economy: Money* (1906)[3]:

> It is true that the exchange of goods effected by money is regulated in the main by those laws: in equilibrium, the supply of, and demand for, every commodity must still coincide; the marginal utility of a commodity, to every individual consumer, will still remain proportional to its price. But money itself has no marginal utility, since it is not intended for consumption, either directly or at any ascertainable future time. It has, perhaps, an *indirect* marginal utility, equivalent to the goods which we could obtain in exchange for it, but this depends in turn on the exchange value, or purchasing power, of the money itself and it thus does not itself regulate the latter. Similarly, "supply" and "demand", expressions so conveniently applied to almost everything under the sun, become obscure and, in reality, meaningless when applied to money.
>
> (Wicksell, [1906], 1978: 20)

A contrasting view is developed by Kemmerer, who from 1903 onwards argued that the law of supply and demand cannot determine the price of goods without introducing money.[4] Prices are determined by a bargaining process between buyers and sellers, each having "his subjective valuation of the commodity in terms of his subjective valuation of money, the common measure of value." (Kemmerer, 1903: 5).[5] This leads Kemmerer to consider "those principles which change the value of money *per se*, and consequently affect general prices." (Kemmerer, 1903: 12). He further introduced the equilibrium condition between "monetary demand" and "monetary supply" (Kemmerer, 1903: 16)[6]; between the "demand for the circulating medium" (or "media") and its "supply" (Kemmerer, 1903: 101 & 112). In 1907, Kemmerer published his thesis, clarifying and improving his treatment of this topic, introducing further revision in the second edition published in 1909. The last paragraph of the book is unequivocal:

> We therefore conclude that the value of money is determined, like the value of other commodities, by the fundamental law of demand and supply, but that *caeteris paribus*, a change in market prices can only find expression, and therefore only take place, through proportionate changes in the relative supply of circulating media…
>
> (Kemmerer, 1909: 150)

In Kemmerer's view, the quantity theory of money[7] is integrated into the general law of supply and demand.

The missing equation afforded by Kemmerer's quantity theory

The first three chapters of Kemmerer's thesis (the first two chapters of the versions published in 1907 and 1909) analyse the functioning of markets for goods. Here, he criticised the dichotomy drawn by the Laughlin School between the law of supply and demand determining the prices of goods on one side and the law of their circulation (against money) on the other. Taking Eugen von Böhm-Bawerk's (1889) analysis of the horse market as a model,[8] Kemmerer shows that the dollar price of the horse cannot be determined if the purchasing power of the dollar is not determined. Indeed, the bargaining process involves "the subjective valuation placed upon (the horse) divided by the subjective exchange valuation placed upon the money unit" (Kemmerer, 1909: 7–8). In this sentence, the valuation placed upon money depends on its "purchasing power over other commodities" (Kemmerer, 1909: 4, ft. 1).

In the diagram below, the functions giving the quantities of horses supplied Q_h^s by the sellers and demanded Q_h^d by the buyers do not only depend on the dollar price of the horse P_h but also on the general price level of goods in dollars, i.e. the inverse of the purchasing power of the dollar. In Kemmerer's example, given a general price level P, the market clears with five horses sold at $106 per horse (cf. equilibrium E_P).

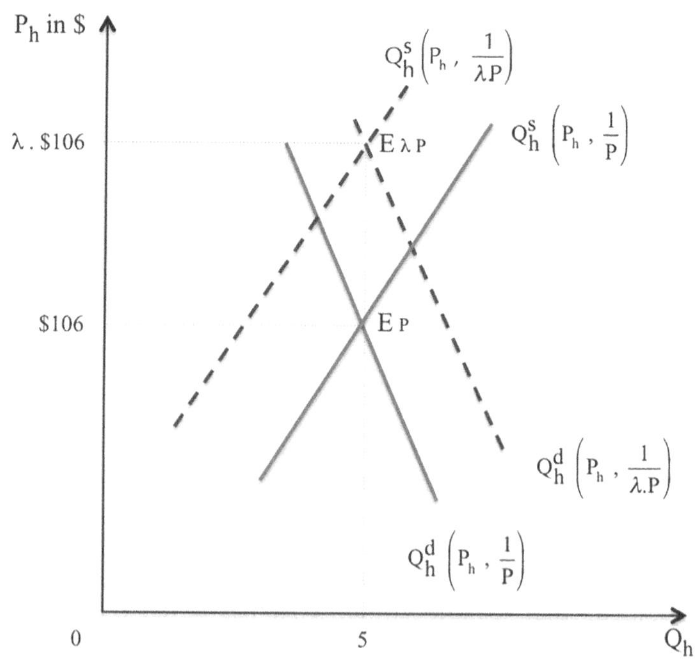

Market price of horses (P_h) and general price level (P)

A change in the general price level leads to shifts in the demand and supply curves. These shifts are not described by Kemmerer himself but by Fisher in his *Elementary Principles of Economics* ([1912], 1997: 274–7).[9] If the price level P is multiplied by $\lambda > 1$, there are a rightward shift of the demand curve and a leftward shift of the supply curve. Indeed, for a given price for one horse, an increase in the general price level means that for the buyer, the marginal utility of the money he gives for the horse decreases, whereas the marginal utility of the horse remains unchanged: he will ultimately buy the horse by selling fewer other goods. Therefore, his demand for horses rises. Symmetrically, for the horse seller, the increase in the general price level means that the marginal utility of the money he receives for one horse decreases, whereas the marginal utility of the horse stays unchanged: by selling the horse, he will ultimately buy fewer other goods. Therefore his supply of horses falls.

If, following Fisher, we add the hypothesis that the demand and supply functions for any good i are homogeneous of degree zero in prices[10]:

$$Q_i^d\left(\lambda.P_i\,,\,1/\lambda.P\right) = Q_i^d\left(P_i\,,\,\frac{1}{P}\right) \quad \text{and} \quad Q_i^s\left(\lambda.P_i\,,\,1/\lambda.P\right) = Q_i^s\left(P_i\,,\,\frac{1}{P}\right)$$

Then, the equilibrium price of the horse would be multiplied by λ; we would obtain five horses sold at λ.\$106 per horse (cf. Equilibrium $E_{\lambda P}$). For $\lambda = 1{,}6933$, the price is \$179,49 per horse.

However, Kemmerer concluded that neither \$106 nor λ.\$106 is the equilibrium price for a horse as long as the price level P or λ.P is not determined. Interestingly, there is one equation missing: for any good i, we have two unknowns - P_i and 1/P - but only one equation for an equilibrium between supply and demand: $\left[Q_i^d\left(P_i\,,\,1/P\right) = Q_i^s\left(P_i\,,\,1/P\right)\right]$. In order to remove the indeterminacy of equilibrium in all the markets of goods, Kemmerer proposed to introduce the missing equation for equilibrium between monetary demand and monetary supply.

Kemmerer's notion of "monetary demand" is a particular one[11]: it is a demand for "money work to be done", defined in each market for goods. For example, if five horses are sold (and bought) at \$106 per horse, this gives rise to a monetary demand equal to \$530. The global monetary demand is obtained by aggregating the "monetary demands" of goods markets. Noting Q^d_{ij} the quantity of good i [$i = 1$ to n] demanded by agent j [$j = 1$ to k], the global monetary demand is $PQ \equiv \sum_{i=1}^{n}\sum_{j=1}^{k} P_i\, Q^d_{ij}$, where P is the price level and Q is the volume of trade. On the other side, the monetary supply is the quantity of money and credit available for the "money work to be done"; it is a nominal quantity of money and credit multiplied by their respective velocity of circulation. Using Irving Fisher's (1911) well-known nomenclature, we note M the quantity of money in circulation and V its velocity of circulation as well as M′ the quantity of credit and V′ its velocity. The monetary supply is M.V + M′.V′ so that the missing equation is M.V + M′.V′ = P.Q.

We have now $(n + 1)$ equations for $(n + 1)$ unknowns: $P_1, \ldots.., P_i, \ldots.., P_n$ and P.

- n equations for n goods i: $\sum_{j=1}^{k} Q^d_{ij}(P_i, 1/P) = \sum_{j=1}^{k} Q^s_{ij}(P_i, 1/P)$.
- one equation for money: $M.V + M'.V' = P.Q$

In Kemmerer's words, the $(n + 1)^{nth}$ equation – the equilibrium between monetary supply and monetary demand – is the "algebraic expression of the quantity theory" (Kemmerer, 1909: 13).

While Kemmerer quoted (75) Fisher's article "The Role of Capital in Economic Theory" (1897), it is however worth noting that in this article, Fisher did not identify $M.V+M'.V'=P.Q$ as the equation for equilibrium between the demand for and the supply of money. It rather expresses two "sorts of exchange"[12]: "money against goods, and deposits against goods" (Fisher, 1897: 516). On the left side of the equation, we have monetary factors and on the right side, we have quantity of goods, and the equation shows that $((M.V+M'.V')/(M + M'))$ and Q have to be constant for P to be "directly proportional to" $(M + M')$,[13] a proposition that corresponds to "the quantity theory" (518). This is a proposition that anti-quantity theorists considered to be a truism, i.e. the equivalence between the money and credit expended by buyers and what they buy.

In Kemmerer's theory, the algebraic expression of the quantity theory is more than a truism:

> If the above statement is true, it is little more than a truism to say that in a society of the kind we have assumed every exchange would involve the transfer from the buyer to the seller of the amount of money represented by the price.
>
> (Kemmerer, 1909: 13)

The missing equation seems to be crucial to determining the equilibrium market price of goods.

Accounting prices and relative prices.

Kemmerer's reasoning is disputable. First, because the determination of equilibrium relative prices (and quantities exchanged) has to be distinguished from the determination of the equilibrium level of prices and second, because accounting prices are different from money prices.

a. Determinacy of relative prices but indeterminacy of the price level

If there are two unknowns for only one equation in the case of the isolated horse market, giving rise to an indeterminacy of the quantity of horses bought (and sold), we do not obtain the same result when we consider n markets for n goods. The reason is that the price level is not a market price. It is an average of the n market prices of goods:

$$P = \alpha_1 P_1 + \alpha_2 P_2 + \ldots \alpha_i P_i \ldots + \alpha_n P_n \quad \text{or} \quad P = \alpha(P_1, \ldots P_i \ldots, P_n)$$

Therefore, we can rewrite the n equations of equilibrium for n markets by substituting $\alpha(P_1, \ldots P_i \ldots, P_n)$ for P:

$$\sum_{j=1}^{k} Q^d_{ij}\left(P_i, 1/\alpha\left(P_1, \ldots P_i \ldots, P_n\right)\right) = \sum_{j=1}^{k} Q^s_{ij}\left(P_i, 1/\alpha\left(P_1, \ldots P_i \ldots, P_n\right)\right)$$

Here, there is no longer an $(n + 1)^{ish}$ unknown. Nevertheless, the system cannot determine the n prices. Indeed, as Fisher understood in his 1891 thesis "Mathematical Investigations in the Theory and Value of Prices", published as an article in 1892 (58–9) (and not quoted by Kemmerer),[14] these n equations are linked by the equation of aggregation of the k budget constraints of the k agents, known as the Walras Law:

$$\sum_{j=1}^{k}\sum_{i=1}^{n} P_i\left(Q^d_{ij}\left(P_i, 1/\alpha\left(P_1, \ldots P_i \ldots, P_n\right)\right) - Q^s_{ij}\left(P_i, 1/\alpha\left(P_1, \ldots P_i \ldots, P_n\right)\right)\right) = 0$$

Therefore, we have only (n − 1) independent equations. We are short of one equation crucial to determine the n prices. However, the equilibrium quantities exchanged may be determined. Indeed, if we divide the price of $(n - 1)$ commodities by the price of one commodity – for example the last commodity – and rewrite the equations with the relative prices $P_{i,n} = P_i/P_n$, we obtain the following n equations:

$$\sum_{j=1}^{k} Q^d_{ij}\left(P_{i,n}, 1/\alpha\left(P_{1,n}, \ldots P_{i,n} \ldots, P_{n,n}\right)\right) = \sum_{j=1}^{k} Q^s_{ij}\left(P_{i,n}, 1/\alpha\left(P_{1,n}, \ldots P_{i,n} \ldots, P_{n,n}\right)\right)$$

Since $P_{n,n} = P_n/P_n = 1$, we have only $(n - 1)$ unknowns – $(P_{1,n}, P_{2,n} \ldots P_{i,n} \ldots, Pn{-}1, n)$ – for $(n{-}1)$ independent equations. The choice of one commodity as a "numéraire" (Walras, 1900: 119) allows us to remove the indeterminacy of the relative prices, hence of the equilibrium quantities. Thus, it appears that to determine the price level is not necessary to determine the real equilibrium.

For example, let us define four goods ($n = 4$) – oil, gold, horses and corn – with their respective units of quantity measurement – barrel (b), Troy ounce (oz), horse (h) and quintal (q). Because corn is the numéraire, there are three relative prices of goods that are quantities of quintals of corn. Suppose we have the following equilibrium relative prices:

($P_1/P_4 = 5$ q/b; $P_2/P_4 = 2$ q/oz; $P_3/P_4 = 10, 26$ q/h)

These equilibrium relative prices are compatible with an infinitum of vectors of accounting prices: ($P_1 = 10$; $P_2 = 4$; $P_3 = 20, 52$; $P_4 = 2$), or ($P_1 = 2, 5$; $P_2 = 1$; $P_3 = 5, 13$; $P_4 = 0, 5$), or ($P_1 = 10.\mu$; $P_2 = 4.\mu$; $P_3 = 20, 52.\mu$; $P_4 = 2.\mu$) … etc. Equilibrium market relative prices – hence the quantities – are determined, but accounting prices (and the so called "general price level") remain indeterminate.

b. Determinacy of accounting prices in Fisher (1892)

Accounting prices are not determined but gold prices are. Indeed, the gold price of a good *i*, that is P_i/P_2, is equal to P_i/P_4:P_2/P_4. For example, P_1/P_2 = 2,5 oz/b. We have also P_3/P_2 = 5,13 oz/h and P_4/P_2 = 0,5 oz/q. If gold coins – Napoleon in France, Sovereign in England, Eagle or Indian in the USA – are used as currency, the money prices are determined. However, here again, the accounting prices remain undetermined.

As Fisher understood it, in order to determine the accounting prices, "(...) we need one more equation. We may let: P_1 = 1" (Fisher, 1892: 59)[15,16]

In fact, in this instance, the prices P_i are "dollar prices".[17] Hence, we have P_1 = \$1; this means \$1 per barrel of crude oil. Then, we can deduce the dollar price P_i of every good *i* from the P_i/P_n relative prices expressed in the numéraire "corn": $P_i = (P_i/P_4 : P_1/P_4)$. \$1. We obtain: P_1 = \$ 1/b; P_2 = \$ 0,40/oz; P_3 = \$ 2,052/h; P_4 = \$ 0,20/q. The indeterminacy of the accounting prices – i.e. the dollar prices – is avoided.

Now, we can fix the dollar price of the gold ounce instead of the barrel of oil.

- With P_2 = \$1/oz, we would have: P_1 = \$ 2,5/b ; P_2 = \$1/oz ; P_3 = \$5,13/h ; P_4 = \$0,5/q

  Or
- With P_2 = \$20,67/oz[18]: P_1 = \$51,675/b ; P_2 = \$20,67/oz ; P_3 = \$106/h ; P_4 = \$10,34/q

The price of gold being fixed at \$20,67 per oz, the equilibrium price of a horse is \$106. If the price of gold were to increase to \$35 per ounce, then the price of a horse would be \$179,49. Here, the quantity equation is not required to determine the level of accounting prices.

Two equations for one price level

Is the "algebraic expression of the quantity theory" – $M.V + M'.V' = P.Q$ – more[19] than a truism? If equilibrium – that is to say, the quantities exchanged, the relative prices and the price level - can be determined without this equation, then it is not. Insofar as fixing \$20, 67 as the accounting (dollar) price of one ounce of gold is sufficient to remove the indeterminacy of the price level, cannot we conclude that the quantity equation is a mere truism?

Fisher did not consider this question in the articles from 1892 and 1897 that have already been cited nor in his 1896 article "Appreciation and Interest" nor in his 1907 book *The Rate of Interest,* where he summarised and improved Alfred Marshall's ideas about the nominal interest rate and inflation. But he did explicitly consider this question in Chapter VIII of *The Purchasing Power of Money* ([1911], 1913). His answer is somewhat equivocal.

First, he admitted that the equation of exchange may be seen as a truism, but he argued that a truism may be useful:

> While the equation of exchange is, if we choose, a mere "truism," based on the equivalence, in all purchases, of the money or checks expended, on the one hand, and what they buy, on the other, yet in view of supplementary knowledge as to the relation of M to M′, and the non-relation of M to V, V′, and the Q's, this equation is the means of demonstrating the fact that normally the p's vary directly as M, that is, demonstrating the quantity theory. "Truisms" should never be neglected. The greatest generalizations of physical science, such as that forces are proportional to mass and acceleration, are truisms, but, when duly supplemented by specific data, these truisms are the most fruitful sources of useful mechanical knowledge. To throw away contemptuously the equation of exchange because it is so obviously true is to neglect the chance to formulate for economic science some of the most important and exact laws of which it is capable.
> (PPM, [1911], 1913: 157)

A few pages later, not quoting Kemmerer but quoting his own 1892 article, Fisher surprisingly argued that the equation of exchange is the missing equation, i.e. the equation "is needed in each case to supplement the equations of supply and demand"[20]:

> Those who place such implicit reliance on the competency of supply and demand to fix prices, irrespective of the quantity of money, deposits, velocity, and trade, will have their confidence rudely shaken if they will follow the reasoning as to price causation of separate articles. They will find that there are always just one *too few equations* to determine the unknown quantities involved*. The equation of exchange is needed in each case to supplement the equations of supply and demand
> (Fisher, [1911], 1913: 174)
>
> *Cf. Irving Fisher, "Mathematical Investigations in the Theory and Value of Prices", *Transactions of the Connecticut Academy of Arts and Sciences*, Vol. IX, 1892: 62.

This quotation raises two considerations. First, whereas Fisher quoted Kemmerer on the statistical test of the quantity theory on several occasions, he did not mention him in connection with the missing equation. Nevertheless, Kemmerer's influence is obviously there. Second, Fisher's reference (in footnote *) to his 1892 article is relevant, concerning the need for an equation to supplement the equations of supply and demand in order to determine the price level. However, it is not relevant for the supplementary equation proposed. The 1892 article introduced $P_1 = \$1$. not $M.V + M'.V' = P.Q$.

In his 1911 *Purchasing Power of Money*, Fisher did not substitute the equation of exchange for the equation fixing the price of the ounce of gold; he instead added it. There are therefore two equations for one price level. Indeed, Fisher rediscovered and summarised Aneurin William's (1892 a &1892 b) ideas for stabilising the price level, i.e. the compensated dollar plan.[21] This relies on the equation presented in 1892 – P_1 = \$1– to change the legal price of the ounce of gold in order to compensate for the influence of the quantity of money on the price level analysed with the equation presented in 1911: M.V + M′.V′ = P.Q. Fisher's colleagues, such as Oliver Sprague, Benjamin M. Anderson or Knut Wicksell, were disconcerted by this.[22]

Acknowledgements

First version, April 2013, for the 17th ESHET Conference, 16–18 May 2013, Kingston University, London.

Notes

1 "La question de la valeur de la monnaie est secondaire; une seule question importe, c'est sa ""Geltung"* (opposée à "Werth"), c'est à dire la force libératoire que lui donne l'Etat, "ce à quoi elle donne droit » en vertu de la loi". (Rist, [1938]: 362). * In a footnote, Rist added, " Le mot *Geltung* est intraduisible en français. *Gelten,* c'est "passer pour". Un homme passe pour honnête, *er gilt für ehrlich*. La *Geltung* de la monnaie, c'est donc "ce pour quoi elle passé", en vertu de la loi."
2 "La monnaie est une création du droit; elle est apparue au cours de l'histoire sous les formes les plus diverses; une théorie de la monnaie ne peut être qu'une théorie d'histoire du droit". (Rist, [1938] : 362)
3 Quoted by Boyer des Roches (2003) and Gomez Betancourt (2010).
4 See Boyer des Roches and Gomez Betancourt (2013a).
5 See also [1903]: 12, "The price of any commodity is the subjective value of that commodity, divided by the subjective exchange value of money."
6 In Kemmerer ([1907], 1909: 16), the monetary demand is erroneously defined as NE, whereas it is PNE. See p. 101 and also Kemmerer (1909): 13
7 See Gomez Betancourt (2008, 2010).
8 See Béraud (2000: 346–9).
9 Fisher states of the market of sugar, "Let us suppose (...) that the purchasing power of the dollar had been cut in two, or that the level of prices had been doubled. We ought, therefore, to find that the demand and supply of sugar will have been affected so as to double its price" (Fisher, [1912], 1997: 314–5).
10 Patinkin (1965: 601–2) emphasises that "Fisher confused the valid dichotomy between money and accounting prices with the invalid one between relative and money prices" and shows that there is no real balance effect in Fisher's (1912) analysis of the effects of price level in the goods markets.
11 See Gomez Betancourt (2010) and Boyer des Roches and Gomez Betancourt (2013a).
12 Among six, between money, bank deposits and goods.
13 ($M + M'$) is denoted "currency" by Fisher (517).
14 On reciprocal quotations between Fisher and Kemmerer, see Dimand and Gomez Betancourt (2012) and Boyer des Roches and Gomez Betancourt (2013a).
15 Fisher adds, "This makes (the good N°1) the standard of value." It is unclear if Fisher distinguishes the "standard of value" from the "numéraire".

16 See also p. 62.
17 See Fisher (1892: 36).
18 It was the US legal price of gold at the beginning of the twentieth century.
19 Instead of "mere".
20 In France, Rueff and Divisia resumed Fisher's idea of the missing equation (see Béraud, 2013).
21 Cf. Boyer des Roches & Gomez Betancourt (2013b).
22 On Wicksell and Wicksellians see Boianovsky (2013) and Hagemann (2013).

References

Béraud, Alain, (2000). "Les Autrichiens," *Nouvelle histoire de la pensée économique, vol 2, Des premiers mouvements socialistes aux néoclassiques*, Chap. XXVII: 294–343, edited by Alain Béraud & Gilbert Faccarello, La Découverte, Paris, 2000.

Béraud, Alain, (2013). "French Economists and the Purchasing Power of Money," *The European Journal of the History of Economic Thought*, 20 (2), April 2013: 349–71.

Böhm-Bawerk, Eugen von [1889] (1891). *Kapital und Kapitalzins*, vol. 2, *Positive Theorie des Kapitals*, Innsbruck, Wagner. Translated by William Smart, *The Positive Theory of Capital*, London.

Boianovsky, Mauro (2013). "Fisher and Wicksell on Money: A Reconstructed Conversation," *The European Journal of the History of Economic Thought*, 20 (2), April 2013: 206–37.

Boyer des Roches de, Jérôme (2000). La monnaie dans la pensée néo-classique pré-keynésienne. *Nouvelle histoire de la pensée économique, vol 2, Des premiers mouvements socialistes aux néoclassiques,* Chap. XXVII: 572–607, edited by Alain Béraud & Gilbert Faccarello, La Découverte, Paris, 2000.

Boyer des Roches de, Jérôme (2003). *La pensée monétaire, histoire et analyse*, Les Solos, Paris, 2003.

Boyer des Roches de, Jérôme & Gomez Betancourt, Rebeca (2013a). "American Quantity Theorists prior to Irving Fisher's Purchasing Power of Money," *The Journal of the History of Economic Thought*, 35 (2), June 2013: 135–52.

Boyer des Roches de, Jérôme & Gomez Betancourt, Rebeca (2013b). "Origins and Developments of Irving Fisher's Compensated Dollar Plan," *The European Journal of the History of Economic Thought*, 20 (2), April 2013: 261–83.

Boyer des Roches de, Jérôme & Gomez Betancourt, Rebeca (2013c). "Irving Fisher's Restatement of the Quantity Theory," *The European Journal of the History of Economic Thought*, 20 (2), April 2013: 167–73.

Debreu, Gérard (1959). *Theory of Value, An Axiomatic Analysis of Economic Equilibrium*, Yale University Press, New Haven and London.

Dimand, Robert W. (2000). "Irving Fisher and the Quantity Theory of Money: The Last Phase," *Journal of the History of Economic Thought*, 22 (3): 329–48.

Dimand, Robert W. & Gomez Betancourt, Rebeca (2012). "Retrospectives: Irving Fisher's Appreciation and Interest (1896) and the Fisher Relation," *Journal of Economic Perspectives*, 26 (4), Fall 2012: 185–96.

Fisher, Irving [1892], "Mathematical Investigations in the Theory and Value of Prices," *Transactions of the Connecticut Academy of Arts and Science*, 9 (July): 1–124, Reprinted in *The works of Irving Fisher* (1997), vol. 1.

Fisher, Irving [1896], "Appreciation and Interest," Publication of the *American Economic Association*, XI (4): 331–442. Reprinted in *The Works of Irving Fisher* (1997), vol. 1.

Fisher, Irving [1897]. "The Role of Capital in Economic Theory," *The Economic Journal*, **7** (28), Dec 1897: 511–37. Reprinted in *The works of Irving Fisher* (1997), vol. 1.

Fisher, Irving [1907]. *The Rate of Interest*, Macmillan, New York. Reprinted in *The Works of Irving Fisher* (1997), vol. 1.

Fisher, Irving [1912]. *Elementary Principles of Economics*, Macmillan, New York. Reprinted in *The Works of Irving Fisher* (1997), vol. 5.

Fisher, Irving (1997). *The Works of Irving Fisher.* 14 volumes, edited by William Barber assisted by Robert Dimand & Kevin Foster, consulting editor James Tobin, Pickering & Chatto, London.

Fisher, Irving with Harry G. Brown [1911]. *The Purchasing Power of Money. Its determination and relation to credit, interest and crises,* Macmillan, New York. Second edition (1913). Reprinted in Fisher (1997), vol. 4.

Gomez Betancourt, Rebeca (2008). "Edwin W. Kemmerer Money Theorist and Money Doctor," PhD dissertation, University of Paris I. Pantheon-Sorbonne.

Gomez Betancourt, Rebeca (2010). "Edwin Walter Kemmerer's Contribution to Quantity Theory of Money," *The European Journal of the History of Economic Thought,* 17 (1), Feb: 115–40.

Hagemann, Harald (2011). "The Impact of Fisher's Purchasing Power of Money in the German Language Area," *The European Journal of the History of Economic Thought*, 20 (2), Apr 2013: 323–48.

Hegeland, Hugo [1951]. *The Quantity Theory of Money.* A.M. Kelley, New York, 1969.

Helfferich, Karl, [1903]. *Das Geld.* Translated by Louis Infield from the 6th edition (1923), *Money*, The Adelphi Company, New York, 1927.

Kemmerer, Edwin Walter (1903). "Money and Credit Instruments in their Relation to General Prices," PhD Dissertation, Cornell University.

Kemmerer, Edwin Walter [1907]. *Money and Credit Instruments in their Relation to General Prices.* Henry Holt and Company, New York. New edition (1909): New York and London

Knapp, Georg Friedrich (1905). *Staatliche Theorie des Geldes*, Duncker & Humblot, Munich/Leipzig.

Laidler, David (2013). "Professor Fisher and the Quantity Theory – a Significant Encounter," *The European Journal of the History of Economic Thought*, 20 (2), Apr 2013: 174–205.

Patinkin, Don [1956]. *Money, Interest and Prices.* Second edition, 1965, Row Peterson and Company, Illinois.

Rist, Charles (1938). *Histoire des doctrines relatives au crédit et à la monnaie depuis John Law jusqu'à nos jours*, Sirey, Paris, 1938.

Rist, Charles [1940]. *History of Monetary and Credit Theory from John Law to the Present Day.* Reprinted by Thoemmes Press, Bristol, England, 1994.

Walras [1900]. *Éléments d'économie politique pure ou théorie de la richesse sociale*, 4ème éd., Librairie générale de droit et de jurisprudence, 1952.

Wicksell, Knut, [1906]. *Lectures on Political Economy: Money*, English translation based upon the third Swedish edition (Lund, 1926), edited by L. Robbins, London, George Routledge & Sons, 1935. Reprinted by A.M. Kelley, New York, 1978.

Williams, Aneurin (1892a). "A Fixed Valued of Bullion Standard. A Proposal for Preventing General Fluctuations of Trade," *Economic Journal,* 2 (6): 280–9.

Williams, Aneurin (1892b). "A Fixed Valued of Bullion Standard," *Economic Journal*, 2 (8): 747–9.

20 The first steps of the money doctor

Kemmerer's gold exchange standard in the Philippines

Rebeca Gomez Betancourt

The American economist Edwin Walter Kemmerer (1875–1945) stands out as a key figure in the World's – and more specifically Latin America's – history of money and banking for the role he played as a *money doctor*. In the first thirty years of the 20th century, he traveled to over 15 countries, often accompanied by a group of experts on what were known as the Kemmerer missions. Their objective was to solve problems, mainly related to the exchange standard and central banking. In his autobiography, he explains how he became a money doctor.[1]

The aim of this article is to examine the nature of the metallic standard systems proposed by Kemmerer in a number of Latin American countries and colonies as Philipinnes, in particular the *Gold Exchange Standard* system (GES).

The role he had in establishing central banks in the Andean countries has already been studied[2] and is relatively well known. However, his involvement in establishing monetary systems in colonies and small sovereign economies has received less attention. I argue that Kemmerer played a central role both in developing and maintaining the Gold Standard (GS) in Latin America in the 1920s and in establishing the GES in the American colonies prior to the First World War. During his time as a financial advisor for the governments of some colonies or protectorates, Kemmerer usually recommended the establishment of a GES. By contrast, he advocated the GS when he outlined his plan to establish central banks in Latin American countries. Kemmerer believed that one of the main prerogatives of central banks was to ensure the effectiveness of the GS.

Gold standards according to Kemmerer

Kemmerer (1944) identified three types of gold standards, depending on whether all or only some of the characteristics that define the GS are present. I will first give a brief definition of the various systems of metallic standards identified by Kemmerer: the Gold Coin Standard (GCS), the GES and the Gold Bullion Standard (GBS) system. Therefore, I will explain the way they worked before the First World War.

The first system is the GCS, also called Gold Specie Standard (GSS) or GS.[3] In this system, gold coins circulate within the country, banknotes are convertible in gold coins without restrictions and coinage is unlimited at costs generally determined by law.

The second type of metallic standard, which is the focus of my analysis, is the GES. The main purpose of this system is to ensure the stability of the exchange rate. Following Alexander Martin Lindsay, Kemmerer defines the GES as a system in which there is neither free coinage of gold nor domestic gold coin circulation, although the latter does not compromise the effectiveness of the mechanism. Currency reserves consist of short-term interest-raising investments in foreign stock markets.

The third type is the *Gold Bullion Standard* (GBS). It relies neither on domestic gold circulation nor on unlimited gold coinage. Gold is stored in the issuing bank and only serves to maintain the stability of the exchange rate. Banknotes are convertible only above a certain amount (equivalent to a bullion) and exclusively for exportation. This system was developed and presented by David Ricardo (1816) but implemented much later. It served as a transition between the GCS and the GES. In what follows, I compare the first system (GCS) with the second (GES), an analysis already undertaken by Kemmerer.

The establishment of the GES in the Philippines Islands

Kemmerer and the other GES Commission members aimed to propose a system that retained the main advantages of the GCS but could be adopted by economies that either were not able to sustain gold circulation and gold reserves or could not ensure convertibility in bullion. To explain how the system works, let us look at the first GES implemented by Kemmerer in the Philippines in 1903:

The case of the Philippines Islands between 1903 and 1910 represents one of the first illustrations of the GES. When the United States took control of its new colony, a group of economists was sent to develop a plan for monetary reforms and reorganize the financial currency system. In early 1903 the Philippine currency mainly consisted of silver pesos, silver coins and money certificates issued by the government. 100% of this was backed up by the reserves of silver pesos and by banknotes, kept in the government fund. In addition, a small amount of American dollars were in circulation, but virtually none in the form of gold coins. Any Philippines gold coins had been minted since the Philippines became an American colony, and the coins minted under the Spanish dominion were no longer in circulation.

In 1903 the Philippines adopted the reform proposed by the American GES Commission. This reform provided a new monetary unit, with a theoretical weight of 12.9 grain of gold, i.e. 50 cents of American dollar.

Although no coinage was produced, it was clearly stated that all forms of money had to remain on a par with gold. In order to maintain the parity between the Philippines silver coins and gold at this fixed rate, a special reserve fund known as the *Gold Standard Fund*[4] was created. It was a very important institution since there were no central banks in the Philippines, nor even, for that matter, in the United States. The *Gold Standard Fund* consisted mainly of a loan allocated by the United States, but also included profits from the minting of new coins as well as other revenues related to the currency's administration. It was a real reserve fund, distinct from other government funds and used exclusively to maintain the Philippine currency on a par with gold. Under the reform, part of the fund was located in Manila, the other in New York City.[5]

The gold points system under the GES[6]

Kemmerer did not distinguish between the price-specie-flow-mechanism and the gold point mechanism.[7] He always referred to the exchange market when explaining gold movements between countries, but the causes of these movements are always associated with some monetary issue. While I consider his account of the gold points system to be thorough his interpretation was limited to disruptions resulting from an excess or a deficit of the amount of money in circulation.

Kemmerer explained that one of the consequences of trade between countries on the GS was that whenever the balance of payments of one country was in deficit, the exchange rate went down as a result of a relative abundance of the country's money supply and consequently an increase in exported gold. Conversely, if one of the GS countries that were engaged in trade had a favorable balance of payments, then the exchange rate would go up, resulting in a relative scarcity of the local currency, and gold would then be imported.

He then considered the exchange market to explain the workings of the GES system. Under the GES, gold physically remained outside the country (there was no gold in the colonies); nonetheless, the same mechanism was at work as in the gold point system. Redemption was now in the form of dollar drafts in New York City. "The system is just as automatic in its regulation of the money supply as the strict gold standard" (Kemmerer 1916: 321).

The Philippine funds deposited in American banks had to be used in case of a disturbance that threatened to undermine the parity of the currency. Thus, for instance, when the exchange rate of the peso to the dollar fell to the Philippines' gold-export point (of entry to the United States), gold was not literally exported to foreign markets, as it would have been under similar circumstances in the United States and other countries on GCS or GBS. The Philippine Government would actually give to the "gold exporter" (in exchange for their Philippine money in Manila) a *draft*, which entitled them to a convertible deposit in New York.

In other words, whenever the exchange rate reached the gold exit point, the *Gold Fund* would buy the Philippine silver pesos from the exporter and sell gold drafts in New York, or, to put it differently, the exporter would sell silver pesos and buy convertible dollars. For this operation, Kemmerer (1933: 314) explains that the *Gold Fund* took a commission equal to the hypothetical cost incurred in the export of gold bars from Manila to New York, had the exporter chosen to conduct the operation itself. The amount of silver pesos paid in exchange for the drafts in Manila was equal to the amount of gold it would have sent.

If there was a deficit in the balance of payment, Kemmerer added, it would be settled by a transfer of drafts payable with gold deposited in the foreign country (in this case, New York City) thereby indicating that there was an excessive amount in circulation. As a result, it was necessary to export some gold in order to reduce the monetary supply. Silver pesos were often withdrawn from circulation by the government. This had the effect of reducing money circulation as effectively as if an equivalent amount of silver pesos had been exported.

> "When under the prewar Philippine type of the gold-exchange standard a government sold for cash at home drafts on a reserve fund located abroad, it withdrew from circulation the purchase money and contracted the monetary circulation by the amount withdrawn; and when foreign depository of the reserve sold drafts on the reserve fund in the home country, the draft was paid in cash, increasing the monetary circulation by its full amount".
>
> (Kemmerer 1944: 167–8)

Kemmerer (1933: 315) considered that, with respect to trade requirements, the GES had the same advantages in terms of regulating the monetary supply as the GCS or the GBS. However, unlike under the GCS, there was no circulation of gold coins in the Philippines nor was it required that they keep gold reserves as it was necessary under the GBS.

If, on the other hand, the peso exchange rate reached the Philippines' gold-import point (which meant that the exchange rate had risen toward the gold-export point in New York City), custodian banks in New York City gave the gold exporter a draft, granting them the right to the equivalent in pesos in Manila.

In other words, if the peso reached the gold-import point in the Philippines, then depositary banks in New York City would sell silver pesos kept in the *Gold Fund* (in Manila), that is, they would sell silver pesos and buy gold drafts. Moreover, as Kemmerer detailed (1933: 315) that the *Gold Fund* was required to pay a commission in order to cover the expenses it would have incurred (on the GCS) if it had transferred an equivalent amount of gold bars from New York City to Manila. Once the drafts on the *Gold Standard*

Fund reached Manila, they were paid in pesos and withdrawn from the fund, leading to an increase in the circulation of silver pesos.

When the exchange rate fell to the gold-export point, the government announced, "So ... we will sell on demand gold drafts on New York on unlimited quantities at these gold-export point rates, and will relieve the currency redundancy by withdrawing from circulation the pesos paid to us fore these drafts" (Kemmerer 1944: 159). By contrast, when the peso became stronger and the exchange rate reached the gold-import-point, the government stated,

As Kemmerer explained (1933: 316), so far they may fall and no farther, a further decline would signify an appreciation of our peso above its legal gold par if we were on a gold coin standard, and it will be so interpreted under the Gold Exchange Standard, therefore, we will send on demand pesos laid down in Manila in unlimited quantities at these gold (or currency) import-point-rates, to be paid for by gold or its equivalent in New York. This will relieve the currency scarcity in the Islands by pouring pesos into circulation from the Gold Standard fund.

These reforms and the establishment of the GES made it possible for the Philippines to stabilize the exchange between the gold-import point and the gold-export point.

The advantages of the GES

Kemmerer (1933: 316) argued that the GES had several advantages over other metallic standards. This system was better suited to the specificities of the Philippines and other colonies because it allowed for the circulation of the silver coins, which was adequate for the small transactions that prevailed within the colonies.

One important argument supporting the GES was the economical aspect it provided. Many countries could not afford a GCS or a GBS. Under the GES, the only type of money in circulation was fiduciary money, which was much more economical than gold coins. No gold coins or bars were hoarded nor was any reserve kept in order to meet potential demands.

Additionally, Kemmerer pointed to the advantage of concentrating all reserves in one fund: the *Gold Standard Fund*. This was reminiscent of his proposals for the US Federal Reserve System, in which he also suggested centralizing the reserves scattered throughout the United States in order to make them available. In Kemmerer's words,

> wherever dollar can be immediately used in times of need, whereas gold coin in circulation and gold bars in private hands are difficult to mobilize in emergencies, for the very emergency that creates demand for the gold is likely to cause the public to cling to it more tightly.
>
> (Kemmerer 1933: 316)

There were advantages for colonies on the GES because they received a commission for the exchange in which the government sold drafts through the *Gold Standard Fund*. Moreover, interests were raised by the funds deposited abroad.

Finally, the GES facilitated exchanges between the sovereign country and its colonies, which promoted the development of trade between those countries. Importers and exporters are always certain to find the currencies they need at a fixed rate. Making the exchange process easier definitely gave a new impulse to business.

Some political aspects of the GES

Kemmerer believed that, by definition, the GES system required the closest collaboration between central banks. Given the considerable amounts of currencies kept in money-issuing institutions, as well as account and holding institutions located abroad, it was necessary for banks to exchange their views beforehand and align their policies. Under the GES, the central bank has often become a means of political action. It should also be noted that support from public opinion was essential for all of these reforms to be carried out. At the Genoa conference, it was recommended that the control exerted by the central bank should be financial and economic, but not political. Yet financial control has sometimes been a powerful political weapon in foreign as well as domestic affairs. Nevertheless, it was claimed "necessary to keep issuing banks away from all kinds of political influence and make sure that only cautious financial methods are used" (Genoa Conference 1922).

Kemmerer considered the GES to be a temporary system, bridging the gap between inconvertibility and the gold standard. The GES was therefore seen as a means rather than an end. For Kemmerer, the GES was only an attempt to adapt to a financial environment and a means to reach a better system: the *Gold Standard*. In short, the GES was considered a transitory system whereas the GS was the ideal system. One of the reasons for this was that the GS was viewed as a sign of discipline by other countries. Kemmerer described the GS as an international signal of following sound financial policies and discipline. He explained how important it was for peripheral countries to have access to European and American capital markets.

He was sensitive to the relationships of dependence caused by the establishment of a GES. He was aware of a real supremacy and hierarchy established between the sovereign country and the colony, i.e. between the GS-country and the GES-country. Kemmerer admitted that a country lost part of its sovereignty when adopting the GES.

Whenever the country holding the currency of another is economically weaker, whenever most of its trade involves the issuing country as a partner or an intermediary, whenever it does not have its own financial means to allow its business to run smoothly thanks to an autonomous credit policy, the holding country inevitably comes under the issuing country's hegemony.

Indeed, the country had to have developed sufficiently before considering a move to the GES. More specifically, it had to have engaged in sufficient, active international trade in order to justify the need for regulating its exchange and currency. The main exchange flow had to have taken place between the country on the GES and the country on the GS. For Kemmerer, the GES system required a significant exchange flow between the countries involved. The amount and origin of capitals used in the country determined the amount of compensation made by the central banks. From this point of view, the main purpose of the system was to stabilize the exchange rates between countries with different but codependent monetary systems.

Conclusions

Kemmerer drew on Lindsay's work to develop his plan for the GES. Kemmerer's work emphasized the need to create a fund designed to ensure the gold parity of the currency under the GS. He called it the *Gold Standard Fund*. Throughout his explanation, he drew attention to the differences between the fund, the way it functions and a *currency board*, featuring other proposals for monetary reforms and the establishment of a GES. The stabilization fund proposed by Kemmerer was not a currency board but an exchange stabilization fund.

However, Kemmerer follows Ricardo in his quantity theory of money.[8] Kemmerer quotes a passage that he managed to find in Henry Thornton's work and uses it to explicate his conception of a quantity theory. For Kemmerer, as for Ricardo and the economists of the *currency school*, gold is not sent abroad in order to pay debts but to reduce the amount of money. His explanation of the gold point system is thus very similar to the theories of Hume and Ricardo: Gold movements are necessarily caused by a monetary policy, such as overissuing, i.e. excessive issuing of money. For Kemmerer, surpluses of money must be sent out of the country. Note, however, that Kemmerer moves away from Ricardo in two respects. First, in contrast to Ricardo, Kemmerer does not favor the GBS, and second, he proposes neither a currency board nor a national bank for the American colonies. Instead, he proposes a stabilization fund to maintain the exchange stability of the currency. The central bank he envisioned differs significantly from the role proposed by Ricardo: Kemmerer highlights the importance of the elasticity of the money supply (1944: 219). He also draws attention to the possibility for the bank to keep on issuing credits, the political role of the central bank, the necessity for all sectors of the economy to be represented, etc.

The choice of a type of gold standard depends on the specific needs and conditions of each country. For Kemmerer, the substitution of a type of standard for another may be a monetary policy device used to stabilize the value of a currency. From this perspective, the GS (or GCS) is best suited for a wide-open economy. Yet it is considered the most expensive system because it makes gold coin circulation easier. Given that the GES does not require gold coin circulation nor gold reserves, it is the most economical of all standards. The GBS does not require gold either for domestic circulation and prevents hoarding. However, it demands that all gold reserves be maintained and is, therefore, more costly than the GES. Kemmerer takes for granted that rich countries will opt for the gold standard whereas poorer countries will choose the gold exchange standard. Countries in an intermediary position may choose the GBS.

The GES may be considered as a second best solution. The GES is the best system for countries that were eager to avoid excessive fluctuations of their currency on the exchange market but did not meet the conditions required for the adoption of GCS. These countries devised a system that ensured the convertibility of currencies in gold while still using silver or paper money within the country's borders. According to Kemmerer, the GES was required for countries that could not afford the GCS, but it was always considered as a transitory stage towards the latter.

Kemmerer played a central part in promoting the GS and GES systems and convincing the public of the advantages of these systems as proposed in the reforms. His convictions remained with him throughout his life. The purpose of Kemmerer's last book (1944) was to contribute to shaping an enlightened public opinion and convince the Americans of the advantages of re-establishing the GS.

Acknowledgements

Gilbert Faccarello's courses, writings, research methodology and personality have influenced my choice to become a historian of economic thought. I am infinitely grateful toward him.

Notes

1 Kemmerer's Papers. Mudd Library. Princeton University. Box N. 27. For more details see also his autobiography: Kemmerer n.d.
2 It has been documented by Paul Drake (1989).
3 In the United States, the establishment of the gold standard came out of a theoretical controversy between the proponents of the gold standard and the proponents of bimetallism (and those in favor of the silver standard). This debate turned into major political arguments in the early 20th century. See, among others, Bordo, M. and A. Schwartz (1984), Eichengreen (1985) and Gomez Betancourt (2010b).
4 See Kemmerer (1904, 1905, 1916, 1933, 1944).
5 For mote detail on this see Kemmerer, 1933: 312. Lindsay (1878) & (1892) also proposed the creation of a fund aimed at maintaining the currency in par with gold, but it was to be established only in London.
6 Kemmerer 1944 shows that he understood how the gold point system worked under a classical gold standard and under a GES. We find that, from very early on, (Kemmerer 1904, 1905, 1906 and 1916): "Under the gold exchange standard, as it existed in the Philippines in 1905, this same fundamental principle [gold points] applied" (Kemmerer 1933: 314).

7 See Gomez Betancourt (2010b), de Boyer & Diatkine (2008) and de Boyer (2007).
8 See Gomez Betancourt (2010a).

References

Bordo, M. & A. Schwartz (ed.). (1984). *A retrospective on the classical gold standard, 1821–1931.* National bureau of economic research. Chicago: The University of Chicago press.

de Boyer, Jérôme (2007). "Cause and effects in the gold points mechanism: a criticism of Ricardo's criticism of Thornton". *The European Journal of the History of Economic Thought*, vol. 14, no. 1, 2007, 25–53.

de Boyer, Jérôme & Sylvie Diatkine (2008). "British monetary orthodoxy in the 1870s: a victory of the Currency Principle". *The European Journal of the History of Economic Thought*, vol. 15, no. 2, summer 2008, 181–209.

Drake, Paul (1989). *The money doctor in the Andes: the Kemmerer missions, 1923–1933.* Durham, NC: Duke University Press.

Eichengreen, Barry (ed.). (1985). *The gold standard in theory and history.* London University, Paperbacks.

Gomez Betancourt, Rebeca (2010a). "Edwin Walter Kemmerer's contribution to quantity theory of money". *The European Journal of the History of Economic Thought*, vol. 17, no. 1, February 2010, 115–140.

Gomez Betancourt, Rebeca (2010b). "Edwin Walter Kemmerer and the origins of the Federal Reserve System". *Journal of the History of Economic Thought*, vol. 32, no. 4, December 2010, 445–470.

Kemmerer, Edwin W. (1904). "A gold standard for the Straits Settlements". *Political Science Quarterly*, vol. 19, no. 4, December 1904, 636–649.

Kemmerer, Edwin W. (1905). "The establishment of the gold exchange standard in the Philippines". *The Quarterly Journal of Economics*, vol. 19, no. 4, August 1905, 585–609.

Kemmerer, Edwin W. (1906). "A gold standard for the straits settlements II". *Political Science Quarterly*, vol. 21, no. 4, December 1906, 663–698.

Kemmerer, Edwin W. (1916). *Modern currency reform. A history and discussion of recent currency reform in India, Porto Rico, Philippine Islands, Strait Settlements and Mexico.* New York: Macmillan.

Kemmerer, Edwin W. (1933). *The gold exchange standard.* Section from economic essays in honour of Gustav Cassel. London: George Allen & Unwin LTD.

Kemmerer, Edwin W. (1944). *Gold and the gold Standard.* New York: Macmillan.

Kemmerer, Edwin W. (n.d). *The autobiography of a money doctor.* Manuscript. Kemmerer's papers at Princeton University. Mudd Library.

Lindsay, A. M. (1878). "A gold standard without a gold coinage in England and India. A step towards an International Monetary System". *Calcutta Review*, vol. LXVII, no. 67. no. CXXXIV, October 1878, 820–838.

Lindsay, A. M. (1892). *Ricardo's exchange remedy: a proposal to regulate the Indian currency by making it expands and contracts automatically at fixed sterling rates, with the aid of the silver clause of the Bank Act.* London: E. Wilson.

Ministère des Affaires Etrangères (1922). *Conférence économique Internationale de Gênes*, 9 avril-19 mai 1922. Documents diplomatiques. Paris.

Ricardo, D. (1816). *Proposals for an economical and secure currency.* The works and correspondence of David Ricardo, edited by Piero Sraffa with the Collaboration of M.H. Dobb (Indianapolis: Liberty Fund, 2005). Vol. 4 Pamphlets and Papers 1815–1823.

21 The political economy of Michal Kalecki

Michaël Assous

I came to appreciate the originality, relevance and broad range of Gilbert Faccarello's contribution while writing my PhD thesis. During those formative years, Gilbert was a guide to whom I could turn, from time to time, for words of wisdom and advice in personal and professional matters. I would like to pay tribute to him via an attempt to pursue some aspects of my early research. I thus naturally decided to return to Michal Kalecki. I first provide an interpretation of Kalecki's early vision, followed by an interpretation of how class struggle issues fit that vision.[1]

Kalecki's early vision

During the 1920s and early 1930s, Kalecki participated in the economic discussions of the Polish socialists.[2] The central ideas wrapped around the irrationality of capitalism, mass unemployment and economic depression and the contributions of Rosa Luxemburg came to play an essential part in these debates (Toporowski 2013, p. 46).[3] Kalecki was convinced that Luxemburg was right in regarding aggregate demand as the key issue in capitalism. However, he thought she was wrong to see aggregate demand as the cause of a potential economic collapse. His view, rather, was that capitalist economies were prone to stagnation.

This argument had two strands. The first explained why, in the short run – and as long as the capital stock remained constant – equilibrating forces may stabilize the economy in a position of "quasi-equilibrium" with unemployment (Kalecki 1934 (1990), p. 201). The second explained why, in the medium and long runs, once capital stock is adjusted, "automatic" oscillations occur: the economy moving constantly from "quasi-equilibrium" to some other state. The message was the following: Although globally stable, the economy was locally unstable.

In a nutshell, "automatic" cycles occur because of the twofold nature of investment. Investment has a favorable effect on the economic situation at the time it increases aggregate demand. However, as soon as capital goods are delivered, past investment exerts a negative effect on aggregate demand. That adjustment process then leads the economy to low quasi-equilibrium.

Once the capital stock has fallen significantly, the cumulative downward movement is reversed and turned into a new cumulative upward movement to high quasi-equilibrium. It is clear that any recovery can occur only when the excess production capacity has disappeared. A considerable amount of time may thus elapse, during which unprofitable past investments are eliminated in physical or in value form. Once the capital stock has been reduced far enough to restore the profit rate, there is a return to a more optimistic view.

Basically, there are always automatic factors that are likely to help an economy come out of a crisis. The ambivalence of investment never undermines the reproduction of the system. Certainly, Kalecki agreed that the economy could fluctuate around a situation with high unemployment and underconsumption.[4] But the key point was that the system was not likely to collapse. There are always "internal" forces that eventually move the economy forward. Of course, government interventions can potentially maintain full employment. However, there is no guarantee that political decisions favoring full employment will be implemented. The political obstacles may be so big that none of these policies will be activated on a permanent basis.

Later, Kalecki extended that vision to long-run processes. His point was that in absence of "external" forces, capitalist economies were doomed to fluctuate around a static position. In that respect, he departs totally from Roy Harrod. According to Kalecki, any deviation from long-run paths renders the system stationary – i.e. subject to cyclical fluctuations but no trend. The system "cannot break the impasse of fluctuations around a static position unless economic growth is generated by the impact of semi-exogenous factors such as the effect of innovation upon investment" (Kalecki 1962 (1991), p. 411). Certainly, achieving such a goal required building a theory of the behavior of aggregate demand off an equilibrium path and in particular a thorough analysis of disequilibrium investment behavior. On several occasions, Kalecki tried to elaborate on such a theory, but it is clear that he never managed to achieve a completely satisfactory solution.[5]

In addition, Kalecki denied that self-correcting market mechanisms working through price flexibility could potentially eliminate unemployment and excess capacity. The argument was not simply that the mechanism might fail because of the market power of firms and trade unions. In his early works, the challenge instead was to question the ability of a competitive economy to attain full employment. The issue was not that this process might take a very long time but rather that it would not work. There are circumstances in which a reduction of money wage rates and prices will not succeed in increasing production and employment. Prices would be lower in the same proportion as wages. In short, real quasi-equilibrium of the economy, real wages, real profit margins and unemployment would be unaffected.

However, Kalecki described one mechanism that considerably restricted the generality of that conclusion. In a paper published in 1934, he admits that a stabilizing effect likely to restore full employment might exist. He advanced the "Keynes effect" as a major argument. The mechanism was as follows: At lower money wages, prices and incomes, the supply of money will be larger in real volume. The transaction demand for cash will be smaller; the excess stock of cash will bid up the prices of interest-bearing assets and will lower interest rates. At any lower interest rates, real investment will be higher. Thus, aggregate demand, further boosted by the multiplier, will expand output and employment.

Not until a decade later did Kalecki (1944) really question the efficiency of that mechanism. Meanwhile, Arthur Cecil Pigou and Gottfried Haberler had advanced the real balance effect as an argument for why lower prices and wages would suffice to increase consumption and to restore full employment. First, Kalecki pointed out that Pigou's (1943) real balance effect did not apply to inside money: An increase in the real wealth of depositors is balanced by an increase in the real liabilities of debtors. In addition, if the interest on government bonds is financed by taxation, bonds are also not net wealth. As a result, the real balance effect can only act on the monetary base, a small fraction of the money supply and the national debt. Second, Kalecki noted that a destabilizing effect could come from the increased burden imposed on debtors. Deflation might indeed increase the incidence of bankruptcy, thereby reducing the level of aggregate demand. If the effects on bankruptcy are strong enough, a lower price level may then be deviation amplifying so that the "adjustment"would probably never be carried to the end: if the workers persisted in their game of unrestricted competition, the Government would introduce a wage stop under the pressure of employers" (Kalecki 1944, p. 132).

In other words, the potentially stabilizing effect of price deflation working through the "Keynes effect" and the "Pigou effect" may well be dominated by the destabilizing effect coming from the increased burden that lower prices impose on debtors. Its impact is easily captured in the IS-LM model. A lower price level shifts the LM downward (the Keynes effect), but if the debt effect dominates the Pigou effect, it also shifts the IS leftwards. If the IS shift is sufficiently strong, aggregate demand and output may fall. Moreover, if the economy is at the nominal interest rate floor, then aggregate demand and output are even more likely to fall because there is no shift in the LM schedule. In this case, full employment equilibrium is unstable. It is worth emphasizing here that this argument is independent of the dynamics of the real interest rates that might result from a revision to expected inflation in a deflationary context. Whatever the dynamics of the revision to long-run expectations, a full employment equilibrium may remain unstable.

It is now time to highlight how Kalecki's political concepts, such as "the regime of the political business cycle" or "crucial reforms", fit that economic vision. It is essential, then, to return to Kalecki's understanding of class struggle.

Class struggle

In the absence of any public interventions, class struggle refers to the determination of the markup and analysis of income distribution. Alongside the degree of industrial concentration and the nature of the strategic interactions among firms, Kalecki (1971) claimed that the existence of powerful trade unions may affect the size of the markup and ultimately the profit share. The mechanism is as follows: If markup and profit share are high, trade unions can increase their wage demands, which tends to increase the money wage and hence, costs. It follows that high profit margins cannot be maintained without creating a tendency towards rising prices. Fearful of losing their competitive position, firms may accept a reduction in their profit margins. Thus, the power of the trade unions effectively imposes a limit on profit share fluctuations.

However, as long as the economy is working below full capacity, class struggle does not play a regulator role. This is because there is a strong complementarity between income distribution and income determination, which finds expression in the idea that although the profit share is related to unions' bargaining power, profits are determined by past capitalist expenditures. So, a rise in the markup resulting from the lower bargaining power of workers will be accompanied by a rise in the profit output ratio but no change in total profits because they continue to be predetermined by past decisions.[6] Hence, we come to the very striking Kaleckian proposition that class struggle does not impinge on the course of the cycle by changing firms' markups. This is not to say that it does not affect the time path of Gross domestic product (GDP) A higher value of profit share increases the amplitude of GDP over the cycle. Simply, class struggle has no impact on the profit rate. Class struggle is among these "internal forces" whose influence is neutral on the dynamics, a point that Kalecki attempted to make clear to Alexander Rachjman (a Polish mathematician and member of the communist party) in the 1930s:

> If a student of mechanics riding in a cab concluded that it would be useless to kick the front panel to speed it up, he would be right, since the assumption that the course of the cab is completely determined by its initial position, initial speed, and the influence of outsides forces excludes the possibility of internal force affecting his course.
>
> (Kalecki [1933b] 1990, p. 113)

From a strict economic point of view, capitalists are thus indifferent between high and low level of profit share over the course of the business cycle.

In contrast, from a political perspective, a high enough rate of employment caused by high wage share can strengthen unions and lead to working-class political agitation. Capitalists may thus pressure the government for a cooling off of the economy or even engage in investment strikes (Streeck 2011) in order to reduce unions' political strength.[7]

This leads to the idea of a political business cycle in which GDP fluctuates between an upper and a lower limit. So, in addition to the automatic regulator role of capital stock fluctuations, a political regulator emerges. As employment increases during expansion, unions use their political power to regain control over firms that eventually decide, once the economy has recovered, to stop investing and put pressure on government to cut its spending. In turn, the downturn is checked when unemployment leads to government countercyclical action, and capitalists decide to reinstate investment expenditures. Hence, besides the change in capital stock, the dynamics of political power reinforce the unstable features of capitalism. This is the "regime of the political business cycle" (Kalecki 1943) based on the assumption that continuous, full employment capitalism would undermine the power of business leaders to control workers.

In his last works, Kalecki also considered the possibility of a regime likely to generate continuous growth at full employment, a regime potentially likely to break the impasse of cyclical stagnation. For this to become a reality, a "crucial reform" would be needed to develop new social and political institutions to reflect a substantial participation of the working class. "There will then be a paradoxical situation: a 'crucial reform' imposed on the ruling class may stabilize the system, temporarily at least" (Kalecki 1971 (1991), p. 467).

At the end of an exceptional decade, as was the 1960s, Kalecki thought, one "[has] to do with just a situation in contemporary capitalism." Taming the cycle and maintaining full employment were the first priorities of macroeconomic policies. However, these policies were formulated in a period of economic revival so as to promote long-run growth. The Kennedy administration is a perfect example in that respect. Of course, looking back at how the world economy has developed over the last forty years, one might say that Kalecki's forecast was overly optimistic. Even if it must be conceded, Kalecki admitted at the end of his considerations that some signs of future destabilization could be detected:

> the relative stability of reformed capitalism depends on a high degree of social conformity. One can express the cautious opinion that recent student movements seem to be an omen of the declining ability of the bourgeois power apparatus to manipulate new generations entering the historical scene. This phenomenon is all the more serious since, with the rapid progress in science and technology, intellectuals are beginning to play an even greater role as a social group.
>
> (Kalecki and Kowalik 1971 (1991), p. 476)

Conclusion

In this short paper, I focused on Kalecki's vision and the way his political arguments fit with it. I argued that there is a strong complementarity between the economical and political arguments he raised. From the 1930s, Kalecki developed a vision of an economy prone to stagnation. With the intent to address the issue of class struggle, he came to develop the political business cycle regime that completed and strengthened his initial message.

Later, Kalecki resorted to the notion of crucially reformed capitalism that is likely to break through old dynamics.

Notes

1 Assous, Dutt, A., Fourchard, P. and Pottier, A. (2017) suggest a simplified model designated to pinpoint key aspects of Kalecki's early analysis of (in-) stability.
2 Kalecki never joined a political party but considered himself a socialist.
3 The Polish Marxist Henryk Grossman also contributed to the debate. His message was that expanded reproduction was impossible.
4 Kalecki emphasized the irrational nature of capitalist development in which firms do not invest to satisfy the needs of the population but first and foremost with the aim of making a profit.
5 Kalecki's theory of cycles went through a number of changes over the years, and it is well known that these changes are closely related to changes in his theory of investment (see Steindl 1981).
6 Certainly, while profits remain constant, real wages and real national product will fall because of the fall in aggregate demand, with a consequent fall in output that will adjust just so much that the higher percentage share of profits in output renders an unchanged absolute amount of profits.
7 Furthermore, once full employment is achieved, workers bargaining for higher real wages reduce the profit rate, and there is then a negative relationship between the profit rate the real wage rate.

References

Assous, Michaël Dutt, Amitava, Fourchard, Paul and Pottier, Antonin. 2017. "(In)-stability in Kalecki's Early Macroeconomics."*Journal of the History of Economic Thought,* 39 (1), pp. 69–87.

Kalecki, Michal. 1933a. "Essay on Business Cycle Theory." Reprinted in Kalecki (1990), pp. 65–108.

Kalecki, Michal. 1933b. "'Critical Remarks on One of the Mathematical Theories of the Business Cycle' by Aleksander Rajchman: A Rejoinder." Reprinted in Kalecki (1990), pp. 109–19.

Kalecki, Michal. 1934. "Three Systems." In Kalecki (1990), pp. 201–19.

Kalecki, Michal. 1943. "Political Aspects of Full Employment." *Political Quarterly*. 14 (4), pp. 322–330.

Kalecki, Michal. 1944. "Professor Pigou on the 'Classical Stationary State' a Comment." *Economic Journal*, 54, pp. 131–2.

Kalecki, Michal. 1962. "Observations on the Theory of Growth." Reprinted in Kalecki (1991), pp. 411–35.

Kalecki, Michal. 1967. "The Problem of Effective Demand with Tugan-Baranovsky and Rosa Luxemburg." Reprinted in Kalecki (1991), pp. 451–8.

Kalecki, Michal. 1968. "Trend and the Business Cycle." Reprinted in Kalecki (1991), pp. 435–50.

Kalecki, Michal. 1971. "Class Struggle and the Distribution of National Income." Reprinted in Kalecki (1990), pp. 96–105.

Kalecki, Michal. 1990. *Collected Works of Michal Kalecki*, vol. 1: "Capitalism, Business Cycles and Full Employment." Jerzy Osiatynski (ed.), Oxford: Clarendon Press.

Kalecki, Michal. 1991. *Collected Works of Michal Kalecki*, vol. 2: "Capitalism: Economic Dynamics." Jerzy Osiatynski (ed.), Oxford: Clarendon Press.

Kalecki, Michal. 1996. *Collected Works of Michal Kalecki*, vol. 6: "Studies in Applied Economics, 1927–41," Jerzy Osiatynski (ed.), Oxford: Clarendon Press.

Kalecki, Michal and Kowalik, Tadeusz. 1971. "Observations on the 'Crucial Reforms." Reprinted in Kalecki (1991), pp. 467–77.

Pigou, Arthur. C. 1943. "The Classical Stationary State." *The Economic Journal*, 53 (212), pp. 343–351.

Steindl, Josef. 1981. "Some Comments on the Three Versions of Kalecki's Theory of the Trade Cycle." In J. Los (ed.), *Studies in Economic Theory and Practice. Essays in Honour of Edward Lipinski.* Amsterdam: North-Holland. Reprinted in Josef Steindl, *Economic Papers, 1941–88*, New York: St. Martin's Press, 1990.

Streeck, Wolfgang. 2011. "The Crises of Democratic Capitalism." *New Left Review*, 71, pp. 5–29.

Toporowski, Jan. 2013. *Michal Kalecki: An Intellectual Biography: Volume 1 Rendezvous in Cambridge 1899–1939*, London: Macmillan.

22 Consumption and money-making in Keynes

Enjoyments of life or morbid instincts?

Maria Cristina Marcuzzo

Keynes, like Mandeville, was a dreadful tease.

(Joan Robinson 1964, p. 73)

Premise

In his most famous and influential book, *The General Theory*, Keynes assigned a central role to expenditure on consumption goods, but unlike certain others who had praised the virtue of spending, for instance Mandeville or Malthus, we also have evidence that Keynes denounced the pursuit of money-making as an end in itself; this is particularly apparent in *Economic Possibility for our Grandchildren*, but it also surfaced in several other parts of his work, especially in the mid- and late 1920s.

As the role of expenditure in determining income and employment came to occupy a central role in the development of his mature theory, probably from 1932 onwards,[1] his condemnation of the money-making pursuit – which was the focus of several of his *Essays in Persuasion* – took a different turn. Individual thriftiness and hoarding were stigmatised, not only as psychological pathologies or heritage of Victorian values but as obstacles to solving the problems of unemployment and Depression. They were seen as detrimental to a pursuit of the aggregate level of expenditure necessary to generate a sufficient level of employment and preserve the cultural and moral values that will make a 'better' society. This was indeed a revolutionary approach that was not too easy to digest. As Joan Robinson (1964, p. 73) nicely put it, 'Worse than private vices being public benefits, it seems that the new [i.e. *The General Theory*] doctrine was the still more disconcerting proposition that private virtues (of thriftiness and careful husbandry) were public vices.'

So, rather than two opposite views, Keynes's position in regard to consumption and money-making became two parts of the same whole. The point I will argue in my contribution is that in Keynes, the need both to maintain high-level consumption expenditure and, at the same time, to 'manage' the money-instinct of individuals in such a way as to attain a society in which abundance of material goods is general and not a privilege of the few are complementary components of Keynes's vision, serving the same purpose in his policy recommendations.

The 'fundamental truth'

In *The General Theory*, consumption is seen as the necessary means for the well-being of society; the propellant, so to speak, in the machinery to boost employment and income. However, Keynes sees two major problems related to consumption. The first is satiation, which he believed derived from a 'fundamental psychological law', according to which 'men are disposed, as a rule and on the average, to increase their consumption as their income increases, but not by as much as the increase in their income' (CWK VII, p. 96). It follows that because 'the larger our incomes, the greater, unfortunately, is the margin between our incomes and our consumption', the government must find ways to fill the gap unless it accepts a level of unemployment sufficient 'to keep us so poor that our consumption falls short of our income by no more than the equivalent of the physical provision for future consumption which it pays to produce to-day' (CWK VII, p. 105).

The second problem associated with consumption is how best to bring about the desired increase in the propensity to consume in order to sustain aggregate demand. The means could be found in a fiscal policy aiming at more equitable distribution of incomes, thereby increasing aggregate consumption.[2] However, this is a policy that is bound to come up against opposition and is by no means easy to implement. Alternatively, fiscal policy can be directed to boosting aggregate consumption through public expenditure, entrusting the government with 'the task of adjusting to one another the propensity to consume and the inducement to invest' (CWK VII, p. 380).[3]

This policy recommendation – boosting public expenditure through deficit spending – has been ridiculed as if based on the 'digging holes in the ground' argument: It does not matter how public money is spent as long as it is spent because it will generate income and, through the multiplier, the savings necessary to finance the initial expenditure.

However, Keynes's 'digging holes' suggestion[4] is a paradox meant to illustrate a principle,[5] not to provide an instance in the blueprint of public work schemes; it shows how expenditure on goods that have *no useful* purposes may nevertheless produce the desired effects on income and employment.

Gold-mining, which is just another form of unearthing bottles dug in the ground, or pyramid-building had positive effects on income and employment because they yielded fruits that 'could not serve the needs of man by being consumed' and therefore did not 'stale with abundance'. (CWK VII, p. 131)

There are two points to note here. The first is that 'it would, indeed, be more sensible to build houses and the like; but if there are political and practical difficulties in the way of this, the above would be better than nothing'

(CWK VII, p. 129). The political difficulties arise mainly from 'the education of our statesman on the principles of the classical economics' (Ibid).

Keynes has many scathing comments on the prevailing attitude against deficit spending, which might well be applied to today's defenders of the austerity programs: 'the man who regards all this [loan-financed public works, particularly public expenditure on housing] as a senseless extravagance which will impoverish the nation, as compared with doing nothing and leaving millions unemployed, should be recognized for a lunatic' (CWK XXI, p. 338).[6]

The second point is that expenditure on 'useful things' may not be as effective: 'Two pyramids, two masses for the dead, are twice as good as one; but not two railways from London to York' (CWK VII, p. 129).

The argument is that the decreasing marginal efficiency of investment, 'unless the rate of interest is falling *pari passu*' sets a limit on the possibility of increasing the stock of wealth by means of 'useful' forms of loan expenditure. Waste results not when expenditure is channelled to objects that are not 'useful' but when they are not 'economically' viable. Financial availability is not so much the constraining factor in the augmentation of objects that 'could serve the needs of man'; the constraints are implied by their diminishing marginal utility and supplementary costs to maintain them.

It is not the usefulness of consumption goods that matters but rather their being the outlet of expenditure and therefore of somebody's else income. This is the 'fundamental truth' that we see Keynes invoking again and again to persuade the economists and the public at large.

The 'real values of life'

Keynes's standing on the vital importance of boosting consumption via creation of inducement to private investment and public spending raises the question of what we should make, then, of his remarks in *Economic Possibilities for our Grandchildren*, an essay published only six years before *The General Theory* in which the pursuit of material objects of wealth is seen as a private and public vice and the love of money as 'possession' or as the by-product of a morbid instinct? Should we interpret these remarks as superseded by his advocacy of deficit spending? Or by his later understanding of the necessity of sustaining effective demand?

In fact, consumption took on a prominent role for Keynes when he was devising tools to raise income and employment. This intuition came quite early in the development of his ideas, although it later became a cornerstone in his theory and policy recommendations.

Between 1928 and 1930 – *after* the conception of *Economic Possibilities for our Grandchildren* – a notable advance towards advocacy of public expenditure as a way to increase private expenditure can be clearly detected in Keynes's thought. Although he was to make full use of the multiplier only in the *Means to Prosperity* (1933), when his theory of effective demand was also beginning to take shape, there is abundant evidence that his thinking was moving in that direction much earlier.[7] As Moggridge explains, *Economic Possibilities for our Grandchildren* was conceived in a particular phase in the development of Keynes's ideas:

> [It] was first presented in 1928 as a talk to several small societies including the Essay society of Winchester College and the Political Economy Club at Cambridge. In June 1930 Keynes expanded his notes into a lecture on the 'Economic Possibilities for our Grandchildren', which he gave in Madrid. It appeared in literary form in two instalments in *The Nation and Athenaeum*, 11 and 18 October 1930, in the mid of the slump.
> (Editorial notes, CWK IX, p. 321)

It was published a few months after the publication of *Can Lloyd George Do It*? (10 May 1929) and just before the publication of the *Treatise of Money* (31 October 1930) – two milestones in Keynes's journey towards the views expressed in *The General Theory* – and is therefore to be evaluated bearing in mind the background and the evolution of Keynes's beliefs at the time.

Similar expressions can be found in *The End of Laissez-Faire*, as in 'the dependence upon an intense appeal to the money-making and money-loving instincts of individuals as the main motive force of the economic machine' (CWK IX, p. 293), and in *A Short View of Russia*:

> it seems clearer every day that the moral problem of our age is concerned with the love of money, with the habitual appeal to the money motive in nine-tenths of the activities of life, with the universal striving after individual economic security as the prime object of endeavour, with the social approbation of money as the measure of constructive success, and with the social appeal to the hoarding instinct as the foundations of the necessary provision for the family and for the future.
> (CWK IX, p. 268)

Keynes's denouncement of 'the money-making instincts of individuals' as a 'somewhat disgusting morbidity' may have been influenced by his reading of Freud at the time. The evidence shows that in the late 1920s, Cambridge had become a centre of interest for psychoanalysis, and several of Keynes's friend went to Vienna to be analysed by Freud himself.[8] In August 1925, Keynes wrote a letter to the *Nation and Athenaeum*, defending Freud from his English critics and calling him 'one of the great disturbing, innovating geniuses of our age' whose theories 'appeal "to our intuitions as containing something new and true about the way in which human psychology works"' (quoted in Winslow 1986, p. 550).

But of course, it was his Moore and Bloomsbury credo that drove him to the point a 'better' society is a society where the money instinct is eradicated and substituted by the pursuit of other – more valuable – objectives.[9]

However, nothing is said against consumption in *Economic Possibilities for our Grandchildren*. Rather, Keynes made it clear that 'The love of money as a possession [is] distinguished from the love of money as a means to the enjoyments and realities of life' (CWK IX, p. 329).

In fact, among the 'enjoyments' of life, we may find many objects of consumption, which need not be acquired with monetary expenditure and could be made available in greater abundance after a solution to the so-called economic problem. It could indeed have been that it was the promise of a solution to the economic problem in a not too distant future – in Keynes's wishful thinking – that would make money-making a distasteful and useless pursuit in life. But until the 'economic problem' was solved, expenditure on consumption goods was a vital receipt for the survival of society.[10]

Just a couple of months after *Economic Possibilities for our Grandchildren* was published, in a radio talk that appeared in the *Listener* (14 Jan 1931), Keynes made a passionate plea for more consumption to fight the Depression:

> O patriotic housewives, sally out tomorrow early into the streets and go to the wonderful sales which are everywhere advertised. You will do yourselves good - for never were things so cheap, cheap beyond your dreams. Lay in a stock of household linen, of sheets and blankets to satisfy all your needs. And have the added joy that you are increasing employment, adding to the wealth of the country because you are setting on foot useful activities, bringing a chance and hope to Lancashire, Yorkshire, and Belfast.
>
> (CWK IX, p. 138)

At the end of Keynes's intellectual journey, in *The General Theory*, the money-making motive is no longer depicted as the dark side of the soul but rather as the prerequisite for the full fruition of certain valuable human activities. 'There are valuable human activities', he writes, 'which require the motive of money-making and the environment of private wealth-ownership for their full fruition'. He even warned that

> dangerous human proclivities can be canalised into comparatively harmless channels by the existence of opportunities for money-making and private wealth, which if they cannot be satisfied in this way, may find their outlet in cruelty, the reckless pursuit of personal power and authority, and other forms of self-aggrandisement. It is better that a man should tyrannize over his bank balance than over his fellow-citizens; and whilst the former is sometimes denounced as being but a means to the latter, sometimes at least it is an alternative.
>
> (CWK VII, p. 374)

Consumption as an end, and not as a means to possession, can therefore be accommodated within Keynes's early and mature philosophy. The question remains, however, as to whether the structure of needs will be modified when the Age of the Abundance – deriving from the solution to the economic problem – comes about.

According to *Economic Possibilities for our Grandchildren*'s taxonomy, human needs fall into two classes:

> those needs which are absolute in the sense that we feel them whatever the situation of our fellow human beings may be, and those which are relative in the sense that we feel them only if their satisfaction lifts us above, makes us feel superior to, our fellows.
>
> (CWK IX, p. 326)

While absolute needs may soon be satiated, the desire for positional goods could remain insatiable. But what are the needs underlying the 'real values of life'? They are exemplified in the famous passage of *Economic Possibilities for our Grandchildren*: 'to pluck the hour and the day virtuously and well [...] taking direct enjoyment in things, the lilies of the field who toil not, neither do they spin' (CWK IX, p. 331).

Does 'taking direct enjoyment in things' preclude buying objects of consumption, or does it simply require that we buy things to enjoy the use, not the possession of them? How seriously should we take the scenario presented in *Economic Possibilities for our Grandchildren*?

Skidelsky has argued that *Economic Possibilities for our Grandchildren* 'is a provocation, a jeu d'esprit [...] typical, in its ratio of fancy to hard argument, of his table talk [...]. It sums up many of the ambivalences in Keynes's own thinking and psychology' (Skidelsky 1992, p. 237).

Others disagree, claiming that *Economic Possibilities for our Grandchildren* is an important piece of Keynes's philosophy. For instance, Carabelli and Cedrini (2011, p. 354) state that, 'Keynes focuses on economic possibilities, not on certainties about morals. In other words, he believes that the end of the economic problem will grant human beings the possibility of moral renaissance and the chance of a happy life'.

In fact, according to Robinson,

> what made the *General Theory* so hard to accept [was] its shocking implications [...]. Keynes seemed to be upholding a 'licentious system' that was even more objectionable than Mandeville's had been to Adam Smith. And, of course, Keynes, like Mandeville, was a dreadful tease.
>
> (Robinson 1964, p. 73)

The *Essay* was an attempt to fight the pessimism of the heart and the untruthfulness of received ideas about the virtue of money-making rather than money-spending. In this respect, *Economic Possibilities for our Grandchildren* should be understood as truly Keynesian, in spirit rather than in the letter.

Conclusions

The question of whether the personal accumulation of wealth is a boon or bane for society has a long tradition in the history of economic thought. In reviewing a book on this topic (Perrotta 2008), in which the condemnation of wealth is aptly described as the 'fear of goods', Faccarello reminded us that

> the debates on this question reach back to antiquity. We also know how much they were lively, opposing those who, for moral, philosophical and political reasons were fearful of enrichment (either in general or for particular class(es) of citizens) to those who believed the accumulation of wealth to be clearly positive in its effects and thus to be welcomed.
>
> (Faccarello 2009, p. 111)

He then argues that there are two ways to understand the 'fear of goods' in the history of economic thought. The first is connected with the idea that generalised high-level consumption will put pressure on wages, thereby increasing costs of production and reducing competitiveness; the second understanding is connected to the consequences of the increased affluence for the moral and ethical values of society. These two views have been updated and refined in the course of more than four centuries, and we find them again and again in present times.

The counterarguments to the first case point to the function of wages as demand and not just cost, and to the second case, to the beneficial social effects of the pursuit of self-interest in a market society. It seems to me that Keynes's position is peculiar because, while stressing the need for an affluent society to keep wages high to guarantee sufficient levels of consumption and, at the same time, denouncing the fallacy of the self-interest-based view of the market as a mechanism bending the action of individuals to the pursuit of aims of general interest, he opposes the individual money-making pursuit as an obstacle to the possibility of the acquisition of material goods by society at large. This needs to be accomplished within a market economy where individual choices are guaranteed.

In the final chapter of *The General Theory*, Keynes warns us that 'The task of transmuting human nature must not be confused with the task of managing it' (CWK VII, p. 374), and that the money-making instinct can hardly be expected to be eradicated from the human soul. We can, however, try to confine it and not let it loose:

> Though in the ideal commonwealth men may have been taught or inspired or bred to take no interest in the stakes, it may still be wise and prudent statesmanship to allow the game to be played, subject to rules and limitations, so long as the average man, or even a significant section of the community, is in fact strongly addicted to the money-making passion.
>
> (Ibid)

So, the Keynesian prescription for a better society is the appeal to setting rules and limitations in the market arena, to not letting individual self-interest prevail and to putting some governing bodies in charge of filling the gap when deficient aggregate demand occurs so that the acquisition of material goods and the fruition of the enjoyments of life are not a privilege of the few but the conquest of civilisation.

Notes

1 For the evolution of Keynes's ideas on the importance of expenditure in his journey towards *The General Theory*, see Marcuzzo (2002, 2014).

2 On 24 March 1936, he wrote to R.G. Hawtrey, 'I favour a scheme of direct taxation in order to redistribute incomes in such a way as to increase the propensity to consume' (CWK XIV, p. 16); quoted in García-Lizana and Pérez-Moreno (2012).

3 'The State will have to exercise a guiding influence on the propensity to consume partly through its scheme of taxation, partly by fixing the rate of interest, and partly, perhaps, in other ways' (CWK VII, p. 378).

4 'If the Treasury were to fill old bottles with banknotes, bury them at suitable depths in disused coalmines which are then filled up to the surface with town rubbish, and leave it to private enterprise on well-tried principles of *laissez-faire* to dig the notes up again (the right to do so being obtained, of course, by tendering for leases of the note-bearing territory), there need be no more unemployment and, with the help of the repercussions, the real income of the community, and its capital wealth also, would probably become a good deal greater than it actually is.' (CWK VII, p. 129)

5 It has been rightly noted that 'In the context of the great Depression where saving was seen by many as the greatest virtue, Mandeville's paradoxical statements [promoting of sumptuary, luxurious and 'vicious' consumption] was for Keynes a colourful way to utter his own paradoxical views' (Lagueux 1998, p. 260). See also Robinson (1964, p. 91): 'Keynes fired off his paradoxes to penetrate the thick walls of obscurantism of the old laissez-faire orthodoxy'.

6 See also: 'When we have unemployed men and unemployed plant and more savings than we are using at home, it is utterly imbecile to say that we cannot afford these things. For it is with the unemployed plant, and with nothing else, that these things are done. To have labour and cement and steel and machinery and transport lying by, and to say that you cannot afford to embark on harbour works or whatever it may be is the delirium of mental confusion' (CWK XIX, pp. 765–766)

7 On the basis of some unpublished notes of a speech during the electoral campaign in support of the Liberal Party, Kent convincingly argues that 'although he did make an error in his development [...] Keynes's arithmetic in his 28 May 1929 speech is a multiplier analysis' (Kent 2007, p. 538).

8 'There was a specific group for whom psychoanalysis became of fundamental importance in the period immediately after the First World War up until the end of 1925. In early 1925, this group – James Strachey, John Rickman, Arthur Tansley, Harold Jeffreys, Lionel Penrose and Frank Ramsey – took to meeting to present papers to one another. Half of them were Apostles [...] the distinctive and principal condition of belonging to this informal Society was entirely novel: having been analysed oneself.' (Forrester 2004, p. 4).

9 See Goodwin (2006), Backhouse and Bateman (2009) for the influence of Bloomsbury on Keynes's worldview in general and of capitalism in particular.

10 According to Harrod (1951, p. 399), the purpose of the lecture, taking up the thread of his talk to Winchester College where Keynes had argued that in a not too distant future the economic problem would be solved, was 'to lift his audience out of the prevailing depression'.

References

Backhouse, R. and Bateman, B. (2009). Keynes and capitalism. *History of Political Economy*, 41 (4), pp. 645–671.

Carabelli, A. and Cedrini, M. (2011). The economic problem of happiness: Keynes on happiness and economics. *Forum for Social Economics*, 40 (3), pp. 335–358.

Faccarello, G. (2009). The "fear of goods": two views. *Storia del pensiero economico*, 5 (1), pp. 111–115.

Forrester, J. (2004), Freud in Cambridge. *Critical Quarterly*, 46 (2), pp. 1–26.

García-Lizana, A. and Pérez-Moreno, S. (2013). Consumption and income distribution: a proposal for a new reading of Keynes' thinking. *The European Journal of the History of Economic Thought*, 19 (1), pp. 45–65.

Goodwin, C. (2006). The art of an ethical life: Keynes and Bloomsbury. In: R. E. Backhouse and B. W. Bateman (eds.), *The Cambridge Companion to Keynes*. Cambridge: Cambridge University Press, pp. 217–236.

Harrod, R. (1951). *The life of John Maynard Keynes*. London: Macmillan.

Kent, R. (2007). A 1929 application of multiplier analysis by Keynes. *History of Political Economy*, 39 (3), pp. 529–543.

Keynes, J.M., (1971–1989). E. Johnson and D. E. Moggridge (eds). *The Collected Writings of John Maynard Keynes* (CWK). London: Macmillan.

CWK VII, *The General Theory of Employment, Interest, and Money*;

CWK IX, *Essays in Persuasion*;

CWK XIV, *The General Theory and After*;

CWK XIX, *Activities 1922–29*, Part II;

CWK XXI, *Activities 1931–39*.

Lagueux, M. (1998). Was Keynes a liberal and an individualist? Or Keynes reader of Mandeville. *Cahiers d'économie politique*, 30 (1), pp. 255–263.

Marcuzzo M.C. (2002). The collaboration between J. M. Keynes and R. F. Kahn from the treatise to the general theory. *History of Political Economy*, 34 (2), pp. 421–447.

Marcuzzo M.C. (2014). Whatever happened to the Keynesian multiplier? In: R. Baranzini and F. Allisson (eds.), *Economics and other branches: in the shade of the oak tree. Essays in honour of Pascal Bridel*. London: Pickering & Chatto, 2014, pp. 157–68.

Perrotta, C. (2008). *Consumption as an investment. The fear of goods from Hesiod to Adam Smith*. London: Routledge.

Robinson, J. (1964). *Economic philosophy*. Harmondsworth: Penguin Books.

Skidelsky, R. (1992). *John Maynard Keynes. The economist as savior. 1920–1937*. London: Macmillan.

Winslow E.G. (1986). Keynes and Freud: psychoanalysis and Keynes's account of the 'animal spirits' of capitalism. *Social Research*, 53 (4), pp. 549–578.

23 Foreign trade or international trade?

Daniel Diatkine

Reading *The Wealth of Nations*, we learn that geographic specialisation seems to obey exactly the same principle (the so-called principle of absolute advantage) as the division of labour. And the same general principle operates between London and Portugal as between London and Lancashire. Logically, it seems that there is no analytical difference between local and international trade. In the *Wealth of Nations*, the ordinary differences between local trade and international trade seem only trivial. For example, customs are generally a survival from feudal times[1], and Adam Smith does not seem very concerned by exchange rates. More generally, Tony Aspromourgos' book (2009) shows clearly that no mention of international trade is necessary to expose Smith's ideas about "Opulence and Policy" or "Policy and the system of liberty" because free trade is a general frame that suffices to introduce Smith's ideas on those central issues. As a matter of fact, there is no occurrence of *international* trade in the *Wealth of Nations*. However, we also know that *foreign* trade is very important: For example, the invisible hand supposes that agents prefer home investment to investment in foreign trade.[2] So the question arises: Is the distinction between local and foreign trade really so trivial? Is foreign trade a synonym for international trade? I intend to show that foreign trade is not international trade because, quite paradoxically, the "nation" is not an economic concept in the *Wealth of Nations*. Of course, it was a very important political notion, but it was not the economic unit that it would become in the 19th century. We will see that the basic economic unit here is the "city", a town surrounded by acountry, where rates of profit and wages tend toward natural rates. Capital circulates between cities, and trade between cities is foreign trade. This latter prevents the fall of the rate of profit and expands each city's market. Of course, competition does not equalise the rate of profit and wages *inside the set* of the cities of the world.

I

To grasp the analytical meaning of foreign trade, we have to look at two chapters (Smith 1776–1976, II, v and III, i) that are not often studied. However, they testify that foreign trade is not as trivial as it may seem. Chapter V of Book II (which is entitled "Of the Different Employment of Capitals") describes an economy divided into three sectors. Each of these employs capital differently: The first sector "procures the rude produce", the second manufactures and prepares it, and the third, which is subdivided into local and foreign trade, is concerned with transport. Smith attempts to show that there is a ranking between these sectors. The ratio of employment per unit of capital invested and the ratio of income per unit of capital invested are higher in the agricultural sector than in manufacturing, and they are higher in the agricultural sector than in foreign trade. Of course, the demonstration of this thesis is complex; I shall not discuss it here.

The next chapter (III, i) is crucial to my central thesis. This chapter, entitled "Of the Natural Progress of Opulence", describes a *dynamic model of growth*[3] (see Jeck 1994). In the first step of the model, the accumulation of capital takes place in an economy with only one sector: the agricultural sector. In the second step, the accumulation of capital in agriculture leads to the creation of markets (an effectual demand) for non-agricultural goods. Consequently, manufacturers and towns appear, and a "great exchange" between town and country takes place. During this step, competition generates a tendency for rates of profit to fall.[4] This may be stopped during the third step by the expansion of the market through foreign trade, which seems to "absorb" the capital.

So, during the first step, agriculture is the only sector that exists:

> As subsistence is, in the nature of things, prior to conveniency and luxury, so the industry which procures the former must necessarily be prior to that which ministers to the latter. The cultivation and improvement of the country, therefore, which affords subsistence, must, necessarily, be prior to the increase of the town, which furnishes only the means of conveniency and luxury.
>
> (Smith 1776–1976, III, i, 2)

Therefore, corn ("subsistence") is the only "commodity" produced in the first step of capital accumulation. Of course, goods other than corn (tools, clothing, houses) are used to produce corn. These goods are joint products[5] of corn and *not* commodities because they are not exchanged. Corn is the only "commodity" because *only* corn creates its own demand:

> As men, like all other animals, naturally multiply in proportion to the means of subsistence, food is always, more or less, in demand. It can always purchase or command a greater or smaller quantity of labour, and somebody can always be found who is willing to do something in order to obtain it (I, ix, b, 1).

Consequently, the only "exchange" at this first step of capital accumulation is the fundamental "exchange" between the surplus of corn and the

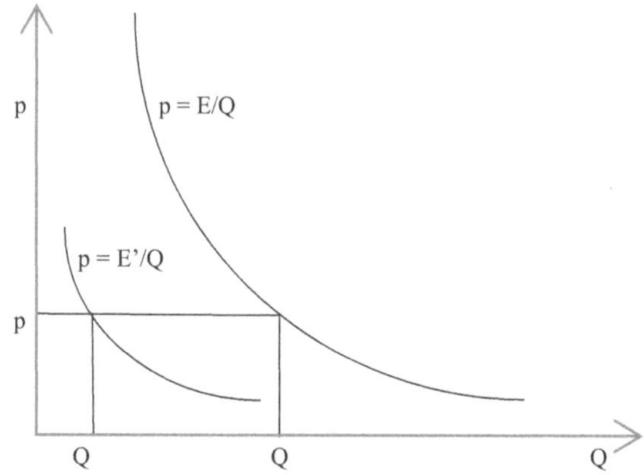

Figure 23.1

demographical surplus, which is the basis of the Smithian definition of real wealth (Smith 1776–1976, I, v). So, "corn", subsistence, and, more generally, food from plants make up a very specific commodity for two reasons: (1) It is the first, and (2) it is the only commodity that *always* commands labour.

The exchange between corn and other goods requires an "extent of their market" sufficient to generate an effectual demand for these goods. The effectual demand must be able to pay the natural rate of wages and the natural rate of profit required to bring them to the market. What exactly does the "extent of the market" and the "effectual demand" mean? This point has been discussed since Pier Angelo Garegnani (1983). The effectual demand is not the quantity Q demanded at the price p as in the modern sense of the term. According to me, the extent of the market means the purchasing power $E = Qp$ present on the market, and the effectual demand is the point D belonging to the extent of the market that associates the natural price and the natural quantity.

On the price-quantity plane, we can represent the *given* extent of the market E ($E = Qp = k$) by a branch of hyperbole.[6]

As Smith explains, from the very beginning of the *Wealth of Nations*, specialisation requires that the extent of the market E must be sufficient to buy the natural quantity Q_n at its natural price (including *natural* profit and wages) p_n. Here, E' is not sufficient because the quantity Q' is inferior to the minimum quantity determined by the division of labour (Smith 1776–1976, I, iii, 2). The shift of the extent of the market from E' to E, resulting from the accumulation of capital in the agricultural sector, describes an element in the process of specialisation. During the same period, towns appear:

> Without the assistance of some artificers, indeed, the cultivation of land cannot be carried on but with great inconveniency and continual

> interruption. Smiths, carpenters, wheelwrights and ploughwrights, masons and bricklayers, tanners, shoemakers and tailors are people whose service the farmer has frequent occasion for. Such artificers, too, stand occasionally in need of the assistance of one another; and as their residence is not, like that of the farmer, necessarily tied down to a precise spot, they naturally settle in the neighbourhood of one another, and thus form a small town or village.
>
> (Smith 1776–1976, III, i, 4)

We are now in the second step of the accumulation of capital. Before pursuing this, I need to recall a very important proposition from this chapter. Smith affirms that at *equal* net rates of profit, an investor will prefer to invest closer to home (in the country) rather than further away from it (in town). We know that this preference is an important component of the metaphor of the invisible hand. Two arguments are used by Smith to justify it. The first involves risk. This proposition is odd, to say the least, if Smith considers the rates of profit net of risk here in accordance with his analysis of risk in Chapters 9 and 10 of Book I.[7] The second is also odd, but it is not contradictory to Smith's analysis for the argument is *aesthetic*. Investing at home is more "pleasant" (Smith 1776–1976, I, 378) than investing far from home. That aesthetics may be used as an argument in an investment function is quite surprising. I will return to this point shortly.

In the *Wealth of Nations*, the rate of profit in town must compensate for this "aesthetic" loss.

Now, "the great commerce of every civilized society" emerges. It "is carried between the inhabitants of the town and those of the country" (Smith 1776–1976, III, i, 1). Here, we have to take this proposition at its face value. The country is the agricultural space that surrounds a town. In the *Wealth of Nations*, as today, the word "country" is equivocal. It can mean this agricultural space, or it can mean the nation. Here, evidently, "country" means the agricultural space.

So, we may suppose that agricultural growth generates an effectual demand (anticipated) for manufactured goods. The exchange between raw products and manufactured products is created, and the crucial relationship between country and town emerges (where artificers work in close proximity). We cannot underestimate the significance of this relationship. It is important for two reasons:

1. It forms the framework of the core of a society or an economy in the *Wealth of Nations*. For example, Chapter VI of Book I begins with this famous sentence, "There is in every society or neighbourhood an ordinary or average rate both of wages and profit in every different employment of labour and stock". And some lines after, "There is likewise in every society or neighbourhood an ordinary or average rate of rent" (Smith 1776–1976, I, vi, 1, 2). Clearly, the words "society" and

"neighbourhood" here refer to the very familiar notion of the city, including the town and its countryside, which was a *normal framework* of the social representation at this time (see C. Tilly 1994; Epstein 2000). The natural ("normal", according to T. Aspromourgos 2009, 68) rate of profit and the natural rate of wage is given in each *city*. Competition concerns each *city*.

2 Smith attempts to theorise the dynamic process of differentiation. Note the great ambition in this attempt to provide a theory of the *genesis*, not only of modern society but also of exchange and the division of labour.[8]

However, this is not the end of the story for this "great commerce" is not symmetrical.[9] Smith supposes that it is possible to conceive of the country without a town, while the reverse is necessarily an exception. This asymmetry is temporally oriented because, as we have seen, subsistence is "prior to conveniency and luxury". Capital movement is oriented from agriculture to manufacture, *and the reverse is not true* (unless the "natural progress of opulence" is not observed). For Smith, as we well know, the accumulation of capital is slower in the country than it is in town because the division of labour progresses more slowly in the first sector (Smith 1776–1976, I, i).

To continue, I need to study another important proposition of the *Wealth of Nations*, namely that *natural* rates of profit tend to decrease under the effect of competition.

While the hypothesis of the preference for local investment would be accepted by David Ricardo, we know the Ricardian and Marxist criticism of the proposition, regarding the falling rate of profit. The natural rate of profit cannot be affected by competition, which only affects the gravitation of market magnitudes and does not concern natural variables. For Ricardian and Marxist critics, Smith confuses two economic phenomena. However, it is possible to provide a very simple explanation of Smith's position.

Smith writes,

> The increase of stock, which raises wages, tends to lower profit. When the stocks of many rich merchants are turned into the same trade, their mutual competition naturally tends to lower its profit; and when there is a like increase of stock in all the different trades carried on in the same *society*, the same competition must produce the same effect in them all.
>
> (Smith 1776–1976, I, ix, 2)

He then clarifies his position:

> As capitals increase in any country, the profits which can be made by employing them necessarily diminish. It becomes gradually more and more difficult to find within the country a profitable method of employing any new capital.
>
> (Smith 1776–1976, II, iv, 8)

The fall of the natural rate of profit is a consequence of the rational choice made by capitalists who favour the more profitable investment *if* the extent of the market is given. The fall of the rate of profit is a consequence of the accumulation of capital, not of some confusion between natural quantities and market quantities. It is possible to describe this situation as a shift in the point of effectual demand along the *unchanged* curve of the extent of the market.

Therefore, we must consider two contradictory effects of the accumulation of capital. On the one hand, the accumulation of capital expands the market, which is good for the rate of profit, the division of labour, and the rate of wages. On the other hand, the accumulation of capital increases competition, which causes the fall of the rate of profit.

Of course, this last hypothesis is difficult to accept, precisely because it is difficult to suppose that the extent of the market remains unchanged with the accumulation of capital. So, we must suppose a sort of ceteris paribus clause, and we have to acknowledge the idea of a *tendency* for the rate of profit to fall, which would enter into effect if no forces (provoking the shift of the extent of the market) were able to oppose that tendency.

If the rate of profit tends to fall in town with the accumulation of capital, what happens next? According to Smith, two paths are possible. The first supposes that land is available, *as is the case in America*. Here:

> When an artificer has acquired a little more stock than is necessary for carrying on his own business in supplying the neighbouring country, he does not, in North America, attempt to establish with it a manufacture for more distant sale, but employs it in the purchase and improvement of uncultivated land. From artificer he becomes planter and neither the large wages nor the easy subsistence which that country affords to artificers can bribe him rather to work for other people than for himself.
>
> (Smith 1776–1976, III, i, 5)

Note that, in this case, our artificer seems to be an independent worker. He acquires stock, which is not capital. This ambiguity is frequent in the *Wealth of Nations* (see for example, the beginning of Book II). However, another difficulty seems to arise, which was later noted by Ricardo (as we know). Why would an artificer acquire more stock or more capital "than is necessary"? It appears to me that the ambiguity here is twofold. It can first be underlined by asking what determines the "necessary" quantity of capital. In the *Wealth of Nations*, the only available criterion is the natural rate of profit. It therefore suffices to complete Smith's phrase in the following manner: "when an artificer has acquired more capital than is necessary *to maintain the natural rate of profit*". So, we may understand that this artificer *anticipates* that pursuing accumulation in the city will cause a fall in the rate of profit. This no longer compensates for the aesthetic loss suffered by investing in the city as opposed to the country. The artificer will thus prefer to return to investing in the country. According to Smith, this was what was happening in America. There, the artificer was faced with a simple choice: Given the same rate of profit in town and in the country, he prefers the country and becomes a planter.

On the other hand, if, as in Europe, land is no longer available, an alternative remains:

> Every artificer who has acquired more stock than he can employ in the occasional jobs of the neighbourhood endeavours to prepare work for more distant sale. The smith erects some sort of iron, the weaver some sort of linen or woollen manufactory. Those different manufactures come, in process of time, to be gradually subdivided, and thereby improved and refined in a great variety of ways, which may easily be conceived, and which it is therefore unnecessary to explain any further.
>
> (Smith 1776–1976, III, i, 6)

It is fascinating to note that here, Smith suggests that it is through foreign trade that the artificer transforms himself into a manufacturer. The "industrial revolution" is sketched in one line, and he does not deem it necessary "to explain any further". Nonetheless, we would like to know a little more about the point of departure of this crucial point!

This passage describes the process whereby the accumulation of capital takes over; the broadening of the scope of the market has thus been established. Because the funds accumulated by the artisan cannot be invested in land, they are invested in a foreign trade, so long as the artisan's products can be sold in more extensive markets, which are hence more distant. We can understand (partially) these phenomena as a move to the right of the curve showing the extent of the market. This move prevents the fall of the natural rate of profit.

So, the accumulation of capital takes place "naturally" (if the mercantile system has not prompted it to take other channels) following this sequence: First agriculture, then manufacturing, and finally foreign trade. Thus, according to *The Wealth of Nations*, the accumulation of capital requires markets to expand; otherwise, the rate of profit will fall. If, for one reason or another, foreign trade should be interrupted, the natural rate of profit, income, and employment would fall.

Thus, Chapter 1 of Book III suggests the outline of a long-term dynamic that begins with the agricultural economy, which experiences the "exchange" of corn for labour, resulting above all in a two-sector economy: Agriculture in the country and factories in the town. It is in the city – the town, surrounded by the country – context that competition tended to impose natural rates of profit, wage, and rent.

And the cities are not isolated. Each of them is directly or indirectly linked to others through foreign trade. I suggest that we call this the "cosmopolitan economy". It would be a global (world) economy if rates of profit and wages tended to be equal on the global scale, which is naturally not the case (this would only be considered by John Stuart Mill at the beginning of his chapter on "International Trade"). This cosmopolitan economy is therefore never at equilibrium. The only barrier to the incessant circulation of capital is the preference for local investment.

However, this idea was to be transformed and intensified by Ricardo (who evoked the "natural disinclination" of investors). According to Ricardo, even if capital circulates between England and Portugal, the rates of profit do not equalise between those two countries as they do between London and Yorkshire:

> These feelings, which I should be sorry to see weakened, induce most men of property to be satisfied with a low rate of profits in their own country, rather than seek a more advantageous employment for their wealth in foreign nations.
>
> [1821–1951, vii, 136–137])[10]

Here, we can find a first step in the identification of an economy – as unified by competition – with the nation, in the modern sense of the word nation. And we know how competition achieves this, according to Ricardo: by means of banks and "moneyed men" [1821–1951, iv, 89]). The economy becomes national at the same time and in the same way as it is unified by the financial market. Between these two nations – two economies – exchanges were thenceforth international. The economy was to become *national* because the financial market unified it, and it was within a national economy that the accounting identity between *national* net income ($Y = C + S$) and the *national* net product ($Y = C + I$) were to become intelligible. This identity was related to the thesis, which Smith nonetheless accepted,[11] that there is no such thing as hoarding, and that all forms of savings are necessarily invested, leading to a formulation of what is known as Say's Law. A strange idea thus emerged that Smith appeared to justify international trade by the necessity of offering a prospective outcome for an excess supply of capital. John Stuart Mill was to liken this to the old mercantilist concept of "Vent for Surplus", and this later gave rise to abundant and regular commentary ([Bloomfield A. I. 1975; Myint H. 1958; Kurz H. 1992; Elmslie B. and Sidgley N. 2002). If I am right, this interpretation is misleading.

Notes

1 "The protection of trade in general, from pirates and freebooters, is said to have given occasion to the first institution of the duties of customs" (Smith 1776–1976, V, I, e, 3). Evidently, Smith knew of the matter.

2 "Upon equal or nearly equal profits, every wholesale merchant naturally prefers the home trade to the foreign trade of consumption" (Smith 1776–1976, IV, 2, 454). I will return to this famous proposition later.

3 As far as I know, the extensive literature about "Smithian growth models" does not use those chapters (Jeck's paper is an exception).

4 *The Wealth of Nations* seems to suggest that the falling rate of profit as a consequence of the accumulation of capital begins at the first stage of the model (1776–1976, IV, ix, 22).

5 See Kurz (1972).

6 Note that point D of this branch represents this effectual demand, which associates the natural quantity Q_n with the natural price p_n (see Garegnani 1983, 312; Aspromourgos 2009, 83). In I, vii, Smith describes the gravitation mechanism. If the quantity Q brought to the market is different to Q_n, the market price p_m will be different from p_n. Then, Smith supposes that the competition affecting the quantities brought to the market will oscillate until the return to equilibrium.

7 Breban and Lapidus (2013). Critics like E. West (1990) often assert that Smith must have forgotten, in the last chapter of Book II, what he had written in Chapter 10 of Book I. I have shown elsewhere (Diatkine 2010) that it is not necessary to imagine such an inconsistency.

8 As we know, neo-Walrasian models and neo-Ricardian models assume that the division of labour is given.

9 On this point, see Jeck (1994).

10 These points are discussed in Faccarello (2015).

11 "What is annually saved is as regularly consumed as what is annually spent, and nearly in the same time too; but it is consumed by a different set of people". (Smith 1776–1976, II, iii, 18) t.

References

Aspromourgos, T. (2009) *The Science of Wealth*, Abingdon: Routledge.

Bloomfield, A. I. (1975) "Adam Smith and the Theory of International Trade", in A. S. Skinner and T. Wilson (eds.), *Essays on Adam Smith*, Oxford: Clarendon Press.

Bréban, L. and Lapidus, A. (2013) "Adam Smith on Lotteries: An Interpretation and Formal Restatement", *PHARE Working Paper.*

Diatkine, D. (2010) "Vanity and the Love of System in Theory of Moral Sentiments", *The European Journal of the History of Economic Thought*, vol. 17: 3, September.

Elmslie, B. and Sidgley, N. (2002) "Vent for Surplus: A Case of Mistaken Identity", *Southern Economic Journal*, vol. 68(3).

Epstein, S. R. (2000) *Freedom and Growth: The Rise of States and Markets in Europe, 1300–1750.* London: Routledge & Kegan Paul.

Faccarello, G. (2015) "Comparative Advantage", in H. D. Kurz and N. Salvadori (eds.), *The Elgar Companion to David Ricardo*, Cheltenham and Northampton: Edward Elgar.

Garegnani P. (1983d) "Two Routes to Effective Demand, in J.A. Kregel (ed) *Distribution, Effective Demand and International Economic Relations*, London: Macmillan. French translation in *L'Hétérodoxie dans la pensée économique K. Marx, J.M. Keynes, J.A. Schumpeter,* études présentées par Ghislain Deleplace et Patrick Maurisson, Paris: Anthropos, 1985.

Jeck, A. (1994) "The Macrostructure of Adam Smith's Theoretical System: A Reconstruction", *The European Journal of the History of Economic Thought*, vol. 1(3): 551–576.

Kurz, H. (1992) "Adam Smith on Foreign Trade: A Note on the 'Vent for Surplus' Argument", *Economica*, vol. 59.

Mill, J. S. (1848–1965) *Principles of Political Economy with Some of Their Applications to Social Philosophy*. Vol. II and III of *The Collected Works of John Stuart Mill*. London: Routledge & Kegan Paul.

Myint, H. (1958) "The 'Classical Theory' of International Trade and the Underdeveloped Countries", *Economic Journal*, vol. 68, June.

Ricardo, D. (1817–1951) *On the Principles of Political Economy and Taxation*, Vol. I of *The Works and Correspondence of David Ricardo* edited by P. Sraffa with M. H. Dobb, Cambridge: Cambridge University Press.

Smith, A. (1776–1976) *An Inquiry into the Nature and Causes of the Wealth of Nations*, The Glasgow Edition of the Works and Correspondence of Adam Smith, Oxford: Clarendon Press.

Tilly, C. (1994) *Cities and the Rise of States in Europe, A.D. 1000 to 1800*, Boulder, San Francisco and Oxford: Westview Press.

West, E. (1990) *Adam Smith and Modern Economics*, Aldershot: Edward Elgar, 1990.

24 The competitive paradigm in spatial economics

Jacques-François Thisse

Introduction

The history of the relationship between spatial economics and general equilibrium theory is both complex and obscure. It is complex because it is fraught with difficulties that have been put aside for simplicity. It is obscure because the several attempts made over the last 50 years to clarify this relationship have befuddled the debate with confusing answers. This state of affairs is all the more surprising given that *trading commodities is spatial by its very nature*. People get involved in trade because they want to consume goods and services that are not produced within their reach. Under these circumstances, agents must bear *transport costs*, which correspond to the expenditures needed to coordinate transactions with suppliers or customers.

The definition of transport costs includes all costs generated by distance and borders: the costs of shipping goods per se but also tariff and non-tariff barriers, communication impediments, cultural differences, and the time needed for the transaction to occur. As a result, transport costs should play an important role in economic theory as they are inherent attributes of exchanges among agents dispersed across locations. Yet it is fair to say that space is ignored by the vast majority of economists. Neither land nor distance is mentioned. Rather, textbooks give the impression that production and consumption take place on the head of a pin as if space had no dimension.

One would expect trade theory to be the economic field in which transport costs occupy center stage. Until the emergence of the "new trade theories," international trade economists dismissed transport costs and privileged the differences of technologies or factor endowments between dimensionless countries. According to Deardorff (1984: 470), "transport costs are almost universally ignored in trade models in the sanguine hope that if included they would not materially affect the results," while Panagariya (1998) views them as "unnecessary complications." As observed by Leamer (2007), all of this implies an intriguing geography: Countries are close enough for the cost of shipping goods internationally to be zero but far enough apart that no workers and capital-owners can find their way from one country to another.

The development of this research strategy is especially surprising because, as stressed by Ohlin (1933, 1968: 97) more than 80 years ago, international trade and location theories are not independent of one another:

> international trade theory cannot be understood except in relation to and as part of the general location theory, to which the lack of mobility of goods and factors has equal relevance.

The most common explanation for this negligence is that the value of transport costs has declined considerably since the middle of the 19th century. Even though transport costs must be positive for space to matter, one should not infer from this observation that location matters less when transport costs decrease. Quite the opposite: By making them more footloose, lower transport costs make firms more sensitive to minor differences between places. As a result, a tiny difference may have a big impact on the geographical distribution of economic activity. Moreover, the cost of shipping some goods remains high. The puzzle that constitutes the gravity equation confirms the idea that distance still matters (Anderson, 2011): On average, *doubling distance halves trade flows*. Consequently, the lack of attention paid to space in economic theory cannot be justified by the fall in transport costs.

Krugman (2007: 33) summarizes this neatly:

> one vision [is] the traditional vision of international trade theory, in which countries are discrete economic points, whose location in space is irrelevant. Another [is] the pure geography vision, in which location in space is all and borders are irrelevant. Finally, there [is] the vision of a spaceless, borderless world in which distance had been abolished—not a world that yet exists, but possibly one just over the horizon. What seems to have emerged from the empirical work of the past dozen years is a compromise vision. Distance matters a lot, though possibly less than it did before modern telecommunications. Borders also matter a lot, though possibly less than they did before free trade agreements. The spaceless, borderless world is still a Platonic ideal, a long way from coming into existence.

This is not yet the end of the story. Despite Econ 101 leading off with the claim that land, labor, and capital are the three main factors of production, land is largely forgotten. Nevertheless, empirical evidence reveals that a growing share of high-value activities is concentrated in large metropolitan areas (Moretti, 2012). As Lucas (1988: 39) put it, "What can people be paying Manhattan or downtown Chicago rents for, if not for being near other people?" Otherwise, how can such high rents in cities be explained? In the most habitable regions of the globe, the supply of land vastly exceeds the demand for land. Therefore, if there is no need for proximity, land should (almost) be a free good. This makes the case for proximity very strong, at least for some activities. Contrary to the opinion widely spread in the media, even with the Internet and other new communication devices, face-to-face contact remains important. To understand why this is so, one must keep in mind that the information transferred by means of modern communication tools must be structured according to schemes and codes that are clearly defined and known to all. Only formal and precise information can be transmitted in this way. On the other hand, information that is diffcult to codify can often be transmitted only through face-to-face contacts. For example, the preliminary stages in the development of a new technology or product require repeated contacts among those involved, and such contacts are much easier and less costly when these people are in close proximity.

Given the importance of the above-mentioned issues, the following question comes to mind: *Why is space peripheral to economic theory?* Because the optimal location of an agent depends on the locations chosen by the agents it interacts with, locational decisions are "interdependent" and consequently must be studied within a general equilibrium framework encompassing the whole range of choices made by firms and households. As the competitive model is the starting point of any study in which the market plays an important role, one should naturally try to understand what can be accomplished in spatial economics by using this paradigm.

The essence of the competitive model lies in the impersonal nature of exchanges: When agents make decisions regarding production or consumption, the only information they need is the price system given by the market, something over which they have no influence. The most elegant and general model of a competitive economy is undoubtedly that developed by Arrow and Debreu (1954). It can be briefly described as follows: The economy is formed by agents (firms and households) and by commodities (goods and services). A firm is characterized by a set of production plans, each production plan describing a possible input-output relationship. A household is identified by a relation of preferences, a bundle of initial resources, and some shares in firms' profits. When both consumers' preferences and firms' technologies are convex, there exists a price system (one price per commodity), a production plan for each firm, and a consumption bundle for each household. These satisfy the following three conditions: At the prevailing prices, (1) markets clear, (2) each firm maximizes its profit subject to its production set, and (3) each household maximizes its utility under the budget constraints defined by the value of the household's initial endowment and shares in firms' profits.

In the Arrow-Debreu model, a commodity is defined not only by its physical characteristics but also by the place where it is made available. For example, in *Theory of Value*, Debreu (1959: 30) insists that "a good at a certain location and the same good at another location are different economic objects, and the specification of the location at which it will be available is essential." Given this convention, the choice of a commodity must also entail the choice of a location. For example, when individuals choose a consumption good or a type of work, they also choose where to consume or where to work. Within the Arrow-Debreu model, spatial interdependencies are integrated in the same way as other market interactions. In other words, this model seems able to cope with the formation of a space-economy without having to consider additional specificities.

However, things are not that simple. The essential question is whether the competitive price mechanism is able to explain the large disparities that arise at different spatial scales—the continent, the country, the city, or the neighborhood. According to Lösch, Isard, and others, new models—fundamentally different from those found in standard general equilibrium—are needed when the spatial distribution of activities becomes itself a variable. However, these authors do not explain why more general models are needed and fail to develop such alternative models.

In this respect, Starrett (1978) has made a fundamental but—strangely enough—almost unnoticed contribution by showing that the introduction of space in the Arrow-Debreu model has a crucial implication[1]: *Total transport costs in the economy must be zero for a competitive equilibrium to exist.* This, in turn, means that the competitive framework cannot explain the formation of big cities and large trade flows. Phrased differently, it seems that the competitive model cannot be used to study a spatial economy. Of course, very much like in standard trade theory, inhomogeneities across space may save the competitive model. Nevertheless, most of these inhomogeneities are not exogenous. Instead, they are the outcome of market and non- market interactions among agents and must be explained rather than assumed.

The remainder of this paper is organized as follows: In Section 2, the inadequacy of the competitive assumption for economic geography is illustrated by means of a simple example. The robustness of the conclusions drawn from this example is then examined in Section 3 where the *spatial impossibility theorem*—stating that no competitive equilibrium involving trade exists when shipping goods across space is costly—is discussed. Note that this result is especially meaningful insofar as it is internal to the theory itself. Section 4 briefly explores the role of spatial inhomogeneities. Section 5 concludes.

The quadratic assignment problem

We begin the discussion by considering the *quadratic assignment problem* introduced by Koopmans and Beckmann (1957). Assume that m firms are to be assigned to m locations. Every firm must be assigned to a single location, and every location can accommodate only one firm. Each firm produces a fixed amount of good and uses one unit of land as well as fixed amounts of goods produced by the other firms. Suppose further that the technology used by each firm is not affected by the chosen location. Finally, shipping a good from a location to another location involves a positive cost.

We now show that any feasible assignment cannot be sustained as a competitive equilibrium. In order to illustrate the nature of the diffculties encountered, we restrict ourselves to the simple case of two firms, denoted $i = 1, 2$, and two locations, denoted $\ell = A, B$. Without loss of generality, we may assume that firm 1 is assigned to location A and firm 2 to B. Firm i produces q_i units of good i and purchases q_j units of good j from firm $j \neq i$ regardless of its own location. It also receives a revenue $a_i > 0$ from other activities with the rest of the world, which does not depend on its location. Finally, each good i can be shipped from its place of production to the other location at a given cost $t_i > 0$.

Let $p_{i\ell}$ be the price of good i at location $\ell = A, B$ and R_ℓ be the land rent to be paid by a firm for using land at location ℓ. Firm 1's profit in location A is thus defined as follows:

$$\pi_{1A} = a_i + b_A + p_{1A}q_1 - p_{2A}q_2 - R_A$$

while a similar expression holds for firm 2 at location B. If this price system sustains the foregoing configuration, then the equilibrium prices $p_{i\ell}$ must satisfy the following conditions (Samuelson, 1952):

$$p_{1B} = p_{1A} + t_1, \tag{24.1}$$

$$p_{2A} = p_{2B} + t_2. \tag{24.2}$$

These equalities mean that the price of good 1 (2) in location B (A) is equal to its price in location A (B) plus the corresponding unit transport cost $t_1(t_2)$. Accordingly, total profits are equal to

$$\pi_{1A} + \pi_{2B} = a_1 + a_2 - (t_1q_1 + t_2q_2 + R_A + R_B),$$

which are always positive when a_1 and a_2 are suffciently large.

We now show that it is impossible to find values of R_A and R_B such that both firms 1 and 2 maximize their own profit at locations 1 and 2, respectively. Without loss of generality, assume that $R_A \geq R_B$. Then, if firms behave competitively, it is readily verified that firm 1 would earn a strictly higher profit by setting up at location B. Indeed, if firm 1 sets up at location B, its profit is

$$\pi_{1B} = a_1 + p_{1B}q_1 - p_{2B}q_2 - R_B.$$

Using (24.1) and (24.2), it is then readily verified that

$$\pi_{1B} - \pi_{1A} = t_1q_1 + t_2q_2 + R_A - R_B > 0. \tag{24.3}$$

In other words, firm 1 would be better off at location 2 and, therefore, has an incentive to move. In other words, *in the quadratic assignment problem, no feasible location pattern of firms can be sustained as a competitive equilibrium.* Observe that, in the above argument, firms are price-takers, and therefore, they believe that "changing place" does not affect the prevailing prices of goods and land rents.

It is tempting to attribute this negative result to the many specificities of the quadratic assignment problem, especially the assumption that firms cannot be located in the same location. In the next section, we show that a breakdown of the competitive price mechanism holds for a general spatial economy.

The spatial impossibility theorem

Consider now a spatial economy formed by a finite number of locations. Each location is endowed with a positive amount of land and can accommodate a large number of firms and households. The economy involves n mobile goods and one immobile good: land. Shipping goods requires the use of resources. Specifically, the transport of a good between any two locations is performed by a profit-maximizing carrier who purchases this good in a location at the market price prevailing there and sells it in the other location at the corresponding market price. To do so, it uses goods and land in the in-between locations.

A typical firm produces in a small number of places. Likewise, a household has a very small number of residences. It is, therefore, reasonable to assume that each firm (household) chooses a single location and engages in production (consumption) activities there. This means that *agents are not ubiquitous* and, therefore, have an "address" in space. Although firms may run several production plants, armchair evidence shows that they concentrate their production at a few sites only. Observe that this assumption is tantamount to what Koopmans (1957: 154) wrote long ago:

> without recognizing indivisibilities—in human person, in residences, plants, equipment, and in transportation—urban location problems, down to those of the smallest village, cannot be understood.

Such indivisibilities are needed for the existence of firms and even of trade. However, both firms and households are free to choose the location in which they want to conduct their activities and the amount of land they use.

Last, space is said to be *homogeneous* if (1) the utility function of each consumer is identical no matter what her location and (2) the production set of each firm is independent of its location. In other words, firms and households have no intrinsic preferences over locations. The reason for making such an assumption is that we aim to identify pure economic mechanisms that generate cities and trade independently of any natural endowment of locations. This was the starting point of Lösch (1940: 105 English translation):

> Among all the factors that can create an economic region we shall select the economic. We shall consider market areas that are not the result of any kind of natural or political inequalities but arise through the interplay of purely economic forces, some working toward concentration

> and other toward dispersion. In the first group are the advantages of specialization and of large-scale production; in the second, those of shipping costs and of diversified production.
>
> In the following derivation we start from radical assumptions in order that no spatial differences may lie concealed in what we assume: that economic raw materials are evenly and adequately distributed over a wide plain. Our area shall be homogeneous in every other respect as well, and contain nothing but self-suffcient farms that are regularly distributed. How can this starting point lead to spatial differences?

Following a line of reasoning similar that used in Section 2, Starrett (1978) has shown that, for any allocation involving costly trade across space, the global incentives to move across agents are always strictly positive. Therefore, we may conclude as follows[2]:

The spatial impossibility theorem. Assume a spatial economy with a finite number of locations. If space is homogeneous, transport is costly, and preferences are locally nonsatiated, then there is no competitive equilibrium involving transportation.

What is the meaning of this *a priori* unexpected result? Whenever economic activities are perfectly divisible, the spatial impossibility theorem implies that the mobility of production factors is a perfect substitute for trade. Such a result is hardly surprising because every activity can be carried out on an arbitrarily small scale in every possible place without any loss of effciency. Firms and households are then induced to suppress all distance-related costs by producing exactly what they need where they are. Mills (1972: 4) very suggestively described the "world without cities" that would result from an economy operating under constant returns and perfect competition:

> each acre of land would contain the same number of people and the same mix of productive activities. The crucial point in establishing this result is that constant returns permit each productive activity to be carried on at an arbitrary level without loss of effciency. Furthermore, all land is equally productive and equilibrium requires that the value of the marginal product, and hence its rent, be the same everywhere. Therefore, in equilibrium, all the inputs and outputs necessary directly and indirectly to meet the demands of consumers can be located in a small area near where consumers live. In that way, each small area can be autarkic and transportation of people and goods can be avoided.

Clearly, such a space is the quintessence of autarky.

However, as observed by Starrett (1978: 27), when economic activities are not perfectly divisible, the transport of goods or people between some places becomes unavoidable:

> as long as there are some indivisibilities in the system (so that individual operations must take up space) then a suffciently complicated set of interrelated activities will generate transport costs.

In this case, the spatial impossibility theorem tells us something really new and important: Whenever agents are mobile, there is no competitive equilibrium (hence "impossibility" in the name of the theorem) such that goods are traded between locations. In other words, *factor mobility and trade are incompatible in a pure competitive setting.* This is clearly a surprising result that requires more explanations.

When locations are not in autarky, some goods must be traded across locations. By implication, the price system must perform two different jobs simultaneously: (1) support trade between locations (while clearing markets in each location) and (2) prevent firms and consumers from relocating. What the spatial impossibility theorem says is that it is impossible to hit these two birds with one stone. The equilibrium prices supporting trade carry the wrong signals from the viewpoint of locational stability. In the quadratic assignment problem, when a good is exported from A to B, the associated positive price gradients induce the producer located in A (who seeks higher revenue) to relocate to B, while the firm already in location B (who seeks lower prices) want to relocate to A. The transport of goods from B to A encourages such "cross relocation." The land rent differential can discourage the relocation in one direction but not in both.

Thus, as long as trade incurs positive transport costs, some agents will always want to relocate. As a consequence, the price system does not convey all the information needed by agents because they must also know where those it interacts with are located. This situation bears some resemblance to that encountered when externalities prevent agents from taking effcient price-guided decisions. The spatial impossibility theorem shows that the same holds in a spatial economy. In a more formal way, the reason for the spatial impossibility theorem lies in the non-convexity of the set of feasible allocations caused by the existence of transport costs and the fact that agents are mobile but not ubiquitous. Given the role played by the competitive model in economic theory, there can be little doubt that the diffculties highlighted by the spatial impossibility theorem acted as an impediment to the development of spatial economics until the monopolistic competition revolution of the 1980s.

In contrast, as illustrated by the literature developed in spatial price theory, standard general equilibrium remains relevant and useful for the study of commodity flows across space when both firms and households have *given* locations (Labys and Yang, 1997). To the best of my knowledge, the first spatial price equilibrium model was developed by Cournot (1838, Chap. X) and was rediscovered and extended by Samuelson (1952). There are several sources and destinations—which need not be different—that are connected by an interregional transport network. Firms' and consumers' choices are aggregated into elastic demand and supply functions, while shipping the good from a source to a destination is costly. The issue is to determine simultaneously the quantities supplied and demanded at each region and the local prices at which the good is supplied by firms and bought by consumers. Trade being driven by spatial arbitrage, in equilibrium, the price of a good in one region depends on the price for the same good in other regions as arbitrage limits the price difference to the shipping cost of the good. To be precise, the equilibrium is reached when the consumer price equals the producer price plus the transport cost for all positive flows; if the consumer price is less than the producer price plus the transport cost, then no trade flow occurs.

When transport costs are high, each region operates under autarky. Once transport costs have decreased suffciently, trade across regions comes into play. As the integration process gets deeper, some regions stop producing the good to become importers because the domestic producers are less efficient than their foreign competitors. In other words, these firms are driven out of business because they have lost "the most effective protection of all tariff protections, namely, that provided by bad roads" (Launhardt, 1885: 150 English translation). Thus, market integration, technological progress in transport, or both redraw the geography of production with some regions producing more and others less.

This simple model highlights the importance of the three major forces stressed in modern trade literature: (1) the size of markets through regional demand schedules, (2) their accessibility through the transport cost matrix, and (3) the heterogeneity of producers through the regional supply schedules. This model could have been used to develop a trade theory with transport costs, which came into being much later on with the new trade theories.

It is, therefore, the combination of two assumption—*trading goods involves positive transport costs while producers* and *consumers are mobile but not ubiquitous*—that leads to the breakdown of the competitive paradigm in a homogeneous space.

Spatial inhomogeneities

The main critical assumption in the spatial impossibility theorem is the homogeneity of space. Relaxing this assumption may help restore the existence of a competitive equilibrium involving the transport of goods.

Exogenous inhomogeneities. In order to gain insights about the effect of spatial inhomogeneities, consider the 2 firm-2 location example in Section 2. More specifically, we assume that location A is now endowed with an exogenous attribute beneficial to firm 1 only (whereas firm 2 experiences a similar advantage in the sole location B). Whatever the reason for it, this attribute gives rise to an additional earning equal to $b_A > 0$ when firm 1 is at A. Under these circumstances, firm 1's profit at location A is as follows:

$$\pi_{1A} = a_1 + b_A + p_{1A}q_1 - p_{2A}q_2 - R$$

whereas π_{1B} is unchanged. Measuring again the incentive to move from A to B by the difference in profit at A and B, we obtain

$$\pi_{1B} - \pi_{1A} = t_1q_1 + t_2q_2 + R_A - R_B - b_A$$

which is always negative when b_A is suffciently large. If the same holds for firm 2, we may conclude that *a competitive equilibrium involving trade may exist when firms have strongly diverging preferences for location attributes.* However, this does not really save the competitive paradigm. Indeed, as Hamilton (1980: 38) put it,

> Stability is lent to the system by having plants differ from one another in their preferences for the sites *qua* sites, and instability arises from a large volume of trade among plants.

Though analytically convenient, this approach does not help us to understand why firms 1 and 2 have divergent preferences about locations. Modern economies are replete with footloose firms, connected by large trade and communication flows. Therefore, although exogenous inhomogeneities and historical circumstances may explain *where* large cities are built, they do not say *why* cities exist.

There has been a revival of the Ricardian approach in the form of spatial quantitative models (Diamond, 2016; Redding, 2016). These models account for various types of mobility costs but assume that locations are endowed with given reduced forms of comparative advantage.

Endogenous inhomogeneities. The assumption of a homogeneous space may also be relaxed when firms, say, benefit from agglomeration economies. Ever since the work of Marshall (1890, Chap. X) and Hoover (1937, Chap. VI), it has been documented that the spatial concentration of firms in cities generates various benefits that are not mediated by the market (Duranton and Puga, 2004). One of the most illustrative examples of this is provided by Ogawa and Fujita (1980), who show that, in an otherwise homogeneous space and perfectly competitive economy, the presence of informational spillovers among firms leads to the emergence of a central business district when commuting costs are low, information spillovers are strong, or both. In this case, *there exists a competitive equilibrium involving workers' commuting.* At the other extreme of the spectrum, when commuting costs are high, information spillovers are weak, or both, the market outcome involves a complete integration of business and residential activities. In other words, there is *backyard capitalism.* Of course, the presence of externalities implies that the market outcome is ineffcient: Firms are insuffciently concentrated because they care only about their roles as "receivers" and neglect their roles as "transmitters."

A new strand of literature focuses on heterogeneous workers whose combinations generate different types of agglomeration economies (Behrens et al., 2014; Eeckhout et al., 2014). However, by assuming that cities produce the same good, or, equivalently, different goods traded at zero cost, these models fail to recognize that cities are anchored in specific locations and embedded in intricate networks of trade relations.

Concluding remarks

When producers and consumers are free to choose their locations, the price system must (1) clear markets in each location, (2) support trade between locations, and (3) prevent firms and households from relocating. The spatial impossibility theorem tells us that, in a homogeneous space, the price system is unable to satisfy all of these requirements. Without external factors that drive firm and household locations, such as a strong preference for particular locations or the presence of spatial externalities, a sound spatial economic theory cannot be built by differentiating goods through their locations and adding land as a new commodity. If firms interact together and those interactions are costly, a firm's profits depend not just on its own location but also on the location decisions made by the other firms. As a consequence, the relative advantage of a location for a given firm depends on the locations of other firms. In such a context, each one must know (or guess?) where the firms it interacts with are located. Adding such a requirement violates the competitive assumption. This issue may be tackled from a different angle: *Is a market coping with the accessibility across agents missing?* The land rent is supposed to play two roles, that is, it must reflect both the scarcity of land and the accessibility to suppliers and/or customers. One solution to this problem of overdetermination is to imagine an economy in which agents would know the land rents associated with all possible location patterns of activities. But such information is not provided by the market. Hence, there seem to be "missing" markets.

By contrast, the presence of exogenous inhomogeneities provides agents with the signal that is missing in a homogeneous space. An illustrative and powerful example of this is provided by the canonical model of land use. Insofar as goods and transactions must take place in a market town, as in the von Thünen model (Launhardt, 1885; Samuelson, 1983), or jobs are concentrated in the central business district, as in the monocentric city model (Alonso, 1964; Fujita, 1989), the competitive paradigm permits the development of a rich analysis of the spatial distribution of activities when *the location of the center is given*. This is because the interdependence between producer or worker locations is replaced by their sole accessibility to an exogenous center whose impact can be captured unequivocally by a competitive land rent profile.

Somewhat ironically, this state of affairs is reminiscent of the main diffculty encountered in the standard model of growth, as summarized by Romer (1992: 85–86):

> The paradox...was that the competitive theory that generated the evidence was inconsistent with any explanation of how technological change could arise as the result of the self-interested actions of individual economic actors. By definition, all of national output had to be paid as returns to capital and labor; none remained as possible compensation for technological innovations.... The assumption of convexity and perfect competition placed the accumulation of new technologies at the center of the growth process and simultaneously denied the possibility that economic analysis could have anything to say about this process.

All of this has a major implication. If we want to explain the formation of cities or the existence of large differences between regions or nations in an otherwise homogeneous space, we must explicitly consider *externalities* or *imperfect competition*. In other words, to explain the most salient feature of the space-economy, that is, the presence of a large variety of agglomerations of economic agents, we have to appeal to non-market interactions among agents or to imperfectly competitive markets (Fujita and Thisse, 2013). The choice of a particular modeling strategy depends on the spatial scale under consideration. Because their extent is geographically limited, spatial externalities are mainly relevant for studying issues arising on a small scale. As for issues arising on a large scale, market-based approaches are more appealing. They range from general equilibrium models with monopolistic competition to partial equilibrium models with oligopolistic competition. In both cases, increasing returns and imperfect competition are integrated within a single framework. What is more, because the location of the cluster is endogenous, it is no surprise that the corresponding setups generate multiple equilibria.

To sum up, the modeling constraints have led economists to concentrate—probably for too long—on the combination involving constant returns and perfect competition. In a sense, it does not seem to be an exaggeration to say that the ability of the general equilibrium setting to tackle various issues, and, especially, the absence of alternative models, generated a lock in effect that economists had a lot of trouble escaping. It is, therefore, not surprising that the renewed interest in spatial economics brought about by Krugman (1991) is concomitant to the monopolistic competition revolution. Trading in Hotelling's (1929) footsteps, several authors have used space as a metaphor to study heterogeneous agents in game-theoretic terms in domains as different as industrial organization and political science. Thus, space seems to have moved from the periphery to the center of economy theory.

Notes

1 The low impact of Starrett's paper in spatial economics is shown by the fairly small number of citations by scholars working in this field.
2 See Fujita and Thisse (2013) for more details.

References

Alonso, W. 1964. *Location and Land Use*. Cambridge, MA: Harvard University Press.

Anderson, J.E. 2011. The gravity model. *Annual Review of Economics* 3: 133–60.

Arrow, K. and Debreu, G. 1954. Existence of an equilibrium for a competitive economy. *Econo- metrica* 22: 265–90.

Behrens, K., Duranton, G. and Robert-Nicoud, F. 2014. Productive cities: sorting, selection and agglomeration. *Journal of Political Economy* 122: 507–53.

Cournot, A. 1838. *Recherches sur les principes mathématiques de la théorie des richesses*. Paris: Hachette. English translation: *Researches into the Mathematical Principles of the Theory of Wealth*. New York: Macmillan (1897).

Debreu, G. 1959. *Theory of Value*. New York: Wiley.

Deardorff, A.V. 1984. Testing trade theories and predicting trade flows. In: R.W. Jones and P.B. Kenen (eds.), *Handbook of International Economics. Volume 1*. Amsterdam: North-Holland, 467–517.

Diamond, R. 2016. The determinants and welfare implications of US workers diverging location choices by skill: 1980–2000. *American Economic Review* 106: 479–524.

Duranton, G. and Puga, D. 2004. Micro-foundations of urban increasing returns: theory. In: J.V. Henderson and J.-F. Thisse (eds.), *Handbook of Regional and Urban Economics. Cities and Geography*. Amsterdam: North-Holland, 2063–117.

Eeckhout, J., Pinheiro, R. and Schmidheiny, K. 2014. Spatial sorting. *Journal of Political Economy* 122: 554–620.

Fujita, M. 1989. *Urban Economic Theory. Land Use and City Size*. Cambridge: Cambridge University Press.

Fujita M. and Thisse, J.-F. 2013. *Economics of Agglomeration. Cities, Industrial Location and Globalization. Second Edition*. Cambridge: Cambridge University Press.

Hamilton, B.W. 1980. Indivisibilities and interplant transportation cost: do they cause market breakdown? *Journal of Urban Economics* 7: 31–41.

Hoover, E.M. 1937. *Location Theory and the Shoe and Leather Industries*. Cambridge, MA: Harvard University Press.

Hotelling, H. 1929. Stability in competition. *Economic Journal* 39: 41–57.

Koopmans, T.C. 1957. *Three Essays on the State of Economic Science*. New York: McGraw-Hill.

Koopmans, T.C. and Beckmann, M.J. 1957. Assignment problems and the location of economic activities. *Econometrica* 25: 1401–14.

Krugman, P. 1991. Increasing returns and economic geography. *Journal of Political Economy* 99: 483–99.

Krugman, P. 2007. The new economic geography: where are we? In: M. Fujita (ed.), *Regional Integration in East Asia from the Viewpoint of Spatial Economics*. London: Macmillan, 23–34.

Labys, W.C., and Yang, C.W. 1997. Spatial price equilibrium as a foundation to unified spatial commodity modeling. *Papers in Regional Science* 76: 199–228.

Launhardt, W. 1885. *Mathematische Begründung der Volkswirtschaftslehre*. Leipzig: B.G. Teubner. English translation: *Mathematical Principles of Economics*. Aldershot: Edward Elgar (1993).

Leamer, E.E. 2007. A flat world, a level playing field, a small world after all, or none of the above? A review of Thomas L. Friedman's *The World is Flat*. *Journal of Economic Literature* 45: 83–126.

Lösch, A. 1940. *Die Räumliche Ordnung der Wirtschaft. Jena: Gustav Fischer. English trans- lation: The Economics of Location*. New Haven: Yale University Press (1954).

Lucas, R.E. 1988. On the mechanics of economic development. *Journal of Monetary Economics* 22: 3–42.

Marshall, A. 1890. *Principles of Economics*. London: Macmillan. 8th edition published in 1920.

Mills, E.S. 1972. *Studies in the Structure of the Urban Economy*. Baltimore: The Johns Hopkins Press.

Moretti, E. 2012. *The New Geography of Jobs*. Boston: Houghton Miffin Harcourt.

Ogawa, H. and Fujita, M. 1980. Equilibrium land use patterns in a non-monocentric city. *Journal of Regional Science* 20: 455–75.

Ohlin, B. 1933. *Interregional and International Trade*. Cambridge, MA: Harvard University Press. Revised version published in 1968.

Panagariya, A. 1998. Do transport costs justify regional preferential trading arrangements? No. *Weltwirtschafliches Archiv* 134: 280–301.

Redding, S. 2016. Goods trade, factor mobility and welfare. *Journal of International Economics* 101: 148–67.

Romer, P. 1992. Increasing returns and new developments in the theory of growth. In W.A. Barnett, B. Cornet, C. d'Aspremont, J.J. Gabszewicz and A. Mas-Colell (eds.), *Equilibrium Theory with Applications*. Cambridge: Cambridge University Press, 83–110.

Samuelson, P.A. 1952. Spatial price equilibrium and linear programming. *American Economic Review* 42: 283–303.

Samuelson, P.A. 1983. Thünen at two hundred. *Journal of Economic Literature* 21: 1468–88.

Starrett, D. 1978. Market allocations of location choice in a model with free mobility. *Journal of Economic Theory* 17: 21–37.

Index

For Product Safety Concerns and Information please contact our EU representative GPSR@taylorandfrancis.com Taylor & Francis Verlag GmbH, Kaufingerstraße 24, 80331 München, Germany